KOREA BRIEFING 2000– 2001

Society

Asia Society is a nonprofit, nonpartisan public education organization dedicated to increasing American understanding of Asia and broadening the dialogue between Americans and Asians. Through its programs in policy and business, the fine and performing arts, and elementary and secondary education, the Society reaches audiences across the United States and works closely with colleagues in Asia.

The views expressed in this publication are those of the individual contributors.

KOREA BRIEFING

2000– 2001

First Steps Toward
Reconciliation
and Reunification

Kongdan Oh
Ralph C. Hassig
Editors

Published in cooperation with
the Asia Society

An East Gate Book

M.E.Sharpe
Armonk, New York
London, England

An East Gate Book

Library of Congress ISSN: 1053-4806
ISBN 0-7656-0953-3 (hardcover)
ISBN 0-7656-0954-1 (paperback)

Printed in the United States of America

The paper used in this publication meets the minimum requirements of
American National Standard for Information Sciences
Permanence of Paper for Printed Library Materials,
ANSI Z 39.48-1984.

BM (c) 10 9 8 7 6 5 4 3 2 1
BM (p) 10 9 8 7 6 5 4 3 2 1

Contents

Preface

Korea Briefing: First Steps Toward Reconciliation and Reunification discusses major events on the Korean peninsula from 1999, when the last *Korea Briefing* was published, to the middle of 2001. The pivotal event in this time period was the first-ever summit meeting between the leaders of the two Koreas, an historic encounter that spawned an encouraging variety of contacts between South and North Koreans. Whether the summit will prove to be a watershed in inter-Korean relations or a symbolic event lacking substance is discussed by nine Korea experts who contribute chapters on South Korean politics, inter-Korean economic cooperation, North Korean affairs, the two Koreas and their neighbors, U.S.-Korean relations, Korean and German reunification, and North Korean defectors to South Korea.

Chapter authors present cogent and penetrating insights about Korea and North-South reconciliation during a period of initially raised, and then dashed, hopes for peace on the Korean peninsula. President Kim Dae-Jung, who staked his reputation on his Sunshine Policy of inter-Korean engagement, never wavered, even as he lost the support of many South Koreans. Economic difficulties following a partial recovery from the financial crisis of 1997 compounded disappointment in South Korea over inter-Korean engagement. In North Korea the economic situation continued to deteriorate, and enthusiasm for serious progress seems to have waned. In sum, *Korea Briefing* asks and seeks to answer one of the central questions of our times: How well prepared are the South Koreans and how eager are the North Koreans for reunification?

The Asia Society would like to thank Kongdan (Katy) Oh and Ralph Hassig for conceptualizing and leading the process to create another *Korea Briefing*. They have skillfully brought together a team of authors who were diligent in perfecting their chapters for publication. As editor, Richard Fumosa did yeoman duty in smoothing out sentences, paragraphs, and chapters, for which the Asia Society is deeply grateful. From the Asia Society staff, Hee Chung Kim diplomatically and graciously oversaw all of the administrative matters associated with producing the volume. Lai Montesca designed the cover for *Korea Briefing*. Many thanks to Patricia Loo and Doug Merwin at M.E. Sharpe, who have supported the series for so many years. We are also grateful to The Korea Society for allowing us to use their materials for the chronology that appears at the end of this volume. Most important, we thank the Korea Foundation, without whose support and generosity this volume would not have been possible.

Nicholas Platt
President
Asia Society

Robert W. Radtke
Vice President, Policy and
Business Programs
Asia Society

December 2001

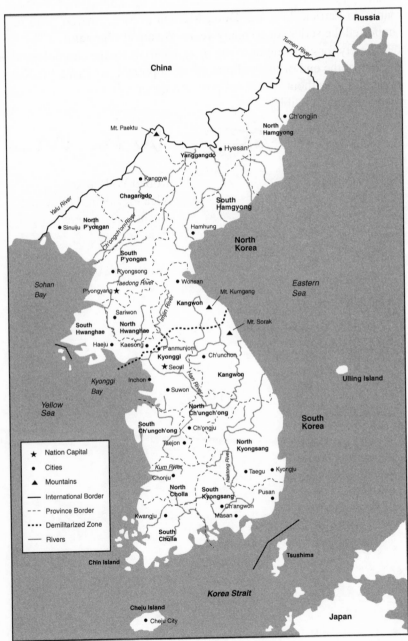

Korea

KOREA BRIEFING 2000– 2001

Introduction: Toward the Elusive Goal of Reconciliation and Reunification

Kongdan Oh and Ralph C. Hassig

In the previous edition of *Korea Briefing*, covering the period from 1997 to mid-1999 and subtitled "Challenges and Change at the Turn of the Century," the biggest challenge was the 1997 Asian financial crisis, and the most important change was the inauguration of President Kim Dae-Jung, the first president of the Republic of Korea (ROK, or South Korea) elected from an opposition party. With the support of the International Monetary Fund, President Kim inaugurated major reforms that put the Korean economy back on its feet within a year. But, as it turns out, that was only the first half of the economic story, because the economy stalled in 2000, and, three years after the financial crisis, South Korea's legacy of financial insecurity remains an important issue facing the electorate.

In the 1999–2001 time period covered in this volume, the economic story was old news, whereas the first inter-Korean summit of June 2001 was a truly new and spectacular event, eclipsing all other news stories. It is this story, with the economic story as a subtext, that is the focus of the following chapters. In one sense the summit meeting was a mirror image of the financial crisis. During the months following the economic crisis, the South Korean spirit was at low ebb, but the crisis was seemingly overcome within a year. In contrast, for several months following the inter-Korean summit, the South Korean spirit was at high tide, but hopes of an early reconciliation faded before the year was out.

The summit meeting gave the Korean people an emotional roller-coaster ride. Three subsequent reunions of separated families unleashed what the press called a "sea of tears" in the South; how much the North Korean public was moved is more difficult to tell in the absence of a free North Korean press. But these strong emotions were soon followed by disappointment and bitterness, as it became apparent that inter-Korean relations were once again taking a step backward. Although this was the first inter-Korean summit to be realized in fifty-five years of Korean division (a summit had been scheduled for August 1994 between South Korean president Kim Young-Sam and North Korean president Kim Il-Sung, but the North Korean leader died just weeks before the scheduled meeting), it was not the first time that the two Korean governments had talked to each other or signed agreements. The July 4, 1972, North-South Joint Communiqué and the Agreement on Reconciliation, Non-aggression, and Exchanges and Cooperation signed in late 1991 also included provisions for tension reduction and inter-Korean social contact, but neither agreement was implemented.

The Joint Declaration of June 15, 2000 differed from its predecessors in that it was signed by the leaders of the two Koreas. On the theory that the will of these two leaders could overcome the many obstacles to cooperation, expectations were high for the Joint Declaration, a case of hope triumphing over experience. It is difficult to determine the truth of this leader theory, insofar as the North Koreans never clearly indicated why they turned away from the declaration later in the year. Did conditions in South Korea and outside the Korean peninsula overwhelm the desires and intentions of North Korean leader Kim Jong-Il, or did Kim himself block implementation to elicit more aid or to keep the North Korean people from having too much contact with their brothers and sisters in the South?

The prospect of reconciliation and reunification raises many important issues. First, how prepared is South Korea politically, socially, and economically? The South Korean public, especially the younger generation, has become impatient with the old, leader-based regional party politics, which has failed to solve economic and social problems and is making only limited headway on Korean reconciliation. The public wants to see South Korea's political house put in order before embarking on the perilous journey of inter-Korean reconciliation. Nor is the South Korean economy in good shape, although it has improved since 1997. Millions of hardworking Koreans feel their livelihood is at the mercy of decisions made by government officials and big-business conglomerates, and subject to the unpredictable forces of the international economy. The promise of economic benefits from a reunified Korean economy lies in the distant future. Most South Koreans do not believe they are wealthy enough to extend substantial economic assistance to a North Korean regime that blocks inter-Korean contact and holds fast to failed economic policies.

And what of the North Korean people, for whom years of deprivation have lowered expectations? Surely they must be deeply skeptical of the Kim regime's recent call for them to renew the entire economy with the latest technology, which they must create for themselves. Rather than pursue such a seemingly impossible goal, they are preoccupied with living from day to day, and by that token they cannot achieve the kind of coordinated, nationwide economic advance that the Kim regime hopes for. Nor do they have the business experience or global mentality necessary to participate in the twenty-first-century international community.

Controlling their own destiny has long been the goal of all Koreans, nestled as they are among the world's great powers: China, Japan, and Russia, with a strong U.S. presence in the region. Despite brave words about achieving reunification by their independent efforts (most recently enunciated in the Joint Declaration), Koreans are well aware of the important role these surrounding powers play in Korean affairs.

The seven chapters in this seventh edition of *Korea Briefing* take up these themes and more, providing a 1999–2001 overview and analysis of important events that have occurred on the Korean peninsula as they relate to inter-Korean reconciliation and reunification. In the first chapter, Scott Snyder looks at how South Korean politics are involved in Korean reconciliation. He finds that the democratization of politics in the last decade has made politicians and the public active players in the formulation of North Korea policy, a fact that may not be sufficiently appreciated by President Kim Dae-Jung, and almost certainly not by Chairman Kim Jong-Il. Given the incompatibility of interests involved, is it possible for the South Korean government to craft a North Korea policy that appeals to the North Korean leaders as well as to the South Korean public? President Kim's pursuit of reconciliation without reunification is promising in principle but problematic in practice: can the two Korean peoples live side by side in separate societies, the one capitalist democratic and the other communist authoritarian?

In the second chapter, Doowon Lee brings readers up to date on the performance of the South and North Korean economies. Inter-Korean economic cooperation, primarily in the form of South Korean aid and investment for North Korea, is the engine driving Korean reconciliation, because that is what North Korea, which has veto power over reconciliation, demands. But North Korea's reluctance to reform its impoverished economy and open its borders is drawing sharp criticism from an increasingly vocal South Korean public, which is trying to cope with its own economic problems. How much is South Korea willing to contribute to the North Korean economy, and what will be demanded in return? How dependent is North Korea willing to become on South Korea, and at what point will the North Korean regime sacrifice its economy and the welfare of its people by refusing further economic cooperation and aid?

In the following chapter, we (Ralph Hassig and Kongdan Oh) search for signs of change in North Korea. Indications of political change, at least in the direction of openness and reform, are difficult to find. The economy has changed to a greater degree than the political system, but not enough to make a dent in North Korea's economic problems. New foreign relations, on the other hand, have been actively pursued. Two important questions need to be answered. First, do North Korea's baby steps toward openness and reform signal a strategic shift in the Kim regime's policies, or are these efforts merely reluctant and perhaps temporary adjustments made to accommodate changes in North Korea's environment? Second, to what extent can changes in North Korea be attributed to South Korea's engagement policy?

The authors of the next two chapters turn their attention to Korea's international environment. Samuel Kim begins his analysis by noting the complicated geographical position of Korea, situated among China, Japan, and Russia. Since China's normalization of relations with South Korea in 1992, Beijing has consistently pursued a two-Korea policy. After withdrawing into itself in the aftermath of the breakup of the Soviet Union, Moscow is now trying to develop its own two-Korea policy. Tokyo has maintained a workable relationship with Seoul, but after a decade of intermittent negotiations the former has failed to improve its relations with Pyongyang. What do Korea's surrounding countries want in terms of Korean reconciliation and reunification, and what can they do to influence the course of events on the Korean peninsula?

In the second chapter on Korea's international environment, Edward Olsen explores America's influence on inter-Korean relations. Olsen believes the United States owes it to the two Koreas on moral grounds to support reunification, for it was both the Americans and Russians who divided Korea after the Japanese occupation. But in Washington, politics trumps morality almost any day of the week, and policy makers in the George W. Bush administration are focused on how Korea policy supports their more important China and Japan policies. The Bush administration is also concerned about how North Korea, as a designated terrorist-sponsoring state and presumed nuclear and missile threat, can be deterred or disarmed. How can the United States pursue the specific security goals of eliminating North Korea's nuclear weapons and missile capabilities, along with the broader goals of making the world safe for democracy and capitalism, and at the same time support the Kim Dae-Jung government's engagement policy, which accepts North Korea for what it is?

The last two chapters examine policy issues of central importance to the process of reunification. Dieter Dettke views the challenges of Korean reunification with the hindsight of the German reunification experience. Koreans, in the North and the South, have carefully studied the German experience as a guide to the process, costs, and benefits of Korean reunification. Despite many obvious differences between the German and Korean cases, the German experience suggests important lessons for both Koreas. Dettke believes that President Kim Dae-Jung has learned that preparation for reunification may take decades, and that Chairman Kim has presumably learned that reunification will mean the defeat of communism. But what lesson should Koreans learn from the fact that reunification so suddenly came upon the German people, who were more surprised than prepared for it?

Reconciliation and reunification as policy choices translate into social interaction between the 46 million South Koreans and 23 million North Koreans. Kelly Koh and Glenn Baek's description of the experiences of North Korean defectors to the South illuminate the human side of reunification. The authors ask: Are South Koreans ready for the open North Korean borders that so many of them say they want? Is there a better way to introduce North Korean defectors to life in South Korea? Will the vaunted homogeneity of the Korean people be able to overcome the economic disparity between the two Koreas and a half-century of socialization under different political systems?

Underlying the fate of the reconciliation process is the stark fact that reconciliation and reunification involve serious trade-offs for all concerned. Whereas a reunified Korea will benefit in the long term from a stronger economy, greater security, an enhanced sense of national pride, and uncountable emotional benefits for reunited families, in the short- to medium-term, the South Korean people will have to bear significant economic costs. Presumably the North Koreans anticipate high costs as well. Kim Jong-Il and the elite must fear the loss of their political positions; they may even face indictment for crimes committed against the Korean people. Thanks to years of propaganda, the North Korean masses may fear enslavement by the American imperialists (whom they are told run South Korea for their own benefit). All North Koreans will have to swallow the costs of years of hardship in fruitless pursuit of a socialist society.

South Koreans are not prepared for reunification, although President Kim Dae-Jung has worked single-mindedly to put the reconciliation process on track, even while admitting that the two Koreas may not achieve reunification for another twenty years. It is more difficult to divine the reunification attitudes of North Koreans, but it seems likely that the majority of the poverty-stricken people in the DPRK would welcome an early reunification, while their leaders seek to avoid it at all costs unless it can be achieved on communist terms. As for the regional powers, despite their public pronouncements of support for a Korean-led reunification process, political considerations would suggest that no one is looking forward to dealing with the disruptions that a unified Korea would present to regional alignments and power balances.

It is as difficult to imagine that Korea could continue to be divided as it is to imagine that the division of the United States that triggered the Civil War could have been tolerated. But if reunification is inevitable, how can it be achieved? One approach would be to wait until North Korea collapses under the strains of its sick and misshapen economy and falls into the hands of South Korea. But the international community, through the use of foreign aid, is working against such a collapse. Another approach would be to force change in Pyongyang by actively undermining the present regime, but the chaos that would likely follow a regime collapse would impose high costs both on the North Korean people and their neighbors, including South Korea. If the world does not want to see North Korea collapse in economic failure, it certainly does not want to see it collapse in civil disorder.

A third approach is to support the Kim regime by providing aid and opportunities for economic cooperation with the hope that somehow the regime will loosen its control over the economy and the people. Exactly how this might happen is not clear, but something of this sort is happening gradually in China and Vietnam. One advantage of the engagement approach is that it reduces the likelihood of the collapse that nobody wants; another is that it preserves peace in the interim. A disadvantage is that it strengthens and rewards an evil regime; another disadvantage is that it condemns untold numbers of North Koreans to continued suffering, for a disproportionate amount of aid and foreign investment will benefit the ruling class.

To paraphrase the well-known saying, reunification will not be a tea party. The South Korean people realize this, and that realization gives them pause. Most North Koreans do not have sufficient information to make an informed decision. Koreans in both the South and the North would surely agree that in the process of seeking reunification the overriding concern must be to keep the peace. Despite an intense rivalry, the two Koreas have been at peace for almost fifty years—albeit a nervous peace, especially for the North Korean people—but peace nonetheless. Transforming this peace into forward motion toward reunification remains the elusive goal. The inter-Korean summit of June 2000 has promoted better inter-Korean communication, symbolically as well as concretely, even though the path toward reunification has yet to be charted.

The End of History, the Rise of Ideology, and the Pursuit of Inter-Korean Reconciliation

Scott Snyder

The entry into a new millennium, the marking of several key anniversaries, and the unexpected unfolding of an historic meeting between the top leaders of North and South Korea have all offered South Koreans extensive opportunity both to reflect on the past and to focus critically on the need to more fully develop social and political institutions in the future. A half-century after the outbreak of the Korean War in 1950, and roughly a decade following the end of the cold war and German reunification, it is inevitable that Korean reflections on the past might revolve around the issues of incompleteness, loss, and "dividedness" that have fundamentally defined Korean self-conceptions of national identity since the end of World War II. With the remarkable and historic first inter-Korean summit meeting between the Republic of Korea (ROK) President Kim Dae-Jung and North Korea's National Defense Commission chairman Kim Jong-Il in June 2000, Koreans were able to imagine in concrete terms the seemingly intangible possibility that internecine conflicts and national divisions might be overcome. However, the summit also revealed the incredible psychological and cultural distance created by over a half century of separation under opposing systems. By achieving the unprecedented meeting between heads of state, Kim Dae-Jung and his counterpart, Kim Jong-Il, together reawakened a cascade of previously unthinkable hopes and possibilities that came into direct conflict with long-held South Korean conceptions of an identity formed partially in opposition to the North with potentially revolutionary and deeply contested implications for South Korean politics and society.

The opinions expressed in this chapter are personal views and do not necessarily represent the views of The Asia Foundation. I would like to thank The Asia Foundation's Program Officer, Chun Sang Moon, for providing research assistance in the preparation of this chapter.

If the inter-Korean summit spurred new hopes for unification that had long been held in abeyance as unrealistic, it also starkly illustrated the extent to which the respective national agendas of the two societies have diverged during over one-half century of separation. South Korea's vibrant democracy, the achievements and the costs of perhaps the most compressed industrialization process the world has ever seen, and the psychological distance of a younger generation of Koreans from the experiences of division and war have raised questions about just where the project of Korean reunification stands on South Korea's national agenda and just how much South Korea's younger generation of emerging leaders will be willing to sacrifice from its own hard-won economic gains to rehabilitate a failed North Korean economy and political system. Soon, the mantle of leadership will pass for the first time to a post-Korean War generation that does not hold in its consciousness direct experience or memories of the terror, tumult, poverty, confusion, and desperation that accompanied the war.

The failure to develop a responsive South Korean political infrastructure commensurate with a truly democratic and just society is currently the single greatest source of public dissatisfaction within South Korean society. The question of how to deal with North Korea is clearly a second-tier concern for the average South Korean. At first glance, the explosive differentiation of South Korean social and interest groups and the development of civil society that has accompanied democratization suggest irreparable cracks, cleavages, and apparent loss of discipline that threaten social cohesion and upend the traditional vertical relationships on which social order had traditionally been based. "Creative destruction" in the social sphere between the contradictory impulses of tradition and democratization has in part given South Korean society incredible energy, dynamism, and flexibility to become early adapters in a rapidly changing globalized context. Ironically, most hopes for positive progress in inter-Korean reconciliation now hinge on the capacity of South Korea to embrace the leading edge of democracy, economic transparency, and responsive government as a means for winning the necessary domestic and international support to finance North Korea's economic rehabilitation and integration with the international community. South Korean social institutions, economic transparency, and political commitment to democratic institutions must be strong enough to be the "tugboat" that tows the North into the world by enabling the state to also accept greater economic transparency and political openness in its own system; otherwise, the entire project of national integration and eventual reunification will be fated to crumble in failure on the rocks of bitter internal conflict, division, and virtually inevitable failure. If the inter-Korean summit marked the entry onto the road to national reunification, it is likely to be a lengthy, bumpy, and wearying ride to the final destination—and one that will require intensive reflection, foresight, and planning to ensure that the results of such an integration process are commensurate with the high-flying hopes that have accompanied it.

This chapter will examine the historic and recent role of North Korea as an issue in South Korea's domestic politics; the South Korean public response to the historic inter-Korean summit and its implications for the sustainability of an inter-Korean reconciliation process; and the relative impact and importance of South Korea's democratic consolidation, economic prosperity, and development of social infrastructure necessary to support a fully differentiated, industrialized society for future progress in inter-Korean relations. It will conclude with an assessment of the inter-Korean summit and the sustainability of the inter-Korean reconciliation process and its possible impact on South Korean politics and society.

The Significance of North Korea as an Issue in South Korean Domestic Politics

Though most outsiders have become accustomed to the idea of two Koreas with their own strongly competitive respective national identities fighting it out for legitimacy on the international stage, the issue of Korea's national division and relationship with the "other" Korea has always been at its core both an intensely domestic and an intensely political issue that has influenced almost every aspect of Korean society. In part, this situation exists because even the development of separate states in North and South was driven on both sides by the need to build rival systems and national identities in opposition to the other. Just as the constitution of the Democratic People's Republic of Korea (DPRK) continues to hold out a revolutionary ideal that includes the overturning of the South's democratic system, the constitution of the ROK defines the state's raison d'être as "anticommunist" in steadfast opposition to the system of the North. The acceptable ideological spectrum of debate within South Korean politics has as a result consistently been limited to conservative or "anticommunist" positions. A favorite way of attacking opposition candidates has been to label them as left-leaning or overly sympathetic to North Korea. This tactic was a well-worn method that had been used for decades by the establishment to attack popular outsiders from the ruling clique, including longtime opposition leader Kim Dae-Jung.

The manipulation of policy toward North Korea to achieve domestic political gains can be traced as far back as the authoritarian leadership in South Korea under Park Chung-Hee and Chun Doo-Hwan. Although concerns about national security were at the fore in the 1970s and 1980s, these South Korean military leaders also found proposals for new dialogue with the North to be a politically useful tool for distracting the South Korean public from domestic problems or political tensions that threatened to boil over from time to time. Because the authoritarian government routinely restricted information about North Korea from the public, citing national security concerns, reunification proposals or bids for breakthroughs with North Korea were a convenient vehicle for distracting the South Korean public from focusing on their own social or political grievances or to seek legitimacy unavailable through other channels by trying to show that they were moving the nation forward in its aspirations for Korean reunification.[1]

Social changes that accompanied democratization have widened the spectrum of South Korean political debate, as well as drastically reduced the ability of the government to restrict or manipulate information about North Korea and raised public expectations of the role and performance of government. However, the hierarchical institutional structures and legacy of old-style partisan tactics and ossified tactical political maneuvering hewn during the authoritarian period remain holdover characteristics of a political structure that has not advanced sufficiently to satisfy Korean public expectations under democracy. South Korean public dissatisfaction with the democratic process remains as high as 30 percent in recent public opinion polls conducted by democracy specialists.[2] Perhaps the most obvious manifestation of the failure of political parties to shed the habits that accompanied authoritarianism is the well-entrenched perception that the role of the opposition is to oppose whatever

1. Chong Chong-Wook, "Has North Korea Really Changed?" *Korea Focus,* vol. 9, no. 3 (March–April 2001), p. 53.

2. Larry Diamond, "How People View Democracy: Findings from Public Opinion Surveys in Four Regions." Presentation to the *Stanford Seminar on Democratization,* January 11, 2001.

the government does, regardless of whether it is in the national interest, and to offer little in the way of new or alternative ideas or platforms for public consideration.

In addition, the changes in the relative power positions of North and South Korea resulting from the end of the cold war have shaped a South Korean government policy focused more on dialogue and engagement than confrontation toward North Korea. This transformation in approach was initially launched by former president Roh Tae-Woo's *Nordpolitik* policy of engagement toward the North in July 1988, and has been a consistent element of South Korea's policy ever since. Even during the intermittent periods of tension and crisis that characterized the North-South relationship under former president Kim Young-Sam, the South Korean government formally initiated food assistance to the North in 1995 (even this effort was motivated primarily by domestic politics and the mistaken impression on the part of Kim Young-Sam that such a "breakthrough" might assist his party's performance in local elections), and was indirectly criticized for failing to maintain adequate back-channel dialogue with the leadership in Pyongyang.[3] The government's attempts to engage North Korea effectively undermined the salience of the traditional terms of political debate over policy toward North Korea, particularly as public images of North Korea gradually focused not only on the North's continued efforts at confrontation, but also on the deprivation and need of the North Korean people in the context of the failure of the North's economic system. In the minds of most South Koreans, the North has come to occupy the dual identities of "main enemy" and dialogue partner—a formidable, persistent, and potentially deadly military threat, and a people in desperate need of assistance from the outside world.

South Korea's democratization has contributed to the gradual transformation of the position and role of North Korea in South Korean politics. North Korea is no longer solely negatively defined as the "other," which stands in opposition to whatever is "right" in the South Korean system, but has been transformed into a player within the system, or a "card," that may be used for tactical advantage in South Ko-

---

3. The November 1996 edition of *Wolgan Choson* included a series of articles describing the history of secret inter-Korean contacts. The theme of the issue may be seen as a not-so-subtle hint to then-President Kim Young-Sam that such contacts have traditionally been regarded as an important means by which to enhance and assure security and to avoid overheating in the inter-Korean relationship.

rean politics. Both North and South Korean political leaders now calculate how their roles and positions may be used to influence South Korean public perceptions and political outcomes, and much effort has been expended in attempts to cynically manipulate those outcomes to gain short-term political advantage. Ironically, the transition from being the litmus test that negatively defines the limits of acceptable political dialogue to being an object of maneuver and potential vehicle by which South Korean parties seek to gain tactical advantage might arguably be seen as a step toward Korean reunification, in the sense that North Korea's role in South Korean domestic politics is now an active rather than a passive one.

One example of the way in which the North has come to be a background player in South Korean domestic politics revealed itself in the form of the "*buk pung,*" or "North Wind," scandal that broke open in the months following President Kim Dae-Jung's (popularly known and hereafter referred to as "DJ") election as president of South Korea in December 1997. That scandal involved allegations that the former chief of the National Intelligence Service and representatives of the Grand National Party had tried during the 1997 presidential election campaign to make contact with the North Korean leadership and convince the North to create a military incident along the DMZ in the days preceding the election. Kwon Young-Hae, former director of the National Intelligence Service, was convicted of having undertaken efforts to paint DJ as pro–North Korean, including the staging of a press conference at which a Korean-American businessman alleged that North Korea had attempted to contribute to DJ's campaign fund. Such activities were designed to serve as a reminder of the importance of national security that might cause voters to hesitate before voting for National Congress for New Politics candidate Kim Dae-Jung, who had long been known for his forward-leaning views regarding the desirability of constructive dialogue with North Korea.[4]

Such maneuvering to instigate public awareness of the need for strong national security had been a tried-and-true tactic of the establishment that had usually worked to stimulate turnout in favor of the old ruling elite. For instance, North Korean DMZ incursions prior to the 1996

---

4. See Yonhap News Agency, "Prosecution Says Former Security Director Behind 'North Wind' Plot," April 30, 1998, and John Larkin, "Reforming the 'KCIA,'" *Asiaweek,* July 16, 1999, p. 31.

National Assembly elections had arguably given conservative then-ruling-party candidates a boost as Koreans focused on continuity of leadership during a time of potential danger. However, the *"buk pung"* scandal appears to have been the first instance in which it has become publicly known that the North was directly involved with the South Korean electoral process through contacts with party representatives who requested assistance to influence the outcome of a national election in South Korea. The incident also reveals an astonishing willingness to place party and personal interest above national interest. For the first time, North Korea became a potentially active player in South Korean politics, rather than simply an external observer that could only hope to influence the process from the outside. The headlines in the spring of 1998 regarding the *"buk pung"* scandal also were an indirect reminder of DJ's susceptibility to charges of having an agenda that is too friendly to the North, possibly at the expense of core national security interests.

With the election of Kim Dae-Jung as president, it was inevitable that relations with North Korea would come to the forefront of political discussion in South Korea. Even prior to his election, Kim Dae-Jung issued public appeals for dialogue with North Korea, signaling a major reversal from the policy of his predecessor, Kim Young-Sam, which had antagonized the North Korean leadership by comparing it to a "broken airplane" and had actively prepared for North Korea's collapse following the death of Kim Il-Sung. DJ, on the other hand, made dialogue with North Korea his primary preoccupation, and in his inaugural speech laid out three principles designed to form a new basis for policy toward North Korea based on hopes for cooperation rather than hewing to the rhetoric of zero-sum confrontation. DJ asserted that South Korea would "never tolerate armed provocation of any kind," that the South had no intention of absorbing the North, and that his administration would "actively pursue reconciliation and cooperation between the South and the North."[5]

In addition, DJ set aside the public declaration of any formulas for unification as an issue for future generations to resolve. Abandoning the rhetoric of cold-war confrontation, DJ set out to follow these principles consistently as a means of proving to the North that his administration was acting in good faith. To the extent that Roh Tae-Woo's *Nordpolitik* represented the first stage of a sustained attempt to pro-

---

5. Nicholas D. Kristof, "South Korea's New President Appeals to North to End Decades of Division," *New York Times*, February 25, 1998, p. 8.

mote reconciliation and cooperation with North Korea, the core principles of which were encapsulated in the landmark Agreement on Reconciliation, Nonaggression, Exchanges, and Cooperation negotiated in December 1991 (also known as the Basic Agreement), Kim Dae-Jung's Sunshine Policy merely represented the initiation of a second stage of government-to-government engagement with the North; however, his public articulation of a strategy that is no longer couched in "zero-sum" terms, but rather envisions a "win-win" outcome for North and South Korea, was something new—and contestable—in the South Korean political context. The concrete effort to implement the win-win component of the Sunshine Policy came to be known as the "separation of politics from economics." As President Kim Dae-Jung explained in his address to a joint session of the U.S. Congress during his first official visit to the United States as president, "We are going to promote cooperation in a wide range of areas under the principle of separation of politics and economics. . . . We hope such an approach gives North Korea psychological room to open its mind—and its doors."[6] Finally, DJ's articulation of his new policy has focused on the need to "dismantle the Cold War structure," an articulation of the need to transform the current state of tension on the Korean peninsula into a state of peaceful coexistence.

The South Korean public initially responded well to the articulation of a policy designed to promote cooperation and reduce tension with the North, particularly since the policy held out the prospect for achieving reunions of divided families and satisfied growing South Korean desires to respond to North Korea's humanitarian crisis. More than 90 percent of Koreans polled by the Ministry of Unification (MOU) at the time of DJ's inauguration showed support for efforts to achieve reunions of divided families, more active cultural and academic exchanges between North and South, and "active implementation of the Basic Agreement."[7] One year later, the support rate for the Sunshine Policy remained positive despite little apparent indication up to that point that the North was prepared to respond, with around 56–57-percent rating the policy as good or outstanding (positive, but down from 72 percent

---

6. Republic of Korea President Kim Dae-Jung, "Address to a Joint Session of Congress," June 10, 1998.

7. Bernama (Malaysian National News Agency), "S. Koreans Give Thumbs Up to President's N. Korean Initiatives," February 27, 1998 (from Lexis-Nexis news service).

in August 1998, according to a USIA poll), with only 18 percent criticizing the policy as poor.[8]

The Domestic Political Debate over the Sunshine Policy—Before the Summit

In seeking an expanded opening with North Korea, DJ was not in a position to play the role of U.S. president Richard Nixon, whose conservatism gave him the domestic credibility in the United States to meet with Chinese communists without significant opposition. Rather, DJ was a moderate who had always been painted as sympathetic to the North Koreans and therefore vulnerable to charges that he was overeager or naïve in his pursuit of reconciliation with North Korea. The political attack against DJ's approach as it unfolded focused in two core areas, in line with DJ's inauguration speech: (1) What is the appropriate price South Korea should pay for active pursuit of reconciliation and cooperation with North Korea? (2) Did the Sunshine Policy compromise national defense and national security in any way? To the extent that DJ appeared overeager or overly dependent on North Korean good will in his relentless pursuit of reconciliation, he would be vulnerable to attack by his political opponents.

Given the propensity of past leaders to try to use "breakthroughs" in North Korea policy for their own domestic political purposes, any dramatic progress in policy toward North Korea would automatically be greeted with skepticism among many in South Korea. This is the case for those who saw policy toward North Korea primarily as a tool for pushing a hidden, progressive social agenda, for achieving political dominance by changing the rules of the game, or as a magic bullet to gain widespread political support from the Korean people. This proved to be the major conundrum and the Achilles' heel of the Sunshine Policy: In proportion to the extent of its success, it would be greeted with cynicism by a South Korean public that had grown accustomed to the manipulation of North Korea policy for personal and domestic political gains. Thus, to the extent that the inter-Korean summit brought success and international acclaim to DJ himself, it deepened public cynicism at home regarding his motives in pursuing the Sunshine Policy.

---

8. As cited in David Steinberg, "The Republic of Korea's Sunshine Policy: Domestic Determinants of Policy and Performance," in Chung-in Moon and David Steinberg, eds., *Kim Dae-Jung Government and Sunshine Policy: Promises and Challenges* (Seoul: Yonsei University Press, 1999), p. 61.

a) Down Payment on Peaceful Coexistence: How Much Is Too Much?

The first practical test of DJ's overtures came in government-level fertilizer talks with North Korea held in Beijing in April 1998, the first such official talks since the negotiations that led to the Basic Agreement in 1991. This early meeting provided the North Koreans with an opportunity to assess how DJ's approach might differ from that of his predecessors and to determine whether there might be tangible economic benefits that the North might receive from DJ as a down payment on perceived hope for inter-Korean reconciliation. However, the new government faced a practical domestic political limit on what it could provide to North Korea. Through official channels, DJ could not offer more than the 150,000 tons of rice assistance provided by his predecessor Kim Young-Sam, or he would be subject to charges of appeasement. The talks broke down on the basis of South Korean attempts to link fertilizer aid with progress in addressing the divided family issue (by arguing that both were humanitarian issues). One interpretation of this result is that North Korea effectively rejected South Korean attempts to apply the principle of reciprocity to North-South negotiations.

To gain initial momentum in inter-Korean dialogue without being perceived as paying too high a price, the initiation of a policy of "separation of politics from economics" became a useful means of circumventing initial limits on the extent of generosity toward North Korea that might be seen as politically acceptable. This was particularly so because Hyundai founder and chairman Chung Ju-Yong had a long-standing interest in doing business with the North for sentimental reasons—North Korea was his birthplace. He had explored possible business relationships with the North as early as 1989, but had since been effectively cut out of opportunities to do business with the North as a result of his own involvement in politics as a 1992 presidential candidate and subsequent efforts by the eventual winner, Kim Young-Sam, to punish Hyundai for Chung Ju-Yong's presidential challenge through tax investigations.

Through Chung Ju-Yong's efforts, Hyundai became a convenient channel for the provision of South Korean assistance, first in the form of two shipments of 500 cattle each during the summer of 1998. By the autumn of 1998, Chung Ju-Yong had an unprecedented audience with Supreme Commander Kim Jong-Il through which he was able to consummate a large business deal. Estimates of the price for that meeting go as high as $150 million, including cattle, gifts, and whatever small change might have been in tycoon Chung's pockets on the day he happened to cross into North Korea. The deal projected that North Korea would receive almost $1 billion in cash transfers over the course of the next five years. The negotiation and achievement of the deal in the fall of 1998 constituted a major breakthrough in inter-Korean economic relations and provided much-needed momentum for DJ's policy of engagement just at the point when domestic criticism of that policy was increasing as a result of North Korea's failure to respond in any significant way to official overtures for dialogue.

The Hyundai deal itself was a source of controversy, although it provided a concrete mark of progress that helped to temporarily damp down Korean public skepticism about DJ's Sunshine Policy during late 1998 and the first part of 1999. Although the tours themselves were carefully guided affairs that provided virtually no people-to-people interaction with citizens of the North, the tours did buy time for DJ to seek further progress with the North by providing a beachhead for South Korean access to North Korea that was sufficiently novel in its initial stages to attract a great deal of attention and public interest. Within months, however, the tours proved to be unsatisfying because individual South Koreans were in the end unwilling to pay the tours' relatively high price (Hyundai had agreed to pay North Korean authorities approximately $300 per visitor as an entrance fee) simply for the privilege of walking on North Korean soil without the prospect of increased people-to-people interaction. The restrictions (and fines for noncompliance with North Korean rules) were regarded as excessive, and the project was ultimately not economically viable, requiring at least half a million visitors to reach the break-even point.

Nonetheless, the project did provide the first evidence that North Korea would respond to DJ's engagement efforts—at the right price. Hyundai transferred $25 million each month to a North Korean account in Macao from November 1998 through May 1999, but the terms of the contract reduced the monthly payment to $8 million per month in June 1999. This reduced monthly payment was accompanied by another crisis, the detention of a Korean housewife, Min Young-Mi, who was falsely accused of carrying out spy activity against the North. After approximately one week of negotiations, Ms. Min was released and the Hyundai operation was able to continue, with the establishment of new procedures between Hyundai and the North to avoid recurrence of such incidents. However, this incident also served to sully the image of the Hyundai project in the eyes of the South Korean public, in combination with the West Sea confrontation of June 1999 (to be dealt with more fully below). By early 2001, having paid $330 million to North Korea since December 1998 and under the pressure of mounting debt, even the monthly payment from the Hyundai Asan company to North Korea could not be sustained, and negotiations ensued to revise the terms of the deal.

The Kumgang Mountain Project represented an important step forward for the Kim Dae-Jung administration in its efforts to cooperate with North Korea, but the results were mixed and drew strong domestic criticism on a number of key fronts: (1) Chung Ju-Yong simply made an offer that North Korea could not afford to refuse, rather than being a vehicle for providing evidence of a fundamental change in attitude by North Korea toward dialogue and cooperation with the South; (2) the price of entry for the project was criticized as too high. The provision of cash, which could be used for any purpose—padding the personal bank account of Kim Jong-Il, military modernization of the war-fighting capabilities of the Korean People's Army (KPA), or strengthening the grip of the totalitarian North Korean system—was strongly criticized as wrongheaded by critics of DJ's engagement policy; (3) the Kumgang Mountain Project did not really represent a step forward in cooperation with the North because the barbwire fences and other restrictions provided only an opportunity to walk on North Korean soil, but hardly represented a significant advance in person-to-person exchanges and cooperation; (4) despite heightening opportunities for South Koreans to visit the North, the project actually inhibited other companies from developing economic cooperation with North Korea because the scale and generosity of the Hyundai project, which is not financially viable on its own, effectively set the bar too high for North Korean expectations and other projects to succeed; and (5) finally, despite the high-sounding idea of "separation of politics from economics," there was South Korean government support and guidance from the MOU. The "separation of politics from economics" ultimately was unsustainable precisely because there was not a solid economic rationale for the project, leading to an indirect government bailout of the bankrupt Hyundai Asan effort in June 2001 through the involvement in the project of the Korea National Tourism Organization.

Stimulated by experience with the Mount Kumgang tourism project, the core of the unfolding debate over the success or failure of the Sunshine Policy became an argument over the extent of reciprocity in inter-Korean economic exchanges, and whether incentives to North Korea constituted a "reward" for North Korean bad behavior. The argument of the South Korean government, as articulated by former Foreign Minister Hong Soon-Young, was as follows:

> The greatest criticism of engagement is that it is merely giving without taking. However, aside from purely humanitarian assistance, there is no such thing as one-way, indefinite giving in international relations. We have a clear purpose in trying to engage the north. But, "giving" and "taking" do not necessarily have to occur at the same time. There can be a time delay. The emphasis now is on giving, so as to demonstrate the goodness of our intentions to the north and to get engagement on track. Over time, however, engagement will be a give-and-take process.[9]

Only time would tell whether there would be a sufficient return on the down payments South Korea had made to purchase progress toward inter-Korean reconciliation.

b) Confrontation or Cooperation?: The Sunshine Policy and ROK National Security

One of the fundamental premises underlying DJ's Sunshine Policy has been confidence in South Korean national defense capabilities, along with the perception that a decade of economic contraction and the withdrawal of support for the DPRK from China and the former Soviet Union has resulted in serious difficulties for North Korean war-fighting capabilities. By the mid-1990s, North Korean military-training exercises had been seriously curtailed, with reports that North Korean MIG pilots were getting only a few hours of actual training per year due to fuel shortages. However, North Korean espionage operations against the South continued, and had been a source of major tension with the beaching of a North Korean spy submarine and crew on the South Korean coast in September 1996. Such espionage efforts did not cease in the early part of the Kim Dae-Jung administration, but the response to such efforts was much less strident in the spring and summer of 1998, despite DJ's pledge in his inauguration address "not to tolerate armed provocation of any kind." Two submarine incursions during 1998 received attention, but did not result in a fundamental change or

---

9. See Minister of Foreign Affairs and Trade Hong Soon-Young, "Changing Dynamics in Northeast Asia and the Republic of Korea's Engagement Policy Toward North Korea," The XXVIIth Williamsburg Conference, Cheju Island, ROK, May 7, 1999, published by the Asia Society, 1999, p. 20.

backtracking in South Korea's policy of engagement toward the North. Nonetheless, the failure to respond decisively to such incidents, though demonstrating consistency of purpose in DJ's approach to North Korea, left him open to criticism for failing to respond decisively to North Korean provocations.

The issue of North Korean military provocations came to a head in June 1999, with the onset of crabbing season and the crossing by North Korean fishing vessels, accompanied by military escort, of the Northern Limit Line (NLL), a boundary which has been defended by the South Korean government as the maritime extension and equivalent of the DMZ (the armistice did not actually set down or recognize the NLL, nor has it been formally recognized by the DPRK). After almost two weeks of successive incursions, increasing tension, and rising domestic concern and criticism of the North Korean incursions that had resulted in warnings and attempts to physically block or impede North Korean entry into waters on the South's side of the NLL, a firefight finally broke out, with the manually controlled North Korean vessels thoroughly outmaneuvered by the more modern automatically controlled weaponry of their South Korean counterparts. Although unacknowledged by Pyongyang, the North's fleet had been defeated; the most significant military confrontation between the two sides in decades had provided DJ with an opportunity to demonstrate the limits of tolerance for North Korean "armed provocation." Regardless of whether the North Korean incursions were intended as a test of the Kim Dae-Jung administration, the response showed that there were limits to South Korea's tolerance of North Korean incursions; it also revealed to the North the weaknesses of their own naval capacity against the South, and ironically provided a "bottom line" for the Sunshine Policy by showing limits beyond which the South would not be pushed.

The West Sea confrontation, in combination with the suspension of the Mount Kumgang tourism project due to the detention of Min Young-Mi, led to a barrage of criticism against the Sunshine Policy on grounds that the focus on reconciliation with the North had the effect of weakening South Korean military deterrence, giving North Korea new opportunities to exploit South Korea's lack of political resolve by sending mixed signals about the mission. Opposition Grand National Party leader Lee Hoi-Chang criticized the Kim Dae-Jung administration's "lukewarm attitude" and the party spokesman offered the criticism that the incursion revealed the weak point of Seoul's security and North Korea policy, warning that the government's indecisive and lukewarm response to the incursion of North Korean ships showed a failure to give top priority to national security over other issues.[10] Opposition-party members have further argued that despite the eventual decisive action taken by the ROK military, the toleration of provocation is a cause and a result of a weakening of national defense capabilities and of the National Intelligence Service (NIS) under DJ. In addition, the opposition has continuously speculated on the possibility of a "secret deal" or major under-the-table financial remuneration to North Korea as part of the implementation of the Kim Dae-Jung administration's policy toward North Korea.

c) Breakthroughs with North Korea as a Tool for Domestic Political Advantage

The surprise announcement of a summit with North Korea on April 10, 2000, was a political bombshell in South Korea, the impact of which was heightened by the fact that the National Assembly elections were scheduled to take place only seventy-two hours later, on April 13, 2000. The timing of the announcement might have represented a shared calculation on the part of the respective leaderships in North and South Korea that such an announcement would have significant political repercussions for the ruling party and would strengthen both parties in their efforts to develop momentum for cooperation in key areas.

In fact, the widespread assumption (and suspicion) in South Korea was that the bombshell announcement would have a major impact on the outcome of the National Assembly elections to be held three days later. The projected performance of the ruling Millennium Democratic Party was revised upward, and initial exit-poll information released by the major television networks upon the close of polling unanimously declared that the ruling party had won a decisive National Assembly majority. However, once the ballots were actually counted, the result was quite different.[11] There were many close districts, especially in Seoul, but the opposition Grand National Party did surprisingly well, and came just a few seats short of capturing a National Assembly majority despite the surprise that had accompanied the summit announcement. The biggest loser in the aftermath of the election

---

10. *Korea Times*, "Hawks, Doves Clash on Both Sides of DMZ," June 13, 1999 (as reported by Lexis-Nexis news service).

11. For an assessment of why the exit polls failed, see "Exit Polls Fail to Predict Election Outcome," *Choson Ilbo* (Internet version-WWW) in English, April 14, 2000 (FBIS Doc. no.: KPP20000414000131).

Figure 1   **Sixth General Elections: April 3, 2000**

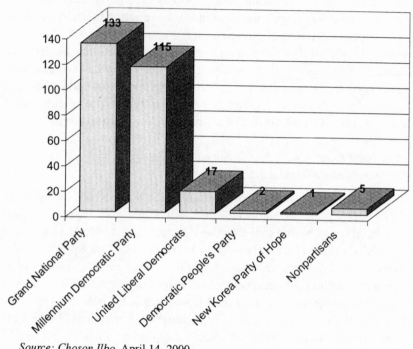

Source: Choson Ilbo, April 14, 2000.

Figure 2   **Exit Poll Accuracy** (Regional Seats Only)

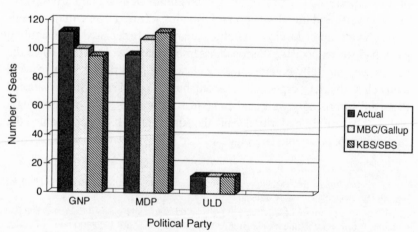

Source: Choson Ilbo, April 14, 2000.

Table 1

Party Support

Region	Total	GNP	MDP	ULD	DPP	NKPH	REP	Dem. Labor P.	Youth Prog. P.	Indep.
Seoul	4,038,289	1,747,482	1,819,735	189,185	52,265	3,862	176	39,568	121,418	64,598
Pusan	1,498,691	904,040	225,160	24,356	223,328	1,449		8,020		112,338
Taegu	931,768	585,974	101,854	95,305	58,163	132	522	4,287		85,531
Inchon	908,502	378,903	368,924	110,120	11,141			6,906	3,664	28,844
Kwangju	490,588	16,144	342,888	1,503	2,015	4,620				128,038
Taejon	494,751	115,186	140,745	169,683	4,607			10,852		49,058
Ulsan	398,534	166,186	38,189	12,277	15,735			68,749		97,398
Kyunggi	3,338,248	1,304,676	1,365,304	413,362	52,426	1,613	3,252	40,909		156,706
Kangwon	689,907	266,136	251,571	70,280	45,076	1,037				55,807
N. Choong	630,364	193,089	197,459	185,920	4,143	5,227				44,526
S. Choong	814,070	141,684	244,128	319,066	9,279	52,678		7,391		39,844
N. Cholla	848,849	30,442	555,462	28,675	1,811					232,459
S. Cholla	1,004,589	41,284	666,697	16,029	4,797					275,782
N. Kyungsang	1,283,448	673,537	188,063	180,031	129,194	4,318				108,305
S. Kyungsang	1,286,285	690,973	151,981	41,948	80,358	2,562		36,579		281,884
Cheju	247,857	109,623	122,465	1,591	1,085					13,093
Total	18,904,740	7,365,359	6,780,625	1,859,331	695,423	77,498	3,950	223,261	125,082	1,774,211

was Kim Jong-Pil's Democratic Liberal Party, which only garnered seventeen seats, not enough to form a parliamentary working group.

Based on these results, one can only assume that the summit announcement had either a negligible or a possibly negative impact on the performance of the ruling party. Perhaps the perception that the timing of the summit was politically motivated led to the expression of deepened regional or anti-DJ feeling as part of the vote, or voters might have presumed that the summit was either a result of overeagerness on the part of DJ and/or had suspicions that an under-the-table deal would have been necessary to achieve such a political victory. Or, perhaps the North Korea "card" has been played so many times as part of election positioning that it was no longer a salient issue for voters, who are much more concerned about their own immediate domestic situation, including the health of the Korean economy, the capacity of the government to deliver needed services, and other issues. Maybe voters were more concerned about immediate problems than about the grand unresolved question of reconciliation on the Korean peninsula.

One result of the strong showing of the Grand National Party was to suggest the need for caution and a bipartisan approach to the summit. Riding high on a better-than-expected National Assembly–election result, opposition leader Lee Hoi-Chang immediately called for the ruling party to observe the "principle of reciprocity," asserting that "investment in North Korea should be implemented under the reciprocity principle, which calls for change and openness in the North corresponding to inter-Korean dialogue and cooperation."[12] By choosing not to oppose the summit though expressing caution about the pace of the process, Lee Hoi-Chang took on a "balancing" and restraining role, cooperating in areas that gained overwhelming support from the Korean people, though playing an obstructionist role on issues where Korean public opinion appeared to be divided. Despite efforts by DJ to woo opposition representatives to join the official delegation to Pyongyang, the opposition decided eventually not to send a representative. This failure to lock in bipartisan support and representation would prove a major disappointment and failure that has jeopardized the consolidation of inter-Korean reconciliation under DJ. The deep divisions among Korean political parties and the public over the significance of the summit and its accom-

---

12. "ROK Opposition May Attempt to Slow Engagement with DPRK," *Korea Herald* (Internet version), April 15, 2000 (FBIS Document no.: KPP20000414000142).

plishments limit prospects for the sustainability of the current reconciliation effort and provide the North with yet another opportunity to exploit political divisions in the South for the sake of maximizing its own position and interests. South Korean public opinion and the domestic political environment in Seoul—influenced both by failures to effectively deliver government services on the part of the Kim Dae-Jung administration and by the broader international environment—have emerged as major factors to be considered in determining the pace of rapprochement with North Korea. South Korean public opinion, rather than the relative eagerness of the incumbent government to strike a deal with the North, has become the lowest common denominator to which Pyongyang must respond if it hopes to give momentum to the peace process, or at least to hold on to the material benefits bestowed on it both from ROK government sources and from the largesse of South Korean NGO efforts to provide help to the North Korean people.

Assessing the Summit and Its Impact on South Korean Politics

An entire nation was riveted to the TV screen on a sunny June morning when DJ made his remarkable visit to Pyongyang. Koreans were astounded at the personal greeting and joint review of KPA troops that Defense Commission Chairman Kim Jong-Il offered upon DJ's arrival at Sunan Airport. These scenes were replayed countless times during and following the inter-Korean summit, but would the images of greeting etched indelibly in the consciousness of every South Korean TV-watcher lead to a lasting change in relations or simply be an ephemeral stage show unaccompanied by substantive progress or institutionalization of an inter-Korean reconciliation process?

The summit and its immediate success posed the greatest challenge for the leadership of the opposition Grand National Party, which, despite its electoral victory of April, had very real worries that the inter-Korean summit and its aftermath would remake the South Korean political landscape in unpredictable ways. Indeed, the weeks following the summit were dominated by a nationwide debate over every aspect of the summit and the North-South declaration, the terms of which generally reflected the themes of price, implications for South Korean national security, and implications for domestic political structure and politics outlined in the previous section. As this debate unfolded, the opposition-party leadership monitored public opinion closely and maneuvered as a counterweight to the euphoria of the ruling party and ROK government. It is worth examining closely the tactical and strategic counterarguments of the opposition as they have unfolded as a means of better understanding how the parties have interpreted trends in South Korean public opinion that will have a critical impact on the pace and direction of the inter-Korean reconciliation process. Also, the restraining role of the opposition and its attempt to counter public perceptions of overeagerness on the part of the DJ government—in combination with the transition from the Clinton to the Bush administration in Washington—have served to give the opposition leadership a great deal of influence on prospects for the Sunshine Policy, which will likely be enhanced as part of the domestic political debate in the run-up to the December 2002 South Korean presidential elections.

a) Opposition Critique of the Summit and Its Aftermath

Reflecting strong public support generated in the immediate aftermath of DJ's visit to Pyongyang and the signing of the inter-Korean Joint Declaration, opposition-party leader Lee Hoi-Chang offered restrained congratulations to DJ upon the president's return to Seoul, while also attempting to lay down a number of important markers and guidelines for pursuing inter-Korean reconciliation in the future. The markers that most clearly defined the opposition position and offered indirect criticism of the summit outcome were as follows: (1) failure of the Joint Declaration to explicitly address tension reduction and establishment of peace; (2) need to pursue reunification policy transparently based on principles of democracy and market economy; (3) failure to discuss South Korean prisoners of war remaining in the North though conceding the release of long-term political prisoners in South Korea; (4) need for reciprocity and transparency in economic dealings with the North; and (5) the need for consultation and deliberation in the National Assembly. Although pointing out additional areas not addressed by the Joint Declaration, Lee emphasized the opposition's passively skeptical attitude toward the North's capacity to fulfill promises made as part of the Joint Declaration ("actions speak louder than words").[13]

As the implementation of the Joint Declaration unfolded, Lee defied

---

13. Grand National Party President Lee Hoi-Chang, remarks made by Grand National Party President Lee Hoi-Chang at a press conference in Seoul, June 19, 2000, on the outcome of the recent summit meeting between South and North Korea (as posted on GNP Web site: www.hannaradang.or.kr).

the hard-line views of some within his party to take a moderate stance, avoiding criticism of DJ in areas where both public support and practical results could be identified. However, Lee also attempted to hold both DJ and the North accountable to a cautious and pragmatic vision of the future not driven either by euphoria or pure obstructionism. Where public opinion doubted the price or pace of reconciliation, Lee voiced the need for restraint and caution, but he did not oppose the process itself or criticize DJ for pursuing reconciliation with North Korea. "As the president of the opposition party, I will make every effort so that the opportunities for dialogue and cooperation, that were opened up with such difficulty by the inter-Korean summit, will bear fruit. Likewise, I will not spare any effort to make constructive criticism and offer advice if there is any problem in the basic principle of inter-Korean relations or in the way it is implemented."[14] Recognizing the achievement of the summit, family reunions, and other cultural exchanges, Lee Hoi-Chang consistently singled out for criticism the failure of the DJ administration to define fully the objectives of the Sunshine Policy; the failure of the summit to address the conventional security situation; the need to use economic assistance strategically as a tool for inducing reforms in North Korea's system; and the need to pursue inter-Korean relations with a spirit of reciprocity. Lee also criticized euphoria and empty symbolism as by-products of the summit: "We must not put emphasis on a cozy South-North relationship for its own sake; rather we seek a relationship that is productive in solving substantive problems of interest to both our countries. Nor do we seek reunification at any cost; rather we pursue a just society for all Koreans."[15]

b) *Domestic Opinion and the Pace of Inter-Korean Relations*

The inter-Korean summit stimulated a nationwide debate in South Korea over the potential impact of reconciliation with the North on institutions and society within South Korea. The prospect of institutional and social change is contentious within South Korean society because it could threaten long-standing vested interests on both an elite and an institu-

---

14. GNP President Lee Hoi-Chang, "Evaluation of Inter-Korean Relations and Future Tasks Following the South-North Summit," remarks at Yonsei University, September 5, 2000 (as posted on GNP Web site: www.hannaradang.or.kr).

15. Lee Hoi-Chang, "Toward Peace and Unification of the Korean Peninsula," *Korea Times*, November 1, 2000.

tional level and because of the difficulties of calibrating necessary institutional change with the pace of rapprochement with the North. In fact, the prospect of rapprochement with North Korea under Kim Jong-Il is truly revolutionary if one considers that, strictly speaking, President Kim Dae-Jung's visit to Pyongyang was a violation of the National Security Law. DJ's statement upon his return from Pyongyang that now there "will be no more war" on the Korean peninsula elicited strong reactions within Korean society and stimulated heated debate on controversial domestic issues related to defense spending, policy, and the question of whether North Korea should be categorized as the "main enemy" in its Defense White Paper. The primary South Korean interlocutor in preparations for the summit was the chief of the National Intelligence Service, Lim Dong-Won, who appeared publicly with Kim Dae-Jung and Kim Jong-Il in Pyongyang, a fact that has stimulated a debate over the future of the National Intelligence Service's intelligence-collection activities directed toward North Korea. The role and purposes of the National Intelligence Service became a matter of controversy, as the NIS assumed the dual roles of primary interlocutor with the North and the chief institution devoted to counterintelligence efforts against North Korea.

The issue of how North Korea should be portrayed in South Korean textbooks has also been raised in the aftermath of the summit with the change in the overall image of the North as a potential partner standing in uneasy coexistence with North Korea's image as an enemy. Surveys of South Koreans show a generational gap in attitudes toward North Korea and prospects for national unification, with older Koreans more skeptical of North Korea but more desirous of reunification, whereas younger Koreans recognize the North as a dialogue partner, but are apathetic about prospects for reunification.[16] How and whether the South Korean media should report critical remarks about North Korea has also become a contentious issue for debate in Seoul, leading to the dismissal of the president of the South Korean Red Cross in December 2000 for remarks that were critical of North Korea and unleashing a broader and more generalized confrontation between the media and the government over management practices and editorial intimidation through a massive tax-probe of the media sector conducted by the National Tax Office

16. Han Mann-Gil, "Role of Education in National Unification," *Korea Focus*, vol. 9, no. 2 (March–April, 2001), pp. 133–46.

in the first half of 2001. Some journalists have even voiced suspicions that the tax-office probe represents an attempt to "tame" the media so as to squelch public opposition or criticism in anticipation of a return visit to Seoul by Chairman Kim Jong-Il.

If the process of reconciliation with North Korea represents the beginning of "the end of history," to borrow Francis Fukuyama's phrase describing the ideational and ideological impact of the end of the cold war, it also means for Korean politics the beginning of ideology as a factor in a national political debate heretofore constrained by anticommunism as de facto prerequisite for participation in political dialogue. Thus, a domestic political debate that has for decades been driven by personality and regionalism is now being infused with ideology just at the moment when in other parts of the world ideology is on the decline as a political force. Ideological division has come to the surface most strongly in initial debates over whether the National Security Law should be revised and in comments made by an opposition-party lawmaker characterizing the Kim Dae-Jung government as a wing of the North Korean Workers' Party. Immediately following the summit in South Korea, there was a torrent of debate over the implications of the summit for South Korean politics, the educational system, the social adaptations that would be required as part of reconciliation with the North, and expectations for what North Korea should do in response. This debate has continued in the context of the impending visit of Kim Jong-Il to Seoul through a campaign to require the Northern leader to apologize for North Korea's invasion of the South and to admit responsibility for terrorist acts attributed to the North such as the bombing deaths of more than half of the South Korean cabinet in Rangoon in the mid-1980s and the downing in 1987 of a Korean Airlines plane prior to the Seoul Olympics.

The ideological division over the intent of engagement is also clearly revealed in rationales that have been put forward for pursuing Kim Dae-Jung's Sunshine Policy. President Kim Dae-Jung himself almost always presents a "liberal" rationale for pursuing engagement with North Korea, arguing that the leadership in Pyongyang has finally recognized the "true intentions" of the Sunshine Policy and has decided that it is possible to trust South Korea. According to this rationale, unconditional giving to North Korea is an essential vehicle for showing good faith, and eventually North Korea will also respond in good faith as trust has been built between the two sides. However, there is also a "realist" rationale for opening a political dialogue as a vehicle for inducing economic dependency and thereby de-fanging the North. This line of argumentation appeals to most South Korean conservatives, but is almost never used by the ROK government, no doubt partially in recognition that such a rationale will only intensify North Korea's mistrust and hesitancy to engage with South Korea. Thus, it is important to recognize that in many respects, Kim Dae-Jung's policies toward North Korea have built on past South Korean efforts to engage with North Korea since President Roh decided to pursue *Nordpolitik* in 1988; however, the liberal justification for engagement is particularly provocative to South Korean conservative elites who suspect that such arguments may represent the leading edge of a progressive ideological wave, possibly revolutionizing South Korean politics and undermining national security.

Although President Kim Dae-Jung's leadership in relentlessly pursuing engagement with North Korea has been critical in achieving an opening in high-level dialogue with Kim Jong-Il, South Korean public opinion remains the critical factor in determining the pace, substance, and sustainability of the engagement process. From May through September 2000, the rapid pace of inter-Korean developments garnered strong support, but also made many Koreans nervous that things were moving too fast; on the other hand, the relative standstill in inter-Korean relations that has developed through the first half of 2001 has yielded higher levels of skepticism about North Korean intentions and disappointment in DJ's management of North Korean policy. The summit unquestionably succeeded in temporarily changing public perceptions of Kim Jong-Il, according to a survey conducted by *Donga Ilbo*.

Prior to the summit, more than 34 percent of Koreans surveyed viewed Kim Jong-Il as a dictator, compared to less than 10 percent immediately following the summit; more than 97 percent indicated that they would welcome a visit by Kim Jong-Il to Seoul.[17] Korean expectations for Korean reunification also rose as a result of the summit, with more than 71 percent of Korean students expressing optimism about the possibility of unification in July 2001 compared to only 59 percent a year earlier.[18] Public opinion polls from the end of 2000 show that almost 80 percent of the

17. *Donga Ilbo*, May 31; June 15, as cited in Lee Geun, "Political and Economic Consequences of the Inter-Korean Summit," presented at the 2001 KAIS International Conference, June 22–23, 2001, p. 11.

18. Han, *Korea Focus*, p. 134.

public supports a policy of cooperation and reconciliation with North Korea, however, they do not necessarily support DJ's generous approach to the North. President Kim's support is running in the low-30-percent range, the equivalent of his core base of regional support from the Cholla region.[19]

One year following the summit, a June 11, 2001, *Choson Ilbo* survey showed that 50.1 percent of those surveyed believe that North Korea has not changed much and that 43.9 percent think that the Kim Dae-Jung government is not managing policy toward the North well, compared to 33.9 percent who believe that the government is doing well.[20] One factor that has influenced a decline in public support for the Sunshine Policy is South Korea's own economic slowdown. Another is the perception that domestic issues, including labor-management issues, public health care, anticorruption efforts within the government bureaucracy, and so forth, have not been well handled by the Kim Dae-Jung administration.

South Korean Democratic Institutionalization and Economic Restructuring

Implications for the Future of North-South Relations

The mixed and uneven record of interaction between North and South Korea in the year following the inter-Korean summit has starkly dramatized the gap between competing systems and separate societies in the South and North. It has also underscored the current incapacity of South Korea to absorb on its own the considerable social and economic costs associated with North Korea's rehabilitation and integration with the South and with the international community. By looking North, many in South Korea have become more aware of the need to consolidate economic and political institutions so as to make them fully capable of withstanding the shocks that may accompany reunification. Strong social and political institutions and continued economic restructuring will be necessary prerequisites if the South is to successfully attract from the

---

19. Yi Tong-Hyon, "Reporter's Note: North Korea Policy Should Stick to Principles," *Joongang Ilbo* (Internet version in Korean), January 2, 2001, FBIS Document no. KPP20010102000094. Gallup Poll Survey on Political Support, December 26, 2000.

20. Lee Geun, "Political and Economic Consequences," p. 11.

international community the support necessary to effectively move in the direction of Korean reunification.

South Korean domestic political support is necessary to effectively pursue reconciliation with North Korea. However, South Korean generosity and support for the Korean government's policies toward the North depend on the extent to which South Korea's own social institutions are working. The widespread public perception that DJ has neglected South Korea's domestic agenda by failing to effectively manage domestic health-care reform, labor-management relations, and the fallout from corporate restructuring, or to gain bipartisan political support necessary to move his agenda, has had a corrosive effect on South Korean support for DJ's Sunshine Policy. The economic slowdown of the fall of 2000 had a doubly negative effect on the momentum of inter-Korean relations. It dried up the economic benefits to the North of reconciliation with the South, also limiting South Korean generosity as a result of the more difficult economic situation in South Korea.

The Mount Kumgang tourist project—endangered following the death of Hyundai founder and chairman, Chung Ju-Yong—could no longer provide subsidies as a result of corporate restructuring, and tourist demand has dropped by at least half since the project began in 1998. Plans to assist North Korea's economic rehabilitation through infrastructure projects such as the inter-Korean railway project also ground to a halt as a result of North Korean noncooperation, further dampening public enthusiasm for investment in North Korea. DJ had pledged in his "Berlin Declaration" in February 2000 that South Korea would provide assistance to rebuild North Korea's economic infrastructure, but his government has struggled through the spring and summer of 2001 to find a way to meet North Korean demands for 2 million kilowatts of energy assistance put forward at ministerial-level negotiations in December 2000. The South Korean public showed a wary reaction to additional giving to North Korea without concrete evidence that the investment would yield a return in the form of concrete steps toward peaceful coexistence. The South proposed a survey of North Korea's current energy needs, but no cost-effective solution to the North's energy problem has yet revealed itself. Moreover, the North Korean proposal raised American concerns that the request for energy from South Korea was a way of sidestepping North Korean nuclear obligations to give up its nuclear program under the Geneva Agreed Framework.

Moreover, as a result of his near-exclusive focus on North Korea, DJ has, in many respects, deepened long-standing political divisions within South Korea rather than healed them. Although Koreans were proud that a Korean was finally awarded a Nobel Prize, they also interpreted DJ's efforts to gain progress with North Korea in the absence of a full-fledged, lasting North Korean transformation as evidence of his own personal ambition, rather than as a project designed to bring lasting national benefit to the Korean peninsula. As one Korean office worker said to a reporter shortly after it was announced that DJ would receive the Nobel Prize, "I'm glad he won the prize this year. Now we no longer have to think he's doing everything just to win the prize."[21]

There is continuing criticism that regionalism and favoritism remain highly sensitive factors in determining who is favored to take plum jobs in government, the media, and business. To the extent that political and social structures and institutions such as the media and the National Assembly, and the policy-making process itself, remain opaque and susceptible to perversion in pursuit of individual gains rather than fulfilling public service, the public remains frustrated, disillusioned, and increasingly cynical and dissatisfied. For instance, efforts to reform the press have been widely interpreted as motivated by a desire to constrain the South Korean media from both reporting truthfully about the North and from making criticisms of government policy. A positive sign for South Korean democratization is that ubiquitous complaints about government attempts to curb critical comments or dampen free speech are refreshing evidence of the extent to which it is impossible to muzzle political criticism in South Korean society today.

As the effort to achieve inter-Korean reconciliation through negotiated cooperation has unfolded, a fundamental dilemma has emerged that underlies the process: South Korea's democratization process has imposed limits on the ability to negotiate with the North over matters that impinge on the freedoms of the South's social and political structure. Thus, confederation or federation proposals are likely to be unworkable, or unacceptable, if they involve compromising the freedoms that have accompanied South Korea's own democratization. In fact, South Korea is more likely to end up being a "tugboat" in the reunification

---

21. Don Kirk, "As the Spotlight Shifts, Doubts Cloud Seoul," *International Herald Tribune*, October 26, 2000, p. 9.

process in the sense that it will be increasingly necessary to assure South Koreans that their own political and social freedoms and quality of life are not being impinged upon in order to gain widespread support for the process of moving toward national unification—if indeed that objective is to be fruitfully pursued and achieved.

Likewise, the agenda for South Korea's economic restructuring has become inextricably tied to the success or failure of the Sunshine Policy. The fate of Hyundai's Kumgang Mountain Project is the best proof that this is the case, because it demonstrates that the economic viability of investment in North Korea ultimately will overshadow political motivations as drivers for providing the inputs necessary to stimulate investment in North Korea. Moreover, foreign capital is unlikely to be available for investment in North Korea without assurances that the economic risk factors have been lowered to a tolerable degree through enhanced standards of transparency and corporate governance among South Korean firms that intend to do business in North Korea. Under current conditions, most international investors would probably interpret intent of major South Korean firms doing business in the North in the absence of an economically viable plan as an irrational and unwarranted assumption of new risk, with no reasonable prospect of return on investment. And the views of international investors are by no means trivial as South Korean *chaebols* remain highly leveraged and must also be increasingly sensitive to foreign investor sentiment as a result of the rising role that foreign investors have been allowed to play in the Korean equities market.

In the short term, the Hyundai project has been directly threatened by economic restructuring efforts as the financial support from sister companies in the Hyundai family is no longer available in the form of cross-share holdings necessary to spread and hide the burden of financial losses generated by the project itself. However, the realization that the project is not financially sustainable has resulted in negotiations that have made progress in the direction of arrangements that may be more in line with economic reality. As part of negotiations in the spring and summer of 2001 that had resulted from Hyundai Asan's nonpayment of the promised monthly fee to the North, both sides agreed to take measures designed to stimulate tourism and to rationalize the project itself, including the lowering of the price of the tour by agreeing in principle to the opening of a land route to Mount Kumgang. The North also agreed to accept its payments on the basis of the number of tourists who visited the tourist site rather than in the form of a monthly fee, regardless of how many tourists participated.[22]

This move in the direction of a more economically viable arrangement between Hyundai Asan and its counterparts from North Korea's Asia Pacific Peace Committee represents a major positive step in North Korea's understanding of the need for the project to be economically viable. However, the deal was also accompanied by provisions that have raised South Korean concerns, as the Mount Kumgang project was in essence partly bailed out by the South Korean government, which authorized the Korea National Tourism Organization (KNTO) to take on responsibilities for implementing the tourism project as a partner of Hyundai Asan as well as to provide financial resources, including $22 million in back dues owed to the North, as a joint venture partner in the project.[23] The South Korean public has been highly critical of these arrangements, which essentially constitute a government bailout of the project and directly contradict the idea of "separation of politics from economics." The DJ government had emphasized from the start of its administration as a key element of its policy toward North Korea. Likewise, Hyundai's economic difficulties have stimulated the Korea Land Corporation (Koland) to take a major role in coordinating any future progress in implementing the industrial-park project in Kaesong that had originally been negotiated by authorities from Hyundai.

Assessing the Inter-Korean Summit:
Is a Korean Peace Process Sustainable?

The inter-Korean summit is clearly a landmark event on the path toward resolution of inter-Korean confrontation, and has allowed unprecedented inter-Korean exchanges in the form of divided family reunions and cultural exchange. At the same time, however, the summit and its aftermath have starkly illustrated the differences between the two Korean systems and the limits that have developed on the two sides as a result of more than fifty years of confrontation and division. Although the summit has opened the way for unprecedented levels of inter-Korean exchange and cooperation, those levels remain limited as both sides seek

---

22. *Hyundai Asan Newsletter,* June 2001, www.hyundai-asan.com, pp. 1–2.
23. *Hyundai Asan Newsletter,* July 2001, www.hyundai-asan.com, p. 1.

to preserve their respective political systems from the aspects of cooperation that could be threatening to core system values on each side.

Both Kim Dae-Jung and Kim Jong-Il clearly have a large stake in pushing forward the reconciliation process they have led. Most remarkable is that both Kims have become politically dependent on each other for cooperation to be able to convince internal critics at home that the process is real. By the same token, many of the measures that have been used in the initial stages of the process have appealed to symbolism and emotion; the core issues of confrontation have not yet been dealt with in concrete terms—nor can they be easily or quickly resolved. North Korea's own recognition of the severity of its economic needs, the political consolidation of Kim Jong-Il, and South Korean president Kim Dae-Jung's consistent and principled pursuit of engagement on terms that would provide North Korea with tangible economic benefits were all necessary conditions for a breakthrough in inter-Korean dialogue. However, the process of moving toward reconciliation will involve considerable institutional adaptation and social accommodation on both sides, a process that, if the German case is any example, is likely to take decades.

There is also a recognition that President Kim's power is beginning to wane as he enters the last year of his administration. In this regard, serious concerns have emerged about the political sustainability of the inter-Korean reconciliation process in South Korea. Despite having achieved successes beyond what almost all Koreans would have imagined possible at the beginning of the year 2000, success has bred not political credit for Kim Dae-Jung but rather the development of higher expectations and the need to initiate more substantive projects that will both induce real change in North Korea and show clearly that North Korea no longer need be considered as an adversary. Despite indications that the opposition party would also favor engagement with North Korea in some form, South Korea simply cannot afford the levels of generosity that have been proffered to the North in the initial stages. North Korea's insatiable demands for assistance are likely to reveal clearly the limits of South Korean capacity to render humanitarian aid. The issue of how to deal with North Korea will inevitably be a major point of debate among future presidential hopefuls as the campaign for a new president kicks off in earnest next year. This is likely to further erode public support for continued one-way government assistance, absent North Korean reciprocal gestures in the direction of rapprochement.

On the North Korean side, it is clear that the political consolidation of Kim Jong-Il's position and North Korea's own economic desperation and increasing dependency on external resources were critical factors that shaped Kim Jong-Il's decision to reach out and invite DJ for the historic summit. In this respect, the foundations for Kim Jong-Il's power and legitimacy in North Korea appear to be different from those of his father. Whereas Kim Il-Sung stood as the founder of the nation and relied solely on ideology as the foundation for legitimacy, Kim Jong-Il's legitimacy appears to be drawn at least in part from economic factors as well as ideology. In other words, North Korea's economic-system failures and its decade-long economic decline have made it necessary for the North Korean leader to raise enough annual external support to ensure the well-being of his core supporters in the party and the military as a vehicle for maintaining his position as the leader. Limited economic cooperation and opening to the outside represent the only available options for drawing in the support necessary for regime survival, even at the cost of greater dependence on external largesse from the outside world, including from South Korea. South Korean public opinion regarding the situation and prospects for change in the North will be the critical variables that are likely in the long term to determine the level of economic assistance available to the North. To the extent that Kim Jong-Il recognizes and responds to his need to maintain a positive image among the South Korean public in the future, the South is gradually developing a powerful lever for catalyzing change and eventually requiring further progress toward peaceful coexistence and the end of military confrontation on the Korean peninsula. The development of this interaction is likely to be the primary driver in the next phase of inter-Korean relations, and will ultimately determine the pace, direction, and shape of progress toward peaceful coexistence and economic and political integration on the Korean peninsula.

The Economic Outlook for Reconciliation and Reunification

Doowon Lee

Introduction

Both sides of the Korean peninsula have experienced internal and external economic changes during the past two years. The historical summit in June 2000 between Kim Dae-Jung, the South Korean president, and Kim Jong-Il, chairman of the National Defense Commission of North Korea, has been regarded as a cornerstone of inter-Korean reconciliation and cooperation. However, despite the initial expectation of full-blossomed economic cooperation between the two sides, no such dramatic change has occurred since the summit. There are several reasons for this, and the weak performance of the South Korean economy is surely one of them.

In an effort to understand the implications of the summit and the current status of inter-Korean economic cooperation, this chapter will analyze three major aspects of the Korean situation: (1) The economic performance of South Korea during the past two to three years. Following its sharp rebound after the outbreak of the financial crisis in 1997, the South Korean economy made a remarkable recovery during 1999 and 2000, then weakened rather disappointingly after the end of 2000. (2) The economic performance of North Korea during the past two years. Despite its limitations, the North Korean economy also rebounded slightly during this period, but not sufficiently to enable inter-Korean economic cooperation to take off, even after the summit. Several factors contribute to this stalemate. (3) External environments that can affect the North Korean economy and inter-Korean economic cooperation.

In analyzing these topics, this chapter will focus more on North Korea than on South Korea, whose economic situation is already well known to outsiders. As it looks to the future, the chapter considers the prospect of reconciliation, not reunification, in the Korean peninsula, because it would be premature to expect any abrupt changes in either side of the peninsula that might lead to reunification in the near future.

Economic Conditions of the Two Koreas and Inter-Korean Economic Relations

Economic Conditions of the Two Koreas

The years 1999 and 2000 can be documented as years of economic recovery in both South Korea and North Korea, even though the causes and magnitudes of recovery were different for the two states. Generally speaking, the South Korean economy went through a more visible and structurally significant recovery, while the North Korean economy experienced rather tenuous and transitory recovery. Table 1 contains recent macroeconomic data for the two sides, and it shows that both enjoyed positive-growth rates with increased trade volume. Particularly noteworthy are the positive-growth rates of the North Korean economy after nine consecutive years of shrinking. Also, the markedly high growth rates of the South Korean economy (which were expanding even faster than its potential-growth rate of 5 to 6 percent) have drawn a great deal of attention both inside and outside Korea.[1] I will examine in further detail how the two sides of the Korean peninsula could enjoy such a recovery—along with potential dangers that lie ahead for these two economies.

The South Korean Economy

The South Korean economy has bottomed out from the deep recession that was caused by the financial crisis of 1997. Particularly impressive were the macroeconomic performances between the first quarter of 1999 and the third quarter of 2000. The South Korean economy was growing at an annual rate of 10.9 percent and 8.8 percent in 1999 and 2000, respectively. It was the giddy growth pace of 13 percent during the second half of 1999 that brought about the so-called V-shape recovery to South Korea. The strong recovery was accompanied by a stable

---

1. The potential-growth rate implies the maximum rate of growth an economy can achieve with its level of labor, capital, and technology stock without triggering inflation.

Table 1

Recent Macroeconomic Data of the Two Koreas

	1997		1998		1999		2000	
	South Korea	North Korea	South Korea	North Korea	South Korea	North Korea	South Korea	North Korea
GDP growth rates	5.0	-6.3	-6.7	-1.1	10.7	6.2	8.8	1.3
Per capita GNI ($)	10,307.00	811.00	6,823.00	573.00	8,518.00	714.00	9,627.00	757.00
Export (billion$)	136.16	0.9	132.31	0.56	143.69	0.52	172.62	0.56
Import (billion$)	144.62	1.27	93.28	0.88	119.75	0.96	160.49	1.41

Sources: The Bank of Korea, *Bank of Korea Information* (July 2000, June 2001); Korea Trade-Investment Promotion Agency (www.kotra.or.kr).

inflation rate and a decreased unemployment rate. There are several causes behind this better-than-expected recovery. One of the major factors for the successful performance of the South Korean economy was a series of painful structural reforms, which were introduced mostly in 1998 and 1999.[2] In particular, the financial sector regained its soundness after a series of government-led consolidations and liquidations were accomplished with the help of injections of public funds. These allowed the corporate sector to lower its debt-equity ratio substantially, and many measures to improve the transparency of the corporate governance system were put in place. It has probably been the labor market that has embraced more changes than the other sectors. The labor market has become much more flexible than before, with fewer people employed full-time and more part-time. The labor market flexibility (measured by Okun's law coefficient) has been enhanced after the crisis.[3] It shows that the labor market responded more actively to the fluctuation of economic growth rates after the crisis than before the crisis.[4] Table 2 summarizes what has been achieved during the past three years.

Thanks to these painful reform efforts, Korean financial institutions and firms now have reached the level of those in Japan, if not the level of those of the United States and the other leading economies, in terms of financial soundness. Tables 3 and 4 compare Korea to other leading nations in terms of its financial soundness in the corporate and financial sectors, measured by the size of NPL (nonperforming loans) and debt-equity ratios. Even though the Korean firms and financial institutions before the crisis could not measure up to those

---

2. See my essay, "South Korea's Financial Crisis and Economic Restructuring" in *Korea Briefing, 1997–1999: Challenges and Change at the Turn of the Century*, edited by Kongdan Oh (Armonk, NY: M.E. Sharpe, 2000).

3. Okun's law states the relationship between unemployment level and economic growth. When an economy grows, the unemployment level falls. Okun's law calculates how much the unemployment level falls when an economy grows. While the additional 1-percent growth rate had lowered the unemployment rate by 10 percent before the crisis, the additional 1-percent growth rate has lowered the unemployment rate by 16 percent after the crisis. Refer to my paper, "In Search for a New Development Model for Korea," presented at the Annual Conference of the American Economic Association, January 2001, New Orleans, U.S.A.

4. Another study also shows more flexible labor-market conditions of Korea. The job-finding rate and job-losing rate of 1997 were 1.79 and 2.09, respectively. In 2000, after the crisis, these rates were 3.0 and 2.75, respectively. They show that it has become easier to hire and fire labor after the crisis. Refer to Samsung Economic Research Institute, "The Changes of the Korean Economy During the 3 Years under IMF Crisis" (January 2001).

Table 2

Summary of Reforms in Four Major Areas

Pre-Crisis Situation	Reform Measures	Changes and Achievements
1) Financial Sector		
1. 14 of the 27 commercial banks below BIS ratio of 8%*	1. Public fund of W 137 trillion injected and 33 trillion retrieved as of April 2001	1. Number of financial institutions dropped from 2,102 to 1,582.
2. Troubled loans are estimated to be W 118 trillion as of March 1998	2. FSC and FSS established	2. Impaired loans (substandard or below) as of end of 2000 estimated to be W 65 trillion, 10.4% of total loans.
3. Lack of proper supervision		
2) Corporate Sector		
1. Highly leveraged firms with debt/equity ratio of 396.3% for manufacturing firms in the end of 1997	1. Five guidelines	1. Debt/Equity ratio dropped: 210.6% for manufacturing firms at the end of 2000.
2. Poor corporate governance: cross-debt guarantees, cross-share holdings	2. Big Deals	2. Cross-debt guarantee decreased from W 11 trillion in 1998 to W 0.2 trillion in 2001 for the largest 5 conglomerates.
3. Lack of transparency		3. Cross-share holding ratio for the largest 30 conglomerates unchanged between 1997 and 2000.
3) Labor Market		
1. Rigid and militant labor union	1. Tripartite Commission established	1. More flexible labor market

(continued)

Table 2 (continued)

Pre-Crisis Situation	Reform Measures	Changes and Achievements
2. Average nominal wage increase rate (13.45%) higher than average labor productivity growth rate (10.37%) from 1992–1996	2. Social safety net hastily set up	2. Average labor productivity growth rate (18.73%) higher than average nominal wage increase rate (5.87%) from 1998–2000.
		3. Productive welfare system
4) Government Sector		
1. Regulation	1. Administrative reform	1. Approximately 400,000 employees are laid off from central and local governments.
2. Inefficient public enterprises	2. Deregulation	2. Number of regulations decreased from 10,717 in August 1998 to 7,156 in July 2001.
	3. Privatization	3. Privatized 6 public enterprises and plan to privatize 5 more as of January 2001.

Sources: Bank of Korea Web site (www.bok.or.kr); Korea Financial Supervisory Commission Web site (www.fss.or.kr); Korea National Statistical Office Web site (www.nso.go.kr); Korea Development Institute Web site (www.kdi.re.kr); Fair Trade Commission Web site (www.ftc.go.kr).

Note: * BIS (Bank for International Settlements) ratio measures the ratio of bank's equity over a weighted average of risky assets. The higher this ratio is, the more financially sound the bank is.

Table 3

International Comparison of NPL (unit: %)

South Korea* (1997)	South Korea* (1999)	South Korea* (2001 June)	United States** (2000)	Japan** (2000)	Germany*** (1999)	UK*** (1999)
6.0	8.3	5.7	1.21	5.44	1.3	2.17

Sources: Korea Financial Supervisory Service (www.fss.or.kr); *The Banker* (July 2000, July 2001), recited From www.seri.org (June 2001) and www.bok.or.kr.

Notes: * Average of all the commercial banks' NPL. Korea has changed its criteria of NPL in 1999 according to international standard. **Average of ten biggest commercial banks' NPL. *** Average of five biggest commercial banks' NPL.

Table 4

International Comparison of Debt-Equity Ratios of Manufacturing Industry (unit: %)

South Korea (1997)	South Korea (2000)	Germany (1996)	Japan (1999)	Taiwan (1995)	United States (1999)
3.96	2.11	0.98	1.74	0.86	1.64

Sources: Krueger, Anne O., and Jungho Yoo, "Falling Profitability, Higher Borrowing Costs, and Chaebol Finances During the Korean Crisis," presented at the IMF-KIEP Conference on "The Korean Crisis and Recovery," May 17–19, 2001, Seoul, Korea (2001). Bank of Korea, *Bank of Korea Information* (June 2001, p. 66).

of the other countries, they do now, after the implementation of financial and corporate reforms, at least as sound as those of Japan.

Even though many structural reforms have been carried out, the South Korean economy still has to struggle with a challenging agenda. In the financial sector, there are still vast amounts of nonperforming loans, even after the injection of an astronomical amount of public funds. Also, as a medium-to-long-term task for the government, there is the issue of reprivatization of many financial institutions, which have been de facto nationalized in the process of reform.[5] Dr. Stanley

5. According to Chopra et al. (2001, p. 55), 36.8 percent of shares of national and regional banks are owned by the government and 33 percent by foreigners, as of the end of 2000. Refer to Chopra, Ajai, Kenneth Kang, Meral Karasulu, Hong Liang, Henry Ma, and Anthony Richards, "From Crisis to Recovery in Korea: Strategy, Achievements, and Lessons," presented at the IMF-KIEP Conference on "The Korean Crisis and Recovery," May 17–19, 2001, Seoul, Korea (2001).

Fischer, the first deputy managing director of the IMF, has urged the South Korean government to get out of the financial sector.[6] In the corporate sector, the fates of several troubled large companies—including Daewoo Motors, Hyundai Engineering & Construction Co., and Hynix Semi-conductor Inc.—still hinge on the decisions that must be made by creditor banks and the government. In the short term, how these several companies are dealt with will greatly affect the credibility of the government-led reform efforts. Also, as an inevitable result of corporate sector reform, the cross-holding of shares among related companies within a conglomerate has been either increased or unchanged, while the cross-debt guarantee has been virtually abolished.[7] In the past, this cross-holding of shares and cross-debt guarantees among related companies within a conglomerate were the cornerstones of control that enabled a single person or a family who actually owned small numbers of shares to control numerous companies. As the internal cross-holding of shares still remains high within conglomerates, the exertion of management power over related companies by a handful of people still occurs. Another mission that has to be undertaken by the financial institutions and corporate sector of South Korea is the improvement of profitability. The probability has still not been improved substantially, but flexibility has left the Korean labor market much more vulnerable to external shocks. In the government sector, deregulation and large-scale privatization are still in progress, and there remains the sensitive issue of whether the government will allow large conglomerates to join the bidding for the sale of large public companies.

While the above-mentioned structural reforms contributed most to the recovery of the South Korean economy in 1999 and 2000, there were other external and internal factors behind the upswing. The first and the most important contributing factor was an impressive export performance, driven by strong demand from the U.S. market. Clearly, the booming U.S. market has been the locomotive of world economic growth in the latter half of the 1990s, and the crisis-hit Asian economies were the biggest beneficiaries of it. The second factor, related to the

---

6. He mentioned that the government should stop guaranteeing bonds that are striking out. Also, he worried that there is a conflict of interest when the government both owns and supervises banks. Refer to *International Herald Tribune* (July 10, 2001).

7. The cross-share holding ratio for the largest four conglomerates (excluding Daewoo) in 1997 was 47 percent. This ratio increased to 55 percent by 1999 and then decreased to 47 percent by 2000.

first, was the role of the booming ICT (information-and-communication technology) industry in both export and investment performance. The ICT industry, which accounts for slightly more than 10 percent of the GDP, has contributed roughly 40 to 50 percent of the economic growth, 30 percent of investment, and 40 percent of total exports.[8] The exports of the ICT industry have enjoyed particularly rapid growth due to the increased demands from the booming so-called new economy sector in the United States. Thanks to this, the ICT sector's exports have grown nearly ten times faster than the non-ICT sector's during the last two years. However, this unbalanced growth of the ICT sector vis-à-vis the non-ICT sector has created the problem of bipolarization of the South Korean economy and has made the South Korean export industry highly dependent upon such external factors as U.S. economic growth. The other sector that enjoyed government support and a high rate of investment growth was the newly emerging venture industry. The outflow of financial and personnel resources after the crisis, along with the strong initiatives taken by the Korean government to develop the ICT sector and venture firms, have created the Korean version of the "new economy." Nearly 10,000 new venture firms have been created during the last two years, and they are employing more than 300,000 as of today.[9]

A third factor is the revival of domestic consumption and investment, in particular equipment investment in the above-stated ICT sector, after the painful efforts of structural reform and easing of the credit crunch. This has something to do with the booming stock market. As the KOSPI stock index jumped from the low of 280 on June 16, 1998, to the peak of 1059 on January 4, 2000, consumption was revived, due in part to the positive-income effect of stock price on consumption (see Fig. 1).[10] Also, many

---

8. Refer to Bank of Korea, *Monthly Bulletin* (in Korean, April 2001).

9. The number of venture firms as of November 2000 was 9,331 with a total employment of approximately 346,000. Refer to *Maeil Business Newspaper* (in Korean, January 27, 2001).

10. In the case of the South Korean economy in the 1990s, a 10-percent increase of a stock's price leads to a 0.4 to 0.6 percent increase of private consumption. Refer to *Bank of Korea Information* (in Korean, March, 2001). Currently, there are three major players in the Korean stock market: individual investors, institutional investors, and foreign investors. The consumption behavior of the individual investors, which accounts for roughly 40 percent of the total stock market, is believed to be influenced by the stock-price variation. Refer to *Bank of Korea Monthly Bulletin* (in Korean, May 2001).

Figure 1   **Stock Index from 1998 to April 2001**

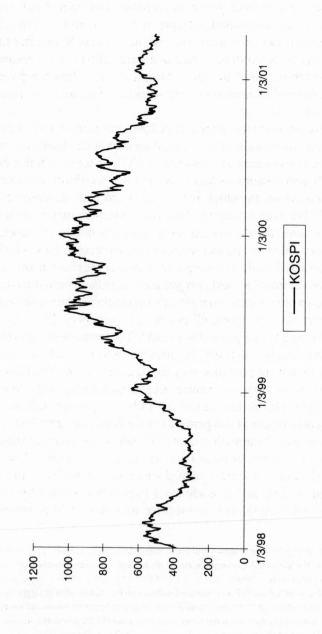

Source: The Korea Exchange (www.kse.or.kr).

firms, particularly the ICT and venture firms, found it easier to raise capital in the stock market.

Lastly, a switch of government policy has helped domestic consumption and investment. Despite the initial advice of the IMF, the government switched to an expansionary stance soon after the onset of the crisis. According to Lee and Park (2001), it is presumed that this switch occurred in April 1998, and since then the government has continued to provide fiscal stimulus and monetary liquidity to the market.[11]

However, since the latter half of 2000, the economic tides have been reversed. There were vivid signs of an economic slowdown, if not recession, from as early as the spring of 2000. As the investment bubble of the ICT and venture sectors burst and the possibility of reform grew more uncertain, the stock market began to head downward in early 2000.[12] The earlier collapse of the Daewoo conglomerate, in July 1999, had triggered the downward trend, not only hitting the stock market hard but also leaving many investment and trust companies, which owned the lion's share of corporate bonds and corporate papers issued by Daewoo, in trouble. Furthermore, such negative external factors as the slowdown of U.S. economic growth, the continued recession of the Japanese economy and rising oil prices came into play. The unexpectedly severe slump took a particularly hard toll in the Korean export industry, especially the ICT industry, because South Korea's reliance on exports had increased substantially over the past three years. The slowdown of South Korean economic growth became undeniable as the fourth quarter of 2000 growth rate turned out to be 4.6 percent, followed by the even worse figure of 3.7 percent for the first quarter of 2001. Particularly low was the growth rate of GNI, which incorporates the effect of deteriorating terms of trade with income data—a mere 1.1 percent for the first quarter of 2001. Coupled with a short-term hike in inflation at the end of 2000 and in early 2001 (which was caused by temporary supply-side factors such as oil-price increases, public-service-charge

---

11. Lee Jong-Wha and Yung Chul-Park, "Recovery and Sustainability in East Asia," presented at the IMF-KIEP Conference on "The Korean Crisis and Recovery," May 17–19, 2001, Seoul, Korea.

12. The burst of the ICT and venture bubbles can be explained best by the dramatic rise and fall of the KOSDAQ index. The KOSDAQ index, which moves almost identically with the U.S. NASDAQ index, with the correlation coefficient of 0.73 in 2000, fell from the peak of 283.44 on March 10, 2000, to a low of 52.58 on December 26, 2000.

increases and exchange-rate depreciation), these figures even led some observers to warn of the possible threat of stagflation.[13]

As the economic situation deteriorated sharply from the fourth quarter of 2000, economists as well as government officials began to reexamine their policies to find out what went wrong. The deteriorating external factors, especially the slowdown of the U.S. economy, were deemed largely responsible[14]—but there were internal factors as well. The most important of these were the lack of structural reform and the initial underestimation of the problems prevailing in South Korea's financial and corporate sectors. As I've emphasized elsewhere, the 1997 economic crisis was not a foreign-exchange-liquidity crisis but a structural one. However, in the process of recovering from the crisis, too much emphasis was given to the provision of monetary liquidity both from domestic and foreign sources. Thanks to these monetary liquidities provided to the market, there have been notable improvements that can be measured by the ratio of short-term foreign debt, foreign-exchange reserve, and lowered interest rates.[15] Relatively speaking, however, structural reform is only halfway done, and there still is the unfinished business of cleaning up the dud loans in South Korea's financial sector—particularly in nonbank financial institutions. Initially, the total amount of troubled loans was estimated to be 118 trillion won, and the 64-trillion-won injection of public funds was thought to be enough to stabilize the situation. However, as companies began to reveal their real financial situations, some of which had long been concealed through tricky accounting practices, more loans turned out to be in trouble. Eventually, the government asked the National Assembly for the establishment of an additional public fund of 40 trillion won, and many skeptics inside and outside the government are wondering whether there may be further need of public funds in the future.[16] Not only are the struc-

---

13. The depreciation of the Korean exchange rate was largely due to the sharp depreciation of the Japanese yen against the U.S. dollar. The yen/dollar rate has been depreciated from 109.00 in October 2000 to 123.88 in April 2001.

14. For the impact of the U.S. economy's slowdown on the East Asian economies, refer to *The Economist* (July 7, 2001).

15. For example, as of May 2001, the total external liability of Korea was $128.7 billion with $42.9 billion short-term debt. Also, the foreign-exchange reserve was $93.6 billion, thus achieving the ratio of short-term debt to foreign-exchange reserve of 45.8 percent. This ratio used to be more than 300 percent at the outbreak of the crisis at the end of 1997.

16. In September 2000, the deputy prime minister, Nyum Jin, asked the National Assembly for the establishment of an additional 40-trillion-won public fund.

tural reforms only halfway done, but the government's appetite for continuing the reform effort seems to have weakened since early 2000. For example, when the government provided support to such troubled giants as Hyundai Engineering & Construction Co. and Hynix Semiconductor Inc. (both saddled with several billion dollars in loans maturing by 2001) through the controversial bond-refinancing program, many watchers inside and outside Korea worried that the government was retreating from the principle of reform.

Aside from this fundamental problem, there are some other strategic factors responsible for the deteriorated economic situation of South Korea. One is the issue of policy overshooting. As Cho Yoon-Je mentioned, the initial high-interest policy of the IMF after the crisis has produced unnecessary victims in the recovery, while the desired effect of stabilizing exchange rates has been minimal.[17] Also, by overly boosting the ICT and venture sectors, the government created a bubble that burst afterward. A second factor is that the sequence of the reform measures is in question. Cho alleged, for example, that asymmetric financial restructuring measures—which reformed bank and merchant banks first, leaving nonbank financial institutions such as investment and trust companies exposed to troubles—have created a moral hazard problem.[18] Thirdly, resistance from vested interest groups such as conglomerates, public enterprises and labor unions increased as the government loosened up its lashes.

From now on, the South Korean economy has to live with new

---

17. Refer to Cho Yoon-Je, "Economic Adjustment Program of Korea after the Crisis: What Have We Learned?" presented at the IMF-KIEP Conference on "The Korean Crisis and Recovery," May 17–19, 2001, Seoul, Korea. There are contradicting views as well. For example, Dr. Stanley Fischer, the first deputy-managing director of the IMF, strongly defended the IMF policy of maintaining high interest rates temporarily in the beginning stage of the crisis. Refer to *The Economist* (October 3, 1998), pp. 19–23. Also, Chung and Kim (2001) provided econometrical evidence on the effectiveness of the high-interest rate policy in stabilizing the exchange rate. Refer to Chung Chae-Schick and Kim Se-Jik, "New Evidence on High Interest Rate Policy During the Korean Crisis," presented at the IMF-KIEP Conference on "The Korean Crisis and Recovery," May 17–19, 2001, Seoul, Korea.

18. The investment and trust companies had not been subject to any corrective actions by the supervisory authorities and allowed to mobilize and manage funds with benignly neglected irregularities in 1998 and 1999. While investment and trust companies were actively purchasing lion's share of CBs issued by Hyundai and Daewoo in 1998 and '99, about 22 percent of CBs, which were issued between December 1997 and December 1999, became defaulted. Refer to Cho (2001), pp. 21–22.

conditions and environments created as a result of the crisis and recovery of the past three years. In terms of the macroeconomic indices, lower investment ratios and lower potential growth rates will
prevail, at least for a while.[19] According to Barro (2001), countries
that experienced currency crises ended up with reduced investment
ratios for a certain period of time.[20] However, he fails to detect a
persisting adverse influence of crises on growth and investment.[21]
Also, Ajai Chopra, et al., estimated that the South Korean economy's
potential growth rate would fall during the period of 2000 to 2005, to
a level of around 6 percent.[22] For an economy like South Korea's,
which has long been accustomed to high investment and high growth
rates, this change would be difficult to cope with, at least for a while.
Another notable change is the highly aggravated income distribution,
measured by the Gini index.[23] According to the National Statistical
Office, the Gini index, whose average value for 1990–97 was 0.286,
deteriorated after the crisis to a level of 0.317 in 2000. In order to
relieve this problem, the South Korean government has to continue to
build a better social safety net system and to develop the means to re-
educate unemployed people.

Other notable changes are the fully liberalized commodity and financial market and the presence of foreign shareholders in the South Korean economy.[24] As a result of this liberalization process, the South
Korean economy is more exposed and vulnerable to external shocks
than it was before. Also, as more foreigners take over shares of Korean

---

19. The average annual investment ratio dropped from 37 percent in 1991–97 to 25.7
percent in 1998–2000. Refer to Bank of Korea, *Bank of Korea Information* (in Korean, June
2001, p. 7).

20. Barro, Robert, "Economic Growth in East Asia Before and After the Financial Crisis,"
presented at the IMF-KIEP Conference on "The Korean Crisis and Recovery," May 17–19,
2001, Seoul, Korea.

21. Also, refer to Lee and Park (2001, p. 52).

22. Chopra, Ajai, Kenneth Kang, Meral Karasulu, Hong Liang, Henry Ma, and Anthony
Richards, "From Crisis to Recovery in Korea: Strategy, Achievements, and Lessons," presented at the IMF-KIEP Conference on "The Korean Crisis and Recovery," May 17–19,
2001, Seoul, Korea.

23. Gini index measures the relative income inequality. This index takes a value between 0 and 1. It goes toward 0 when the wealth is more equally distributed.

24. According to the Korea Stock Exchange, foreigners own 30.2 percent of total stock
market value in Korea as of March 2001. For example, foreigners own 58.4 percent of
Samsung conglomerate's shares and 58.3 percent of POSCO as of May 14, 2001.

financial institutions and leading companies, it is more and more difficult for the government to carry out conventional industrial policies. From now on, the South Korean economy will have to learn to live in this new environment, while it continues to tackle the unfinished business of restructuring.

The North Korean Economy

While the South Korean economy traveled a bumpy road of recovery over the past two years, the North Korean economy was experiencing positive growth rates in 1999 and 2000, after nine consecutive years of negative growth. Even though the dire food-and-energy situations are far from being resolved, there are several signs of economic recovery in North Korea. First, the North Korean authority announced during the Supreme People's Assembly of April 2001 that the material foundation for the four leading industries of coal, railroad, electricity, and transportation had been successfully built, with an industrial production increase of 1.1 times, compared to the previous year.[25] Evidence of a more confident North Korean authority can also be found in the New Year's message of 2001—while it was the first such message to acknowledge the nation's economic difficulties, it also declared that the year 2001 will be the first year that marches into the new millennium after the victory over adversities of the past. There is another symbolic sign that the North Korean leader is paying more attention to economic matters. The frequency of Kim Jong-Il's on-the-spot guided tours regarding economic matters—a tactic frequently used both by Kim Il-Sung and Kim Jong-Il as a major means of bringing about ideological and productive stimulus—is increasingly compared to those of noneconomic matters, shown in Table 5.

Even though these signs are largely symbolic and rhetorical, they still give outsiders, whose access to raw economic data of North Korea is strictly restricted, hints of economic recovery. More concrete evidence can be found in the testimony of North Korean defectors. For example, the price levels of major commodities traded in the wide-spread peasant markets declined between 1999 and 2000. As the peasant-market prices are believed to reflect demand and supply of goods better than prices in the official state stores, lowered price levels here imply

---

25. When the Supreme People's Assembly was held in 1998, after a four-year absence, they designated Kim Jong-Il as the chairman of the National Defense Commission, the highest state body.

Table 5

Frequencies of On-the-Spot Guidance Tours of Kim Jong-Il from 1997 to 2000

	Classification				
Year	Activities related to Army	Activities related to Economy	Activities related to Diplomacy	Etc	Total
2000	21 (28.8%)	25 (34.2%)	16 (21.9%)	11 (15.0%)	73 (100%)
1999	43 (62.3%)	18 (26.0%)	2 (2.9%)	6 (8.67%)	69 (100%)
1998	48 (68.5%)	6 (8.6%)	2 (2.8%)	14 (20.0%)	70 (100%)
1997	40 (67.8%)	1 (1.7%)	2 (3.4%)	16 (27.1%)	59 (100%)

Source: Ministry of Unification (www.unikorea.go.kr).

that the supply situation in North Korea has improved. Table 6 calculates the change of price indices between 1999 and 2000, based on the witness of North Korean defectors. Also, the change of weighted price indices (using the weight of South Korea's consumer price indices of 1975) is calculated. The weight of the 1975 indices can represent the consumption structure of today's North Korea best because the 1975 South Korean per capita income is similar to the per capita income of today's North Korea. According to this calculation, the consumer price index of North Korea dropped by 6.79 percent between 1999 and 2000.

Other concrete signs of recovery have come from the observations of South Koreans. According to the estimation made by the Bank of Korea, the North Korean economy had positive growth rates of 6.2 percent and 1.3 percent in 1999 and 2000, respectively. In particular, the import volume of North Korea has expanded rather rapidly during the last two years. Also, according to pictures taken from the air, the average operation ratio of several selected industrial facilities of North Korea has increased from 46 percent in February 1997 to 77 percent in February 2001.[26] Even though the average operation ratio of the overall North Korean economy is far smaller than these figures indicate, it still shows that there has been some improvement in selected industrial sites.

What factors have made two consecutive years of positive economic

---

26. KDI, *KDI Review of the North Korean Economy* (in Korean, May 2001, p. 51).

Table 6

Price Index of North Korea Peasant Market (unit: %)

Commodity item	% Change of price index	Weights of each commodity	% Change of weighted price index
Cereals	−12.9	0.24	−3.12
Meat	−17.6	0.04	−0.76
Fish and shellfish	−29.6	0.03	−1.01
Vegetables	−14.1	0.06	−0.91
Fruits	−17.3	0.02	−0.37
Condiments	−22.8	0.05	−1.09
Confectioneries	−35.6	0.02	−0.75
Beverages and alcoholic drinks	20.4	0.02	0.36
Meals outside home	−7.0	0.01	−0.10
Furniture and furnishings	−6.3	0.05	−0.31
Clothing	5.0	0.11	0.55
Medical care	−28.7	0.06	−1.66
Stationery goods	23.3	0.01	0.15
Miscellaneous goods	8.3	0.27	2.25
Total	−12.1	1.00	−6.79

Sources: Ministry of Unification (www.unkorea.go.kr); National Statistical Office (www.nso.go.kr).

growth possible in North Korea? Even though there has been some internal effort to mobilize and utilize domestic resources more effectively, the recent upswing of the North Korean economy was by and large made possible through external help. In particular, the inflow of additional hard currencies through the Kumgang Mountain Project with Hyundai, coupled with continued aid from international sources, has played the major role in reviving the North Korean economy. Since the beginning of the Kumgang Mountain Project through the end of 2000, Hyundai has provided $342 million.[27] The provision of hard

---

27. The Kumgang Mountain Project began in November 1998 between North Korea and Hyundai with the promise of providing $942 million by February 2005. Hyundai promised to provide this amount in a lump sum every month with the expectation of attracting 720,000 tourists every year; however, the annual number of tourists until the end of 2000 was merely 180,000. It has caused Hyundai approximately $400 million accumulated loss until the end of 2000. Refer to KDI, *KDI Review of the North Korean Economy* (in Korean, May 2001), pp. 4–5.

currencies from Hyundai to North Korea was definitely a blessing to the cash-stripped North Korean economy, and it has clearly had an impact on the surge of the import volume in North Korea in 2000. In addition to this, international aid—including aid from South Korea— continued to pour into North Korea. Table 7 summarizes the total amount of aid North Korea has received during the past couple of years. It shows that the total amount of outside help provided to the North Korean economy exceeds $500 million and $300 million in 1999 and 2000, respectively. This amount is almost identical to the total export volume of North Korea. Furthermore, it is large enough to finance the current account deficit of North Korea for those two years.[28] Also, when the total amount of investment is calculated based on the budget data of North Korea, the outside help can account for almost 15 percent and 10 percent of the total investments that were made in 1999 and 2000, respectively.[29]

Aside from this external help, North Korea has initiated a couple of new movements during this period. Since 1998, the announced goal of the North Korean regime has been to build a so-called strong nation *(Kangsong Taeguk)*, and by "strong" is implied a strong army and a measure of national wealth.[30] In order to achieve this goal, North Korea is emphasizing two major areas: normalization of its four leading industries, and improving the living standard of the people. In practical terms, this means a new emphasis on science and technology, as represented by "new thought" and "the theory of seed."[31] More concretely, North Korea has built approximately 6,000 small- and medium-size generators in 1998 and 1999. However, realizing that these generators can not help much in easing the energy shortage due to their limited scale and frequent malfunctioning, construction of these small generators drasti-

---

28. Other than this external aid, North Korea is believed to finance its current account deficit through the sales of weapons and drugs, as well as remittances from *Chochongryun.*

29. The expenditure for the people's economy out of the North Korean budget was regarded as the total amount of investment in North Korea.

30. Since it was first mentioned in *Rodong Shinmun*, August 1998, building a strong nation has been the slogan that has been continuously emphasized by Kim Jong-Il as a goal to be achieved.

31. The "new thought" is emphasized to encourage laborers and bureaucrats to abolish old practices and to develop new ideas, new management, and new technology. Also, the so-called 'theory of seed' is to enhance the production efficiency by qualitative improvement of input factors in production. Refer to KDI, *KDI Review of the North Korean Economy* (in Korean, June 2001), pp. 6–7.

Table 7

Total Amount of Outside Help to North Korea and Its Relative Importance

1) Total Amount of Outside Help (unit: million $)

	1995	1996	1997	1998	1999	2000	Total
UN (WFP)	9.27	34.70	157.81	215.87	202.63	90.67	710.95
Red Cross	3.49	4.43	7.56	14.03	8.26	4.20	41.97
Foreign countries and NGO		220.19		88.86	151.72	15.99	476.76
South Korean government	232	26.67	3.05	11.00	28.25	78.63	379.60
South Korean private sector	4.96	8.50	20.85	18.63	35.13	96.97	
Transfer from Hyundai		—		54.00	144.00	144.00	342.00
Total		735.56		398.84	549.43	364.42	2,048.25

Sources: The Bank of Korea (www.bok.or.kr); Ministry of Unification (www.unikorea.go.kr); Korea Development Institute; *KDI Review of the North Korean Economy,* May 2001.

2) Relative importance of outside help (unit: million $, %)

	Total outside help (A)	North Korea export (B)	North Korea investment (C)	A/B	A/C
1999	549.43	520	3,756	105.66%	14.63%
2000	364.42	560	3,812	65.08%	9.56%

Sources: Ministry of Unification, *Weekly Report on North Korea* (www.unikorea.go.kr); Korea Trade Investment Promotion Agency (www.kotra.or.kr).

cally decreased in 2000.[32] The other area Kim Jong-Il has personally emphasized during the last couple of years is to rationalize farm size. By early 2001, beginning in Kangwon Province, North Korea has ratio-nalized 300 km^2 of Kangwon Province, 550 km^2 of North Pyungahn Province, and 300 km^2 of South Hwanghae Province. This land-ratio-nalization movement converts pseudo-private paddy fields, which are scattered along mountainsides, into standardized farmland. By doing so, it aims to maximize productivities of these underutilized lands. How-ever, this effort is very different from the agricultural reform introduced in China or in Vietnam. Rather, it aims to reenforce the collective farm system.[33]

Even though there were some internal efforts to overcome economic adversity during the past two years, these measures were different from market-oriented reform. They were introduced by the North Korean au-thority to reinforce the existing centrally planned economic system. In this sense, these measures can be considered, at best, as a North Korean version of *Perestroika*. In reality, North Korea cannot achieve sustainable economic growth by relying on temporary measures, as their effect will inevitably be short-lived. North Korea is widely perceived to be in the poverty trap, from which it cannot escape without external help.[34] This view is advocated by Nicholas Eberstadt,[35] who notes that it is premature to speak of the stabilization of the North Korean economy, much less its recovery, because empirical evidence for the augmentation of value added due to increased domestic productivity or resource mobilization is still extremely limited.[36] Furthermore, he warns that the severe depletion of human capital during the state's prolonged economic crisis will impair any potential productivity gain the future reform effort engenders.

Even though the macroeconomic indices and some of the microeconomic aspects improved during the past two years, the food

---

32. Refer to KDI, *KDI Review of the North Korean Economy* (in Korean, April 2001), p. 51.

33. Ibid., p. 58.

34. According to Yoon (2001), poverty trap is defined as the situation in which a country's investment rate is barely large enough to cover the depreciation rate. Under such a situa-tion, the real value of capital stock shrinks over time. Refer to Yoon, Deok-Ryong, "The Role of EU in the Korean Peninsular Affair and Its Implication," *KIEP (Korea Institute for International Economic Policy) Issue Analysis* (June 2001).

35. Eberstadt, Nicholas, "Prospects for Economic Recovery," *Joint U.S.-Korea Academic Studies*, vol. 11 (2001).

36. Ibid.

Table 8

Food Shortage Problem of North Korea (unit: 1000 tons)

	1999	2000
Aggregate Supply	3,783	3,472
Aggregate Demand	4,823	4,765
Import Demand	1,040	1,293
Commercial Import	300	300
Food aid	642	370
Shortage	98	623

Sources: WFP Special Report, FAO/WFP Crop and Food Supply; Assessment Mission to DPRK (June 29 to November 8, 1999); Bank of Korea (www.bok.or.kr).

and energy shortage is still the most urgent problem to be resolved. According to WFP, the minimum amount of grain demand in North Korea is 4.76 million tons for 2000. However, only 3.5 million tons were produced in the previous year, and approximately 0.7 million tons were imported from abroad, leaving the amount of absolute shortage at 0.6 million tons.

The North Korean authority has recently released to the international community an internal report that reflects the deteriorated standard of living due to these problems. In the report submitted by the North Korean representative at a meeting of UNICEF, Beijing, China, May 14–16, 2001, the dire economic and social conditions of North Korea were blamed on economic harshness and natural disasters. This was the first time North Korea had ever released such official data internationally. By doing so, North Korea was trying to draw more attention from international society and to maximize the potential for economic aid. This report also noted that 1995 flood damage may reach a cost as high as $15 billion.

Inter-Korean Economic Relations

Since inter-Korean economic cooperation began in 1989, there have been periods of setbacks and expansions. Generally speaking, the overall trade volume between the two Koreas has continuously increased, while the expected flow of investment from South Korea to North Korea is not yet realized. ROK government red tape and institutional barriers that hindered free movement of trade and investment have been largely removed. In particular, the South Korean government's April

Table 9

Report of the North Korean Authority at UNICEF

Category	Period	Data (unit)
Per capita GNP	1993–1999	991 to 457 ($)
Population	1993–1999	21,034 to 22,575 (thousand)
Average life expectancy	1993–1999	73.2 to 66.8 (year)
Birth rate	1993–1999	2.2 to 2.0 (%)
Mortality rate (under 5 years)	1993–1999	27 to 48 (out of 1,000)
Population with access to safe water	1994–1996	86 to 53 (%)
Population with access to vaccination	1990–1997	90 to 50 (%)

Source: Ministry of Unification, *Weekly Report on North Korea*, vol. 539 (in Korean, May 12, 2001).

1998 measure to vitalize inter-Korean economic cooperation has paved the way for South Korean businessmen to get easier access to North Korea without worrying much about the government restrictions. Also, the four signed agreements between South Korea and North Korea— on clearing settlements, investment protection, procedures for resolution of commercial disputes, and prevention of double taxation of income—have built the institutional foundation for the expansion of investment between the two.[37] However, even with these developments before and after the summit, inter-Korean economic cooperation is still lagging behind expectations.

Inter-Korean Trade Relations

After the 1997 financial crisis, the inter-Korean trade volume suffered a severe setback in 1998. Beginning in 1999, inter-Korean trade bounced back, and it reached the historic peak of more than $400 million in 2000. Table 10 summarizes the trends and structure of inter-Korean trade relations.

As Table 10 shows, the overall amount of trade has increased rather rapidly during the last two years. The expansion of OEM trade between the two sides is particularly noteworthy. However, if nontransactional trade is excluded from the overall trade volume, the expansion becomes less impressive. The transactional trade volume for 2000 was only $240 million, which is short of the 1997 pre-crisis level of $250

37. The agreements were made in December 2000 after the fourth inter-Korean ministerial talk that was held after the historical summit of June 2000. Refer to www.unikorea.go.kr.

million. (Nontransactional trade consists of expenditures on the Korean Peninsula Energy Development Organization (KEDO), aid from the Korean government and the private sector, and so on.[38] Including these items in the total trade volume between the two Koreas can be misleading.)

One encouraging aspect of the inter-Korean trade relationship is that the continuous increase of the Original Equipment Manufacturing (OEM) trade now accounts for roughly half of transactional trade. The OEM trade, which is especially concentrated in the area of textiles and the electronics industry, now accounts for 80 percent of transactional trade. According to Lee Sang-Man, OEM trade has many merits over ordinary trade, and it can be beneficial to both sides.[39] Even though it does not yield much profit at present, OEM trade requires more and better communication than ordinary trade, and can thus deepen economic cooperation between the two Koreas. Also, until large-scale investments from South Korea to North Korea materialize, engaging in OEM can be an interim stage between trade and investment. When nontransactional trade and OEM trade are excluded from the trade volume, the balance of inter-Korean trade is still dominated by primary goods such as agriculture and fishery goods.

Inter-Korean Investment Relations

While the inter-Korean trade volume shows the potential for continuous growth, inter-Korean investment relations are still sluggish, even after the historical summit of the two Kims in June 2000. As of December 2000, there had been eighteen approvals of economic cooperation projects; out of these, only ten were actually carried out—and this was accomplished with a total amount of merely $130 million. Only a handful of projects are currently in operation, and no other major companies are yet showing interest in investing in North Korea. The less-than-expected volume of inter-Korean investment is particularly disappointing when compared to the inter-Sino investment relationship between China and Taiwan. According to Ko Jeong-Sik, inter-Sino trade and investment

---

38. For a more detailed classification of non-transactional trade, refer to KDI, *KDI Review of the North Korean Economy* (in Korean, May 2001).

39. Lee Sang-Man, "Current Status of Inter-Korean Economic Cooperation and Tasks to Vitalize It after the Summit," *Proceedings of the 2000 Fall Conference of APEA (Asia Pacific Economic Association)*, November 2000, Seoul, Korea.

Table 10

Inter-Korean Trade and Its Structure (unit: thousands $)

	Import		Export		Total	
	Transaction (OEM)*	Non-Transaction**	Transaction (OEM)*	Non-Transaction**	Transaction (OEM)*	Non-Transaction**
1989	69 (0)	0	18,655 (0)	0	18,724 (0)	0
1990	1,188 (0)	0	12,278 (0)	0	13,466 (0)	0
1991	5,547 (0)	0	105,719 (0)	0	111,266 (0)	0
1992	10,563 (200)	0	162,863 (638)	0	173,426 (839)	0
1993	8,425 (4,023)	0	178,167 (2,985)	0	186,592 (7,008)	0
1994	18,249 (11,343)	0	176,298 (14,321)	0	194,547 (25,663)	0
1995	53,441 (24,718)	10,995	222,855 (21,174)	0	276,296 (45,892)	10,995
1996	55,420 (38,164)	14,219	182,400 (36,238)	0	237,820 (74,402)	14,219
1997	60,020 (36,175)	55,250	190,281 (42,894)	2,788	250,301 (79,069)	58,038

1998	51,530 (29,617)	78,149	92,159 (41,371)	105	143,689 (70,988)	78,254
1999	67,553 (45,883)	144,279	121,482 (53,736)	122	189,035 (99,620)	144,401
2000	93,723 (57,224)	179,052	150,517 (71,996)	1,856	244,240 (129,190)	180,908

Sources: KDI Review of the North Korean Economy (in Korean, May 2001) Korea Trade Investment Promotion Agent (www.kotra.or.kr).

Notes: * OEM stands for original equipment manufacturing. OEM occurs when South Korean firms send intermediate inputs to North Korean partners, and North Korean partners reprocess these inputs and send final products back to South Korea. ** "non-transactional trade" implies exchange of goods and services that are not based on commercial needs.

has soared continuously since 1987.[40] As of 1998, the total volume of inter-Sino trade was $24 billion, according to Taiwan sources, and $20.5 billion, according to Chinese sources. Both sources show a trade imbalance of more than $10 billion in Taiwan's favor. Direct investment from Taiwan to China was reported to be $1.5 billion, according to Taiwanese sources, and $3.1 billion, according to the Chinese. Comparing the case of China to Korea, Ko stated that inter-Korean trade and investment relations would not grow in the short term due to several restrictions that are imposed in Korea vis-à-vis China.[41] Until North Korea adopts a more open-minded policy, as China did two decades ago, it will be considered premature and risky to engage in large-scale investments in North Korea.

The most frequently cited hurdles that lie ahead for inter-Korean investment include: high transportation costs; lack of infrastructure in North Korea, such as insufficient and irregular supplies of electricity; the absence of raw- and intermediate-input supplies inside North Korea; complicated government red tape in South Korea; and the lack of legal and institutional frameworks.[42] For example, the transportation cost between Inchon, the South Korean port near Seoul, and Nampo, the North Korean port near Pyongyang, can be three times higher than the transportation cost between Inchon and Chenjin, the Chinese port near Beijing. Even though inter-Korean trade and investment can be done without the imposition of tariffs, the merit of nontariff transactions disappears when high transportation costs are factored in.

The 1998 measure to vitalize inter-Korean economic cooperation and the December 2000 signing of four agreements removed many legal and institutional barriers, and some expected to see inter-Korean economic cooperation soon. For example, Cho Dongho predicted that inter-Korean economic cooperation would experience a take-off after 2000, following the experimental period of 1989–90, the expansion period of 1991–92, the stalemate period of 1993–94, the adjustment period of

40. Ko Jeong-Sik, "A Comparative Approach of Economic Cooperation between South-North Koreas and PRC-Taiwan," *The Comparative Economic Review*, vol. 7, no. 1 (1999).

41. Ibid.

42. Yoon Deok-Ryong, "Integration and Direction of Investment Market of the Two Koreas: Gradual Integration Approach," *Korean Unification Studies*, vol. 4, no. 2 (2000). Also, refer to Lee Sang-Man, "Current Status of Inter-Korean Economic Cooperation and Tasks to Vitalize It after the Summit," *Proceedings of the 2000 Fall Conference of APEA (Asia Pacific Economic Association)*, November 2000, Seoul, Korea.

1995–97, and the sluggish period of 1998–99.[43] But even after the summit of the two Kims, the hoped-for boom in inter-Korean investment is not visible. The reasons include changes in the North Korea policy toward the U.S. government after Bush was elected president, from a policy of more generous engagement to a strict reciprocity policy. As the chances of North Korea normalizing its relationship with the United States get slimmer, potential investors from South Korea are hesitant to make substantial investments in North Korea. Furthermore, as stated above, the high-profile Kumgang Mountain Project turned out to be unprofitable, and the development of the Kaesong Industrial Zone is still not yet feasible. Since the South Korean government provided financial help to Hyundai, partly because of this loss, public opinion in South Korea regarding inter-Korean economic cooperation has deteriorated severely. Additionally, the mild recession in the South Korean economy that started in the fourth quarter of 2000 makes many South Korean firms reluctant to invest in a country like North Korea, whose long-term prospects are still foggy. Until these obstacles are either removed or minimized so that investing in North Korea can make economic sense, it will be difficult to expect large-scale investment in North Korea from the private sector of South Korea.[44]

Even though inter-Korean economic cooperation in terms of trade and investment is still sluggish, many people agree that there is a great deal of potential to realize large-scale investment from South Korea to North Korea. However, in order to make it happen, the previously stated barriers have to be removed. In particular, the high transportation cost can be dramatically reduced once commodities can be transported overland after the railroad is reconnected between South Korea and North Korea as it was agreed in the summit. This can reduce the transportation cost by two-thirds compared to the current oversea-transportation cost, and can make inter-Korea trade, especially OEM trade, more attractive. Another significant barrier is the lack of proper infrastructure in North Korea, especially in terms of electricity. Due to the lack of electricity, large-scale facilities and factories cannot be operated in North Korea, which restricts business opportunities.

---

43. Refer to KDI, *KDI Review of the North Korean Economy* (in Korean, June 2001).

44. Yoon (2000) calculated that the return on capital invested into North Korea has to be at least 37 percent or higher to make any economic sense for the South Korean investors. Yoon Deok-Ryong, "Integration and Direction of Investment Market of the Two Koreas: Gradual Integration Approach," *Korean Unification Studies*, vol. 4, no. 2 (2000).

Economic Prospects for Reconciliation and Reunification

External Economic Environments

Current external environments for North Korea are full of uncertainties, both economic and political. Generally speaking, North Korea is having a hard time figuring out the real intentions of the new administrations in the United States and Japan, even as it is improving relations with the EU and China. Until these external environments become more favorable to North Korea, any effort by the country to induce foreign investment into its Special Economic Zone (SEZ) would be fruitless. In fact, North Korea has continuously enacted laws related to foreign investment since the mid-1980s, when the open-door policy was first initiated. In the early 1990s, when North Korea designated the Rajin-Sonbong area as a Free Economic and Trade Zone (FETZ), several more laws related to foreign investment were enacted.[45] According to other laws enacted in 1998 and 1999, foreign firms in the Rajin-Sonbong ETZ can enjoy privileges such as no tariffs on imports and exports, three years' tax exemption, and two years' tax reductions of 50 percent. Still, unfavorable external factors and poor internal conditions for foreign investment are prohibiting any massive amount of foreign investment from flowing into North Korea.

The most significant of these external factors is the North Korea–U.S. relationship. The Bush administration's more restrictive reciprocity policy has reduced the chances of the further lifting of the economic sanctions that have been imposed on North Korea since June 28, 1950. Unless these economic sanctions are lifted, any amount of remittance from the United States to North Korea that exceeds $400 (excluding humanitarian aid) will be prohibited. Even worse than the economic sanctions is the inclusion of North Korea in the United States so-called blacklist of countries that support international terrorism. Because of this designation, the United States blocks North Korea's attempt to join international organizations such as the International Monetary Fund (IMF), the World Bank, and the Asian Development Bank (ADB). Also, without normalization of its diplomatic ties with the United States, North Korea will have a hard time normal-

---

45. The North Korean authority dropped the word "free" from FETZ later on, and at present calls it ETZ.

izing its relations with Japan, a connection that could bring North Korea $5–10-billion worth in compensation funds. Fortunately, there are some recent signs of easing tensions between North Korea and the United States.

The case of the normalization of the Vietnam-U.S. relationship can provide some analogies to North Korea's situation. The United States imposed an economic embargo upon Vietnam as the Vietnam War ended in 1975. When Vietnam invaded Cambodia in 1978, western European countries and international organizations such as the IMF, the World Bank, and the ADB joined the embargo, thus making the Vietnamese economic situation similar to today's North Korean situation. However, as Vietnam began its *doi moi* reforms in the later half of the 1980s, its relationship with the United States began to improve. Finally, in 1993, the United States agreed that Vietnam could receive funds from international organizations, and the embargo was lifted in 1994. From this experience, North Korea can learn several lessons. First, North Korea must make its own efforts to reform its economy in order to create favorable external environments, just as Vietnam did with its *doi moi* policy. Second, North Korea needs to satisfy the demands of the United States regarding regional security. In the case of Vietnam, it was the war with Cambodia that bothered the United States; North Korea's nuclear- and missile-development programs are a similar provocation, and any serious movement toward normalized relations with the United States will be hampered without substantial progress in these areas. Third, even if the United States lifts sanctions, North Korea's major trade and investment partner would not be the United States. In Vietnam's case, it was mostly Asian countries such as Japan, Korea, Singapore, Taiwan, and Hong Kong that invested in Vietnam (with an expectation of exporting goods produced in Vietnam to foreign countries including the United States). In North Korea's case, the major trade and investment partner would be South Korea.[46]

One consoling aspect of North Korea's relationship with the United States is that, despite the administration change in the United States, the 1994 Geneva Agreed Framework is still in place without modification. According to this agreement, the United States is providing 500,000

---

46. For the experiences of the Vietnamese open-door policy and the other former socialists' open-door policy, refer to *Research Report* (in Korean, May 2001) of SERI (Samsung Economic Research Institute).

tons of heavy oil to North Korea, and an atomic energy plant is under construction despite many difficulties. So far, about 11 percent of the planned investment has been made.[47] Mr. Desaix Anderson, the executive director of KEDO, recently emphasized the positive economic and political roles of the KEDO project in the context of regional security.[48]

More encouraging signs of favorable external environments come from China and Europe. China has traditionally been a major ally to North Korea not only politically but also economically. Sino–North Korea trade increased substantially last year, from $370 million in 1999 to $488 million in 2000. Most Sino–North Korea trade is in the form of imports by North Korea from China, and these can be classified in three categories: official imports, border trade, and aid. Of these three, the relative importance of aid is decreasing as that of official and border-trade increases, reflecting the economically improved situation of North Korea. Moreover, the expected visit of the Chinese president to North Korea, in return for Kim Jong-Il's visit to China early this year, is likely to further deepen the Sino–North Korea relationship.

Perhaps it is North Korea's relationship with the EU that has produced the most favorable results for North Korea during the past two years. As of July 2001, North Korea had normalized its diplomatic ties with all the EU countries except France and Ireland, and it can expect to receive more development aid from the EU from now on. (So far, the EU has provided mostly humanitarian aid to North Korea through the Food Aid and Food Security Programme, the World Food Program, and NGOs, totaling 168 million euros during the past four years.)[49] By enjoying a better relationship with the EU, North Korea can alleviate pressures from the United States and have better leverage in international negotiations. Having stronger bargaining power in talks with the United States can be crucial to North Korea, especially when the new U.S. government is relying more on hard-line policies.

---

47. Refer to KDI, *KDI Review of the North Korean Economy* (in Korean, June 2001), p. 62.

48. Refer to KDI, *KDI Review of the North Korean Economy* (in Korean, May 2001), pp. 43–47. He claimed that the KEDO project is going on as it is scheduled, and it contributes to the non-proliferation of nuclear weapons. Also, he says that there is no other alternative better than building the atomic energy plant.

49. Yoon Deok-Ryong, "The Role of EU in the Korean Peninsular Affair and Its Implication," *KIEP (Korea Institute for International Economic Policy) Issue Analysis* (June 2001).

Inter-Korean Relations for Reconciliation

One important step in overcoming barriers to inter-Korean reconciliation can be the development of North Korea's Kaesong Industrial Zone near the South Korean capital.[50] According to a presentation made by Hyundai in February 2001, the corporation is planning to develop a Kaesong Industrial Zone of 8 million pyung in three stages over eight years.[51] A rosy scenario released by Hyundai estimates that during the eight-year development period, North Korea will be able to enjoy direct cash income of $2 billion with indirect income of $4.9 billion, while South Korea can reap direct income of $18.5 billion as well as indirect income of $27 billion.[52] However, due to liquidity problems at Hyundai, this ambitious plan had not been launched as of July 2001.

Other barriers to be removed come from the South Korean side. The weakening of the South Korean economy since the fourth quarter of 2000 is a major hindrance, but this will become less important once the South Korean economy rebounds from the current slowdown, as is predicted in a survey done by Yoon Deok-Ryong.[53] A more serious barrier could be a political one. Many conservative people in South Korea, including the opposition party, oppose the idea of pouring money into North Korea, with its die-hard socialist philosophy, in a time of economic hardship in South Korea. Also, they suspect that the government is subsidizing the troubled Hyundai companies, perhaps unfairly, in order to save the Kumgang Mountain and Kaesong Industrial Zone Projects, both of which Hyundai is pursuing. (In order to overcome the stalemate caused by Hyundai's liquidity crisis, the South Korean government stepped in to save the Kumgang Mountain Project through the formation of a consortium that agreed to pay North Korea $6 million a month instead of the $12 million monthly that Hyundai was paying at the end of 2000.) Criticism notwithstanding, the actual amounts of money transferred from South Korea to North Korea in the form of nontransactional

---

50. Kaesong is an industrial city near the DMZ (Demilitarized Zone), and Kim Jong-Il agreed to let Hyundai develop an industrial zone in this city.

51. 1 pyung = 3.3 m².

52. Refer to Hyundai Research Institute, *VIP Report* (in Korean, June 13, 2001).

53. According to Yoon (2000), out of 448 firms responding to a survey, 60 firms said that they would be interested in trading with or investing in North Korea once the economic condition of South Korea improves. Yoon Deok-Ryong, "Integration and Direction of Investment Market of the Two Koreas: Gradual Integration Approach," *Korean Unification Studies*, vol. 4, no. 2 (2000).

trade, aid, and transfers from Hyundai are almost negligible when considered in terms of the overall size of the South Korean economy. As shown in Table 7, these transfers were as much as $250 million in 2000, which is a mere 0.15 percent of South Korean exports and 0.05 percent of the South Korean GDP in 2000. Therefore, the fear on the part of South Koreans of pouring too much money into a bottomless pit such as North Korea is premature. All the same, the lack of better understanding of these North Korean projects and the absence of consensus among opinion leaders inside South Korea can potentially cause a great deal of trouble for the South Korean government.

Generally speaking, even though inter-Korean economic cooperation is still at a stalemate due to the reasons examined above, several positive movements are gestating underneath the surface. One encouraging sign is the increased number of personal exchanges between South Korea and North Korea. The number of South Korean people visiting North Korea has been continuously increasing. From slightly over 1,000 in 1997, this figure reached 7,280 in 2000. The number of family reunions between the two Koreas has also dramatically increased, from 61 cases in 1997 to 558 cases in 2000.[54] If these positive changes go on with more sincere cooperation from the North Korean side, greatly improved inter-Korean economic cooperation will be likely in the future. For example, Hwang (2001) estimates that once North Korea becomes a normal state, the annual investment from South Korea in North Korea could be as high as $190 to $250 million.[55]

Concluding Remarks

This chapter has analyzed the South Korean and North Korean economic situations of the past couple of years from domestic, inter-Korean, and international perspectives. In terms of the domestic economic situations, both economies have experienced positive growth in 1999 and 2000. In terms of inter-Korean economic cooperation, the much-anticipated expansion of trade and investment is not yet visible.

---

54. Refer to *Munhwa Ilbo* (in Korean, June 15, 2001).

55. This estimation is based on the assumption that North Korea's Export to GDP ratio reaches the level of South Korea's and North Korea's monthly wage level stays around $80–110. Refer to Hwang Eui-Gak, "Beyond the Summit: Deepening Linkages," *Joint U.S.-Korea Academic Studies*, vol. 11 (2001).

The South Korean economy has traveled a bumpy road of recovery and slowdown from 1999 to 2001, learning several valuable lessons along the way. Also, owing to changes that occurred in the process of recovery, the internal and external environments of the South Korean economy as of 2001 have been altered greatly compared to those of 1997.

The North Korean economy also achieved positive growth rates in 1999 and 2000. While some of this progress might be attributed to efforts made by the North Korean side, many believe that the positive growth was made possible by external help, including major assistance from South Korea. In many respects, North Korea is still at its core a centrally planned economy, and its future is much in doubt.

Inter-Korean economic cooperation is still sluggish despite the historical summit. The reasons for this include the lack of infrastructure in North Korea, the uncertain future of North Korean reform, the weakened economic situation of South Korea, and the hard-line policy of the new U.S. administration against North Korea. Even though the South Korean government has stepped in to save large-scale North Korea projects such as the Kumgang Mountain Project, the private sector of South Korea does not show much enthusiasm for investing in North Korea.

External environments are also full of uncertainties that affect the North Korean economy. Even though the new U.S. administration has softened its posture more recently, it is still not yet clear how much U.S. policy toward North Korea has actually changed. At the same time, North Korea has succeeded in achieving a better relationship with the EU and preserving and extending its friendly relationship with China.

The New North Korea

Ralph C. Hassig and Kongdan Oh

Since the 1980s, watchers of North Korea have looked for signs that the government in Pyongyang was prepared to undertake practical reforms to rescue its faltering economy and deliver on the promise that its people will "eat rice and meat soup, wear silk clothes, and live in a house with a tiled roof." Each new initiative—the adoption of a foreign joint-venture law in 1984, the signing of reconciliation and nuclear-free agreements with South Korea in 1991, the opening of the Najin-Sonbong foreign trade zone in 1991, the Agreed Framework freezing the North's nuclear program in exchange for economic and diplomatic rewards from the United States in 1994, and the first inter-Korean summit meeting in June 2000—raised the same question: Is North Korea ready to modify or abandon its totalitarian social system and open its borders to South Korea and the international community?

For most Koreans living in the relatively prosperous southern half of the peninsula, the 2000 summit meeting was a convincing sign that North Korea had taken a determined and irrevocable step down the path of reconciliation and reunification, but with a year's hindsight many are no longer confident that the North's quest for economic survival has finally overcome the logic of regime security, which dictates that totalitarian governments place firm economic and political controls on their people and restrict their access to information from foreign sources.

It is impossible to miss the changes that came to North Korea in the last two years of the twentieth century. In 2000, for example, 7,280 South Koreans visited the North, and 706 North Koreans visited the South. The fenced-off tourist preserve set up by South Korea's Hyundai Asan company at North Korea's Mount Kumgang was visited by 213,009 South Koreans. In each of three family reunions, 100 family members from each side crossed the border, enabling a total of 3,630 family members to be briefly reunited. A special program enabled 10,213 persons to discover the whereabouts of separated family members. In another program, 600 people were permitted to send letters to divided family members (who were not permitted to reply). The value of inter-Korean economic exchanges (much of it unilateral aid from South Korea) totaled $425 million, and 652 South Korean companies engaged in inter-Korean trade. The South Koreans sent 600,000 tons of food and 300,000 tons of fertilizer to the North in 2000, with another 200,000 tons of fertilizer in 2001.[1] Representatives of the two Korean governments held over a dozen important meetings, including the first inter-Korean summit. Kim Jong-Il even met with a delegation from South Korea's leading media companies. Hundreds of North Korean officials were sent abroad to study the market economy, and Pyongyang opened diplomatic relations with the European Union (EU) and numerous Western governments.

The North Korea of 2001 is not the North Korea of 1980 or 1990, nor can it compare with today's far more prosperous South Korea. Viewed from the perspective of a half-century of conservative North Korean politics, there is ample reason to suspect that these recent changes are of a tactical nature designed to tide the country over in times of great economic need, rather than a strategic change in policy.

In politics, North Korea changed little in the last two years of the twentieth century, as Kim Jong-Il and the military jointly increased their political power. The impoverished economy rebounded temporarily due to two years of better harvests and a continuing inflow of foreign aid, and the people continued to resort to the unofficial farmers' markets to supplement the meager rations flowing from government warehouses. The most remarkable change occurred in foreign policy, as the Kim government mounted a vigorous diplomatic campaign to repair its relations with China and Russia, while opening relations with Western governments, all the better to gain foreign aid and bolster the government's legitimacy internally and externally. But diplomatic ties were not accompanied by people-to-people relations, as North Korea's borders remained closed.

---

1. Kim Sang-Yon "First Anniversary of 15 June—Inter-Korean Exchanges as Seen by Statistics," *Taehan Maeil*, Internet version at http://www.seoul.co.kr, June 14, 2001. On the occasion of the first anniversary of the summit, the ROK Ministry of Unification issued two publications: *Toward an Era of Peace and Cooperation* reviews inter-Korean relations over twelve months; *Peace and Cooperation*, a white paper, includes a chronology of inter-Korean contacts from 1998 through 2000.

In North Korea it is an article of faith to keep outsiders guessing about what is happening in the country, thereby providing (so they think) a relatively weak country with some small advantage in dealing with more powerful countries. This lack of transparency forces outsiders to draw conclusions based on fragmentary evidence, as is the case in this survey of North Korea.

The Politics of Sameness

Where the Power Lies

How has Kim Jong-Il been able to perpetuate the fifty-year-old Kim dynasty even during periods of appalling hardship for the North Korean people? After his father's death in 1994, the odds against the junior Kim's survival did not look good, at least to many foreign observers. Kim was immediately faced with the challenge of resolving a potentially deadly standoff with the United States over the North's nuclear program. Then, in 1995, heavy summer rains devastated much of the North Korean countryside, destroying crops and villages, and flooding the country's coal mines. The country's GNP continued to show negative growth, foreign trade diminished, and factory operating rates hovered around 25 percent. For the next three years Kim secluded himself from the public, never making a public speech. North Korean officials explained that as a dutiful son, he was honoring a traditional three-year mourning period.

In October 1997, Kim acceded to the position of General Secretary of the Workers' Party of Korea (WPK), and in September 1998 he reappointed himself chairman of the National Defense Commission, from which position he runs the country; the office of president was retired so that his father could be the country's "eternal president." North Korea watchers hoped but doubted that Kim was a closet reformer who would take the country in a new direction now that his father and most of the old guard had passed from the scene. It was not to be. "Expect no change from me" is how the North Korean press quoted Kim,[2] and he delivered on that promise, choosing to rule according to his father's *Yuhun* (be-

---

2. Unattributed talk entitled "Having the Most Sublime Revolutionary Will," Korean Central Broadcasting Network (KCBN), October 12, 1998. KCBN is the domestic broadcasting network.

hest) under the slogan "The great Comrade Kim Jong-Il is today's Comrade Kim Il-Sung."[3]

In the mid-1990s he consolidated his power in the office of the National Defense Commission and gradually moved out of his father's shadow. New slogans and policies such as "military-first" began appearing under his name, as Kim sought to bring the country out of its slump with methods that had served his father well in the 1950s and 1960s.

Kim undoubtedly has more power than anyone else in North Korea, but what is his position with other potential power-holders, especially the military brass? And what is his position with the millions of ordinary North Koreans on whom the fate of the country ultimately rests? The short answer to the first question is provided by former North Korean party secretary Hwang Jang-Yop, who confidently asserts that "Only Kim Jong-Il has real power."[4] Lists of those who accompany Kim on inspection tours and lists of attendees at major events suggest that since his father's death Kim has co-opted the military leadership.[5] By the turn of the century most of the top generals had received their commissions from Kim, and his military-first policy guaranteed the generals a prominent role in government and society.[6]

---

3. The seventeen-page behest was published in volume 44 of Kim Il-Sung's *Collected Works.* As summarized in the South Korean newspaper *Choson Ilbo* (November 18, 1996, p. 9), the instructions advocated building oil-burning power plants, completing the Hungnam fertilizer plant, "normalizing" cement production for export earnings, increasing production at steelworks, building 100 oceangoing cargo ships to promote trade with Southeast Asian economies, permit economic bureaucrats to study business practices, and even visit foreign countries for that purpose, and achieve the socialization and unification of the entire Korean peninsula.

4. Interview with Hwang Jang-Yop, KBS Television, July 10, 1997; translated by the BBC Summary of World Broadcasts, July 15, 1997.

5. In 2000, Kim Kuk-Tae, director of the WPK Cadres Department, accompanied Kim on thirty-seven occasions; Kim Yong-Chun, chief of the KPA General Staff, made thirty-two trips; and Cho Myong-Rok, director of the KPA's General Political Bureau, and Kim Il-Chol, minister of the People's Armed Forces, each made thirty trips. The next most frequent fellow travelers were Generals Hyuon Chol-Hae and Park Chae-Kyong, with twenty-eight trips each. Kim Jong-Il's brother-in-law, Chang Song-Taek, accompanied him on twenty-five trips. See Yi Sok-U, "Who Are Closest to NDC Chairman Kim?" *Taehan Maeil*, Internet version at www.seoul.co.kr, January 11, 2001.

6. Military trappings of governance are nothing new to North Korea: in Kim Il-Sung's day the military was accorded top economic priority, and the most powerful individual after the senior and junior Kims was the top military general, O Jin-U, who died in 1995.

Because the junior Kim is not a professional soldier, and since the economy that funds the military has been on a downward spiral almost every year since his rise to power in the 1990s, Kim's dominance over the military cannot be taken for granted. To bolster his position, he has strengthened political oversight of the military, which is watched by multiple security services all reporting directly to him. The second most powerful person in North Korea appears to be Cho Myong-Rok, the vice marshal who directs the General Political Bureau of the Korean People's Army (KPA).[7] Power in North Korea is invested in people rather than in positions or laws. Kim and his close associates, including members of Kim's extended family such as his first son, Kim Jong-Nam, and Kim Jong-Il's brother-in-law, Chang Song-Taek, seem to have a firm grip on the reins of power.

Kim Jong-Il Up Close

"Thunder roared, lightening struck, and later even a rainbow appeared in the snowy skies above Panmun County and Taehongdan County on the occasion of the great general's birthday, and residents who witnessed these phenomena were unable to contain their amazement . . . noting that this again proves that our general is a great man sent from heaven."[8] Thus did the North Korean press in 2001 mark Kim Jong-Il's fifty-ninth birthday.

South Korean president Kim Dae-Jung is quoted as describing Kim Jong-Il as "perhaps the only one who matters in his country."[9] To the frustration of foreign analysts, Kim until recently has led an exceptionally reclusive life for a man who seems to have been running the government since the early 1980s. Unlike his late father, Kim has rarely met with foreigners. He has never given a public speech. Even the annual New Year's addresses from the leader were discontinued after his father's death, to be replaced by unsigned New Year's editorials.

---

7. Article 59 of the DPRK constitution says the mission of the KPA is "to protect the interests of the working people." The Charter of the WPK clearly states that "The Korean People's Army is the revolutionary armed forces of the WPK in the glorious tradition of the anti-Japanese armed struggle." That the KPA is the army of the leader is made clear in instructions such as "It is the noble view of life of the KPA soldiers that to defend him [Kim Jong-Il] at the risk of their lives is the highest honor of the revolutionary soldiers." See *Rodong Shinmun*, March 14, 2001; quoted by the Korean Central News Agency (KCNA), the official North Korean news agency, on the same date.

8. KCBN, February 17, 2001.

9. Steven Mufson, "Seoul's Kim Presses for U.S. Role," *Washington Post*, March 9, 2001, p. A22.

Over the years, Kim has been portrayed as arrogant, impulsive, decisive, bold, reckless, energetic, fast thinking and fast talking (in a high-pitched voice, often in fragmentary sentences), quick tempered and at times violent, and awkward among strangers. His hobbies are said to include fast cars, fast horses, hunting and shooting, and watching action films from his extensive library of foreign films ("imperialistic propaganda" videos that are forbidden to the North Korean people).

In the year 2000 the foreign public finally had an opportunity to observe Kim firsthand. In broadcasted portions of the inter-Korean summit, which were watched with keen interest in South Korea (the North Korean people saw only brief silent footage of their leader), Kim proved to be a charming, talkative, humorous, and courteous host, not the ogre that many South Korean viewers had expected to see. To quote one news commentator, "For President Kim and his entourage, it was a case of three days of 'Alice in Wonderland,' in which they found themselves dealing with a Kim Jong-Il looking, sounding, and behaving in exactly the opposite ways from his lifelong stereotype."[10]

South Korean public opinion polls taken after the summit documented the "Kim Jong-Il shock." In one survey, the proportion of people holding a favorable view of Kim's leadership jumped from 20 percent before the summit to 64 percent afterwards.[11] In another poll, 54 percent of respondents had a favorable impression of Kim after the summit, compared to only 5 percent before.[12] Another survey asked South Korean opinion leaders about their post-summit impression of Kim. Interestingly, 57 percent of journalists changed their view of Kim, compared to only 24 percent of North Korea experts, who perhaps had held more realistic views of Kim before the summit, or were less impressed by his showmanship.[13]

Two weeks after the summit meeting, Mun Myong-Cha, a Korean journalist based in the United States, became the first foreign news reporter to be granted an exclusive interview with Kim Jong-Il. In a five-hour meeting that included an elaborate lunch featuring swallow's nest

10. Dong-Bok Lee, "Inter-Korean Summitry: Another Indian Game of Elephant versus Blind People?" *Korea and World Affairs*, vol. XXIV, no. 2 (Summer 2000), pp. 207–27; see p. 209.

11. Kim Tack-Whan, "The Image of North Korea after Inter-Korean Summit," *Korea Focus*, vol. 8, vo. 6 (November–December 2000), pp. 114–32; see p. 120. The survey was commissioned by the Korean Broadcasting Institute and originally reported in the *Korea Daily News*.

12. Ibid., p. 120.

13. Ibid., p. 126.

shark fin soup in a coconut shell, broiled beef, fried potato dumplings, pine nut gruel, spiced steamed goose, and crab salad, Kim was frank and knowledgeable about a wide range of subjects. As a reporter who is famously supportive of North Korea (hence her opportunity to visit the republic on numerous occasions), Mun made no judgments about Kim, noting without comment that when asked to list the most important traits of a leader, Kim said, "As the Leader [Kim Il-Sung] once said, a leader should not reign over the people. He should work with them. Bureaucracy prevents the unity between the people and the leader. We have eliminated it, and that was how we could overcome difficulties."[14]

Two months after the summit a delegation of fifty South Korean media chiefs met Kim at a luncheon in Pyongyang, where he displayed the utmost confidence in his power and judgments. Speaking of Korean reunification, Kim said, "It is all up to me. I can tell you that it will happen at an appropriate time. People in high positions can use expressions like this." On relations with the United States, "If I so instruct, diplomatic relations will be established with the United States even tomorrow." On the proposed project to allow South Korea's Hyundai Asan company to develop an industrial zone in the North Korean city of Kaesong: "You could say that I bestowed a privilege on Hyundai."[15]

In regard to Kim's openness, one member of the visiting media delegation observed that "Kim Jong-Il's unexpected way of talking and presenting himself has opened an uncomfortable gap between his attitude and the DPRK regime that remains little changed."[16] Thus the puzzle: Kim is obviously an intelligent man in touch with current domestic and foreign affairs. Yet he remains a dictator of the worst kind, overseeing the demise of his people, if not his country. He lives a life that ordinary North Koreans could not even dream of. Is he a heartless dictator, or is he so isolated from everyday life in his country (and the outside world) that he really believes in his own propaganda?

Kim's trips to China in 2000 and to China and Russia in 2001 provided little direct evidence about his personality, for in these visits he met only with a few officials. In fact, both his trips to China were "secret" in the sense that neither the North Korean nor Chinese govern-

14. Interview by Sin Chun-Yong on July 7, 2000, in Beijing with Mun Myong-Cha, *Taehan Maeil* Internet version at www.seoul.co.kr, July 12, 2000.

15. Yonhap News Agency, August 13, 2000.

16. "DPRK Travelogues by Eight Media Heads: 'Kim Jong-Il Is in a Hurry,'" *Sindong-a*, September 6, 2000. The interviews were anonymous.

ments acknowledged his obvious presence in China until Kim had returned to North Korea. In the absence of a free press in China, few reports of Kim's activities were published. Kim's Russian trip was semi-secret: the North Korean people were not told of his "immortal external revolutionary activities" in Russia (to quote a North Korean television broadcast) until the ninth day of his twenty-day journey. In Russia, as in China, he met only with a small number of Russian officials, keeping well away from Russian journalists and citizens. The Russian press was predominantly hostile toward Kim's visit, viewing it as an unpleasant reminder of the Stalinism of their distant past. The press frequently commented on the tight security surrounding Kim's twenty-one-car train (fifteen cars, some of them armored, came from North Korea but were manufactured in Japan; six cars were added for Russian officials at the border). The governor of Saint Petersburg, who hosted Kim for lunch, saw the sociable side of the reclusive dictator: "[T]here had been much talk that he is an unsociable person closed to the public . . . [but] he takes a lively interest in history, culture and economy, and is not afraid of asking questions."[17] The Chinese and Russian visits seem to confirm that Kim is morbidly concerned about his personal safety, and that he is an elitist who is interested in dealing with VIPs but has little sense of "public" relations.

Reign and Rule

Kim Jong-Il and his late father have employed three methods to instruct their people: "on-the-spot guidance," instruction of managing officials or "functionaries," and mass propaganda.

Although Kim Jong-Il does not appear to be comfortable around strangers—either because of shyness, impatience with them, or fear for his own safety—he has become increasingly active in delivering on-the-spot guidance since his father's death.[18] If one believes the

---

17. This observation of Saint Petersburg mayor Vladimir Yakovlev was published by Interfax, a private Russian information agency, August 7, 2001.

18. Kim made seventy-three public appearances in 2000, approximately the same number as in 1999 and 1998 but more than the fifty-odd appearances made in 1996 and 1997. In 1999, forty-four appearances were at military installations, but the number declined to twenty-one in 2000. An increasing number of visits have been for economic guidance and inspection (twenty-five in 2000), as Kim became more involved in running the economy. Sources: *Korea Annual 2000*, (Seoul: Yonhap News Agency, 2000), p. 266, and the ROK Ministry of Unification. Table 5 in Doowon Lee's chapter in this volume presents a breakdown of Kim's guidance for the years 1996–mid-2001.

North Korean press reports, Kim is invariably more knowledgeable about the work he is inspecting than the managers and workers themselves. Work sites visited by Kim become "sacred," and the few people fortunate enough to shake his hand become socially and economically privileged for the rest of their lives. Kim's instructions at the site are published in the press and become required study material at the political study meetings that all North Koreans attend on an almost daily basis.

Kim also leads by issuing instructions to functionaries. He has encountered considerable difficulty in motivating these intermediaries, whose overriding concern is to avoid making mistakes—the most serious mistake being to utter any word or commit any deed that could be construed as contravening Kim's policies and official ideology. Because officials' salaries in North Korean currency are virtually worthless, many functionaries routinely accept bribes from their underlings and clients for duties performed. The North Korean party newspaper, *Rodong Shinmun*, probably gives an accurate description of typical work habits when it complains about functionaries "doing nothing but lingering in offices, picking up statistics, coming back to organize cumbersome meetings, and giving empty model lectures."[19] Bureaucratic lethargy is punctuated with occasional "speed battles" whose effects are short-lived, giving rise to the phrase "five-minute heat."

In the press, Kim Jong-Il has frequently urged functionaries to go out into the workplace, become acquainted with the workers' problems, and vigorously lead them as a commander leads his troops in battle. Lacking any practical plan for economic recovery, Kim urges economic managers to come up with something themselves: "Strictly speaking, initiative means one has one's own opinion on one's own work, maps out a plan of operation for work and pushes it ahead based on one's own judgment and determination."[20] The practical hazards of pursuing such a course of action in a centrally planned socialist society are obvious. Moreover, there is the political hazard of repudiating years of party guidance, as when managers are told: "When all the functionaries thoroughly free themselves from everything old and conservative and set out on their work with a desire to create something new, something world-renowned,

---

19. "Be the Functionaries the Party Expects Them to Be and the Masses Follow," *Rodong Shinmun*, May 22, 1999, p. 3.

20. Kim Chin-Kuk, "Initiative, Creativity, and Dedication," *Rodong Shinmun*, February 23, 2001, p. 2.

they can make themselves the standard bearer, propelling today's socialist advance under the red flag."[21]

Propaganda Campaigns

The collective efforts of the North Korean people are supposed to be guided by grand ideological campaigns that focus the public's energies on the national tasks of the moment. Most of these campaigns come down to the same things: work harder and endure hardship to preserve socialism and support the party and the leader. In fact, the campaigns are so general in nature that they offer the people little guidance in their daily lives; rather they are meant to provide a heightened level of motivation, although these campaigns probably fail to achieve even this goal.

From the time of Kim Il-Sung's death in 1994, the national struggle for survival was called the "Arduous March," taking the name from the difficult marches that Kim Il-Sung and his guerrilla band endured during their fight with the Japanese in the 1930s. On the occasion of the fifty-fifth anniversary of the WPK in October 2000, it was announced that the Arduous March had been crowned with victory, perhaps referring to the fact that the harvests of 1998 and 1999 had been somewhat better than in the previous three years. According to the North Korean press, "victory" also meant that Kim Jong-Il had officially taken the reins of power: "the greatest victory gained by the 'Arduous March' is that Kim Jong-Il's absolutely authoritative helmsmanship and powerful political system were fully verified and universally recognized."[22] "Victory" was further interpreted to mean that the "imperialists" had failed to eliminate socialism in North Korea: "the people of Korea under [Kim Jong-Il's] leadership have heroically crossed the sea of blood and tears and the death line in their crucial struggle to defend socialism and build a powerful nation."[23] In any case, the people were warned not to expect an early reversal in their fortunes. The 2001 New Year's editorial warned that "We should march through the arduous road of struggle of the new century too."[24]

In 1998, around the time when the Supreme People's Assembly was

---

21. Ibid.

22. KCNA, October 3, 2000; citing a *Rodong Shinmun* article of the same date.

23. Ibid.

24. "Let's Open Up the Road of Advance through the New Century in the Spirit of the Victorious 'Arduous March.'" This is the translation provided by the North Korean–affiliated newspaper in Japan, *The People's Korea*, nos. 1879/1880 (January 27, 2001), pp. 2–4.

convened (the first SPA meeting since Kim Il-Sung's death), Kim Jong-Il decided to bring back two economic campaigns that had worked for his father years before. The *Chollima* campaign—named after a legendary Korean flying horse and first introduced in 1956—urges the people to work harder and faster. In 1998, working at *Chollima* speed was supposed to enable the people to create a *Kangsong Taeguk*, that is, an economically and militarily strong nation. Kim also directed his economic cadres to reemphasize heavy industry, turning away from the agriculture, light industry and trade emphasis of the preceding years. *Chollima*, like the more limited "speed battles" that are a permanent fixture of the North Korean economy, is often enforced at the work site by drumbeating and flag-waving exhortations performed by mobile propaganda teams, and by rousing articles in the press:

> The drum is beating. All of the people run by mounting a swift horse. . . . Our people like to dash ahead while beating a drum. . . . Only an iron-willed brilliant commander [i.e., Kim Jong-Il] who is intelligent and courageous could precisely seize the moment to beat the drum. . . . Today's drumbeat is the drumbeat of a laugh, a joyful drumbeat, and a drumbeat bound for paradise. . . . When the general calls, tens of millions of warriors must echo him on the battlefield.[25]

By 1999 the military had been designated as the model for all fields of endeavor, with party officials commanded to work in "battlefront style."[26] In early 2001, the military-first campaign was given a more political emphasis:

> Military first politics is a unique form of politics presented for the first time in history by the respected and beloved general [i.e., Kim Jong-Il]. When our country instituted it, many people saw it as an effort to cope with the strained military and political situations then prevailing, and simply as aimed at military buildup. However . . . military first politics precisely is a completely new form of politics unprecedented in the political history of humankind and . . . is invincibly powerful.[27]

---

25. "Sound Loudly the Drumbeat of the Revolution," political essay from KCBN, September 28, 1999.

26. Hwang Chang-Man, "The Great Leader Who Leads the Socialist Cause by His Military-First Revolutionary Leadership," *Rodong Shinmun*, February 28, 1999, p. 2.

27. Kim Hong-Yong, "The Basic Requirements of Our Party's Military-First Politics," *Rodong Shinmun*, February 7, 2001, p. 2.

The 2001 New Year's editorial kicked off yet another campaign, the "Socialist Red Banner March of the Twenty-first Century," coupling the usual appeal to work harder with the demand that the work be done more efficiently and scientifically.[28] Workers were called upon to "renew all our factories and enterprises with up-to-date technology," and "introduce basic innovations in improving our ideas, thought, working style, and fighting spirit." Subsequent editorials also emphasized the importance of displaying unity with the leader and the party, possibly in anticipation of an opening of North Korean society to the outside world.

The ideas in the 2001 New Year's editorial were elaborated and expanded over the next several months. Upon returning from a trip to China during which he observed Shanghai's vibrant economy, Kim weighed in with more advice: "A new age demands a new ideological viewpoint and a new struggle ethos. It is impossible to advance the revolution even a step further if we should get complacent with our past achievements or be enslaved to outdated ideas and stick to the outmoded style and attitude in our work."[29] Yet there was no hint that the constraints of totalitarian socialism would be relaxed; rather, the new thinking must be done within the context of socialist ideology.

And so the political picture in North Korea remains largely the same, with Kim Jong-Il dominating 22 million people and taking special care to reward and keep a close eye on the military. The corrupt political foundation on which the country rests is not to be rebuilt. Many of the people who have led the country into failure over the last quarter century remain in power. The Kims, father and son, have tried for fifty years to shape North Korea through "social remodeling, nature remaking, and human remolding," but Kim Jong-Il's "new thinking" focuses only on the second two alterations, leaving North Korea's social structure intact. In addition to the all-too-familiar call for the people to work harder and endure more hardships, Kim Jong-Il in his impatience with North Korea's inability to escape from its depression has embraced the fantastic idea of leapfrogging fifty years of failure into the twenty-first century by employing the latest technology. A large dose of optimism is required to believe that Kim is giving serious thought to loosening his grip on North Korean society as a first step toward reconciling with

---

28. This is the translation provided by the North Korean–affiliated newspaper in Japan, *The People's Korea*, nos. 1879/1880 (January 27, 2001), pp. 2–4.
29. Ibid.

South Korea. The South's successful democracy and strong economy remain potent threats to the security of the Kim regime. In the Joint Declaration that concluded the inter-Korean summit, the two Korean leaders claimed to have found a "common element" in their respective proposals for reunification, but the reunification issue was never pursued, and it is hard to imagine how two such different political and economic systems could be reconciled.

Economic Stirrings

Still Struggling

It appears that during the first three years after his father's death, Kim left economic matters to others, focusing his attention on consolidating his power with the military. In an unpublished speech reportedly made at Kim Il-Sung University in 1997—a speech highly critical of how the cadres were handling the economy—Kim said, "When he was alive, the Leader [Kim Il-Sung] told me not to get involved in economic work. He repeatedly told me that if I got involved in economic work, I would not be able to handle party and Army work properly."[30] But as economic problems worsened, Kim was forced to address them personally. Economic policies attributed to him were presented beginning in late 1998.

The 2001 New Year's editorial boasts that fifty years of socialism have enabled North Koreans to "consolidate our powerful national economy to meet the requirements of the new era." This despite the fact that the North's economic infrastructure has crumbled and millions of its people suffer from disease and malnutrition. Staying the present course guarantees that the people will be on an arduous march for many years to come. Only by soliciting donations of food and energy from other countries—socialist countries during the cold war and capitalist countries since the beginning of the 1990s—has the Kim government been able to avoid a total societal collapse.

The North Korean government does not publish reliable economic statistics, although figures of unknown validity are occasionally released as they benefit the regime, for example in support of appeals for international assistance. A recent example was the disclosure by Deputy Foreign Minister Choe Su-Hon at a UNICEF conference that life expectancy

---

30. *Wolgan Choson*, April 1997, pp. 306–17.

had fallen from 73.2 years to 66.8 years between 1993 and 1999.[31] But for the most part outsiders have to guess at how bad the situation really is. Recent estimates put the North's GNP in 2000 at $19.0 billion, down from $23.1 billion in 1990, reflecting a negative GNP-growth figure every intervening year except in 1999 (up 6.2 percent) and 2000 (up 1.3 percent).[32] Foreign trade dropped from $4.72 billion in 1990 to $1.97 billion in 2000, but still a slight recovery from the mid-1990s. North Korea's trade balance has been negative for several decades. Net foreign debt stands at around $11.9 billion (62 percent of the country's 2000 GNP), in default since the 1980s.

Despite this dire situation, North Korea's officials and press hold to the line that although the economy is encountering temporary setbacks, socialism is bound to triumph and capitalism is doomed. Years of economic hardship do not seem to have created widespread resentment of the Kim dynasty, and the recent modest upturn in economic conditions may have inspired hope in the people. Because the people have never experienced economic plenty, and even their basic wants have been unsatisfied for the last twenty years, expectations are very low. As long as they can keep from dying— and stay free from the clutches of the dreaded "imperialists"—they seem to be satisfied. Such low expectations provide the Kim government with considerable room for political maneuvering, enabling the North Koreans to engage in long, drawn-out negotiations with foreign governments.

From one year to the next the lists of economic priorities published in the annual New Year's editorial hardly vary. In 1999 the priorities were listed as agriculture (potato farming, double-cropping, the seed revolution, and land rezoning), electricity (building large, medium, and small power plants), coal, railways, and consumer goods. Priorities in 2000 were electricity (large, medium, and small power plants), coal, metals,

---

31. Minister Choe also reported higher mortality rates for children, a decline in the availability of potable water, a reduction in vaccinations, and deaths of 220,000 attributed to hunger since the 1995 famine—although the latter figure is assumed by most foreign observers to be far too low. "Life Expectancy Plummets, North Korea Says," *New York Times*, May 16, 2001, p. A6. See also Table 9 in Doowon Lee's chapter in this volume. Another case of self-serving statistics was the North's request in 1997 for a reduction in its UN dues, citing a fall in per capita GNP from $547 to $239 between 1993 and 1995 (Yonhap News Agency, June 23, 1997). In 2001, Minister Choe cited GNP figures of $991 in 1993 and $457 in 1999, which are close to the estimates of foreign observers.

32. Figures from the Bank of Korea as cited by Yonhap News Agency, May 28, 2001, and from the ROK's Ministry of Unification.

railways, consumer goods, agriculture (the seed revolution, potato farming, double-cropping, livestock raising, fish breeding, land rezoning, and tree planting). In 2001 the government called for advances in electricity (large power plants), coal, metals, railways, light industry, and agriculture (seed revolution, potato farming, double-cropping, livestock raising, fish breeding, land rezoning, and culture and welfare projects for rural residents). Specific economic goals as outlined in the annual national budgets (which are not published annually) are usually abandoned and replaced by new goals in the following year without acknowledging any failure, as indeed it is difficult to admit failure for the leader and the party who set the plans are supposed to be infallible.

Persistent Problems

The Kim government officially attributes its economic problems to bad weather: drought, floods, heat waves, cold spells, and typhoons, according to the year and the season; that is, the extremes of nature that are part of any normal weather pattern. The American economic embargo and the collapse of socialist economies with which the North engaged in (subsidized) trading have also been blamed. In the domestic press, North Korea's own economic officials are criticized for their lackadaisical work attitude, and the masses are reproached for failing to exhibit revolutionary zeal.

But the real problems, easily recognized by outsiders and presumably by some of North Korea's economic technocrats, reside in the fabric of the North's socialist society. First is the impossibility of coordinating an entire economy from the center, especially if the center is dominated by ideologically minded bureaucrats. Second is the weakness of socialist ideology as a work ethic, because it deprives individuals (except Kim Jong-Il and the elite) from directly profiting from their efforts.[33] Third is the folly of trying to create a self-sufficient economy

---

33. The North Korean leaders have always recognized the motivational problem of socialism, but they are caught in an ideological trap. Excerpts from a recent article in the party newspaper show how they try to deal with this issue: "Even in the socialist society there can be a great deal of old ideological and cultural legacies. . . . If egalitarianism is applied to distribution, pushing aside material appreciation of the fruit of labor, it will lower the working people's zeal for production activities and cause the society trouble by creating an atmosphere where people are less willing to work and want to get more distribution even though they have put in less amount of effort. . . . In the socialist society, the lever of incentive should be utilized only on the basis of giving priority to the political and moral incentive." *Rodong Shinmun*, July 22, 2001, p. 2.

in an interdependent world, a fact that Kim Jong-Il seems to have finally recognized. Fourth is the wastefulness of the military-first policy, which redirects the first fruits of the economy to a military machine whose primary task is to confront the outside world, not to develop the domestic economy (although a relatively small sum of foreign payments can be extracted by making veiled military threats, as in the case of the KEDO nuclear agreement).

As a result of these problems, North Korea's infrastructure has been in decay for many years and the people have learned inefficient economic practices. During the arduous march the people were called upon to mine their "inner reserves," which were largely spiritual in nature, the better to "grow flowers on rocks." But without the more mundane economic resources such as food, fuel, electricity, steel and technology, willpower proves woefully insufficient. The old North Korean economic plan can sustain a subsistence economy, especially with the addition of some foreign aid, but it cannot lift the economy out of its depression.

Minor Adjustments

North Korea's official position is that its economic principles are the most superior ever formulated, leaving no need for economic reforms. Yet economic adjustments have always been made, going back to the adoption of local management and accounting systems in the 1960s. But all of the adjustments remain well within the boundaries of a socialist command economy. The adjustments are of three types: minor changes in domestic economic procedures, relaxation of regulations, and limited opening to foreign economies.

In the late 1990s one change in domestic procedures has been to grant the military managerial control over some civilian enterprises, presumably on the theory that military discipline can whip these failing domestic enterprises into shape. Another adjustment has been to break up large industrial combines (in late 1998), and then recombine them two years later, although the reasons for this switch are not known.

One significant relaxation in economic regulations in the 1990s gave the people more freedom to buy and sell in the farmers' markets that have sprung up in towns and cities across the country. Under the watchful eyes of local officials (who can be easily bribed), vendors sell or barter all manner of goods at prices 10 to 100 times above the official government rate.[34] Goods come from household possessions, private garden plots, pilfered stocks of government organizations, and imports from China. During the lean period of the year when the harvest stocks are depleted and government rations are severely curtailed or suspended, these markets are a necessary source of sustenance for those who have cash or something to trade. As much as 60 to 70 percent of North Koreans' food and daily necessities are purchased in these markets, with private enterprise constituting as much as a quarter of North Korea's total economy.[35] Reports that the government is closing some of the markets have surfaced from time to time.[36]

In 1984 North Korea drafted its first foreign-investment law. In 1991 a foreign-investment zone was opened at Rajin-Sonbong in the isolated northeastern corner of the country. Few foreign investors have been attracted by either inducement because of North Korea's lack of reliable legal procedures and the isolated location and poor economic and social infrastructure. The founder of South Korea's Hyundai companies, Chung Ju-Yong, who, in June 1998, reached an agreement with North Korea on operating what turned out to be a money-losing tourist attraction in the southeast corner of North Korea, signed a contract with North Korea in August 2000 to build a large industrial park in the city of Kaesong, conveniently located on the more populous western side of North Korea between Pyongyang and the South Korean border. Plans initially called for projected industrial output of $2 billion, $6 billion, and $12 billion

---

34. North Korean refugees in China report having traded in the following goods in farmers markets: food (61 percent), clothes (13 percent), fuel wood (11 percent), daily necessities (6 percent), furniture (5 percent), liquor (4 percent), and other items including medicine, cigarettes, coal, and cosmetics. *Understanding and Responses of the North Koreans on the Social and Economic Condition of North Korea*, Seoul: Good Friends, 2000, p. 33.

35. Chung Chung-Gil and Jeon Chang-Gon, "The Farmers' Market in North Korea: The Seed of Capitalism?" *East Asian Review*, vol. 12, no. 1 (Spring 2000), pp. 101–15. An interesting firsthand account of the largest market in Pyongyang is given by a Swedish reporter who slipped away from his North Korean security detail. According to his description, the market area was bustling, in contrast to the rest of Pyongyang, and foods of every description were being sold and traded. Also on sale were many useless items, attesting to the desperation of some venders to trade household goods for food. Pahl Ruin, "Private Markets Are Appearing," *Dagens Nyheter*, April 24, 2001.

36. Replying to a Japanese report in 1999 that "free markets" were being closed, KCNA denied that "free markets" had ever existed in the DPRK, "where the socialist independent national economy has been established and, accordingly, the 'tendency towards a system of market economy' cannot exist at all." "KCNA on Japan's False Propaganda," September 8, 1999.

in the three stages of development spanning 2001 to 2008, but Chung's death and the large losses that Hyundai Asan has incurred in its North Korean tourist business at Mount Kumgang have dampened investor enthusiasm for the Kaesong site.[37]

Because the most desperate need of the North Korean people in recent years has been food, Kim Jong-Il and his officials have devoted considerable attention to increasing the food supply within the constraints imposed by socialism and North Korea's inhospitable climate and geography. As is well recognized outside the socialist mindset, to improve agricultural production the collective farms should be broken up into private farms, as they were in China twenty years ago, rather than nationalized, as the Kim regime intends. Some recognition of the advantages of privatization is reflected in the government's allocation to each farmer of a small plot of land to cultivate as a sideline occupation. Travelers to the North can easily see the difference between these lush little garden plots and the leaner collective fields. The government has also experimented with letting collectives keep surpluses beyond what is owed to the state. There are even unconfirmed rumors that a general shift toward acceptance of greater private enterprise on collective farms may be in the offing.

The Kim government's proposed solutions to the food problem are better land management (leveling land so it can be cultivated by machinery, if the machinery were available), double-cropping, production of better seeds (the "seed revolution"), a switch away from rice (which is unsuited to the North's relatively cold and hilly land) to potatoes and other hardy crops, and a new emphasis on the alternative sources of nutrition provided by catfish farms, goat farms, ostrich farms, rabbit hutches, and the like. These initiatives are in their early stages, and often go against traditional eating habits, which center around rice, vegetables, and meat, pork, and fish (but not catfish). Two important means to alleviate the food shortage in recent years, neither one easily recognized by the Kim government, are to resort to "alternative foods" such as edible grasses, seaweed, roots, bark, berries, mushrooms, and acorns; and to aggressively solicit food aid from the international community.

Throughout the 1990s North Korea's grain production has fallen significantly below domestic needs; since 1995 the shortfall has been on

---

37. Nam Sung-wook, "Theory and Practice: Kaesong and Inter-Korean Economic Cooperation," *East Asian Review*, vol. 13, no. 1 (Spring 2001), pp. 67–88; see p. 79.

the order of 2 million tons a year out of minimum demand of 5 million tons a year. Because the government lacks money to pay for large amounts of imports, substantial grain donations have been made by the international community through the UN's World Food Program, with leading donors being the United States, Japan, South Korea, and the EU. The cost of this foreign food aid has been in the range of 200–300 million dollars annually since 1995. Foreign economists see no prospect that the North will be able to become self-sufficient in food in the foreseeable future. Although the 1998 and 1999 North Korean harvests were somewhat better than in previous years, the poor 2000 and 2001 harvests brought renewed hardship on the people.

"New Thinking" for the Economy

It is obvious to everyone, including even Kim Jong-Il, whose ample girth testifies to his immunity from the failure of socialist economic policies, that the above-mentioned adjustments in North Korea's industrial and agricultural sectors will never bring the economy up to the level of South Korea's. In recognition of this fact, the "new thinking" in politics has been applied to the economy. It could be argued, however, that by avoiding necessary changes in totalitarian socialism, Kim is merely replacing the useless white elephants of socialist economics with the pink elephants of self-delusion.

If taken literally, the pronouncements in early 2001 about new thinking are decidedly promising. Kim is clearly fed up with the inefficiency and waste of the socialist economic system, which provides equal rewards (such as they are) to the productive and the unproductive. Consider this practical admonishment in a March 2001 *Rodong Shinmun* article: "If the results of economic activities barely compensate or cannot compensate at all for materials consumed for production, compared to expenditure, and if products failed to have utility value or give negative influence to labor conditions, living conditions, and living environment, no matter how great the results of economic activities may be, we cannot say that such results actually contributed to the nation's development and prosperity and to promoting the people's living."[38] The press even makes the highly unusual admission of economic problems: "Every sector and every factory and enterprise of the national economy are,

---

38. *Rodong Shinmun*, March 29, 2001, p. 2.

without exception, left unable to make headway even a step without modernizing and renovating their obsolete processes, equipment, and production methods."[39]

The prescription to escape decades of economic stagnation is to modernize everything from the ground up by employing the latest science and technology (S&T). For despite years of *Juche* ("national self-reliance") propaganda insisting that North Korea's ideological strength can overcome all obstacles, it is now admitted that "One's subjective desire alone is not enough to enable him to follow the intention of the party or to carry out his work in compliance with the requirements of the new century or to fulfill his duty successfully."[40] North Koreans are told to follow closely the words and deeds of Kim Jong-Il in adopting the new technology, in which Kim is said to be the supreme authority. Yet when the news media cite.the technological advances that Kim has made in recent years, the accomplishments listed are trivial: poultry plants, catfish farms, instant-noodle plants, cosmetics plants, potato-starch plants, and foodstuff plants.[41]

If Kim Jong-Il's S&T revolution were implemented systematically, over a long period of time, starting with a correction of the basic flaws of the socialist economy, significant results would be achieved. But without repairing the foundations of the economic system, the S&T campaign will turn out to be yet another "five-minute heat." It is highly doubtful if socialism is fertile ground for rapid advances in information technology, despite claims such as this in the North Korean press: "Socialism of our own style has decisive advantages in developing the information industry. . . . Since the planned economy is in force, the creative strength of the masses can be broadly organized and tapped."[42]

Motivation remains a dilemma in the socialist model. According to North Korea, "real science" cannot be found in the capitalist world, "where science's lifeline is tied to money and where companies fight bloody battles between themselves." Real science can only be created in a socialist society. "It is the respected and beloved Comrade Kim

---

39. Kim Myong-Chol, "The Central Tasks in This Year's Socialist Economic Construction," *Minju Choson*, February 22, 2001, p. 2.

40. Kim Chin-Kuk, "The Proper Skills for the Information Age," *Rodong Shinmun*, May 8, 2001, p. 2.

41. Kim Myong-Chol.

42. Yi Un-Chan, "General Understanding of the Age of Information Industry," *Rodong Shinmun*, April 22, 2001, p. 4.

Jong-Il who, through the great power of the *Juche* science, is the heaven-sent great one who is creating a world of true science for human kind."[43] The same article notes that North Korean scientists do not emigrate as do scientists in other countries. Even in hard times they rise up to "defend their great leader with the do-or-die spirit." Their motivation? "Scientists' pure conscience devoted to the fatherland is as pure as soldiers' conscience." Such statements provide an example of the seriously flawed economic model that is supposed to guide North Korea into the information age.

The great mystery is where bankrupt North Korea expects to find the resources to make over its entire industry with the latest technology. There are probably no more than 100,000 computers in the entire country of 22 million people, and five telephones for every 100 people, few of them in private residences.[44] Electrical current is undependable. A few local area networks have been operating in Pyongyang since the early 1990s, and the networks have recently been extended to several other important industrial sites, but there is no link to the World Wide Web except through foreign-owned long-distance lines, which are available to very few people. The official government Web site originates in Beijing. In any case, it is hard to see how Kim Jong-Il could permit wide access to the Web given his need to keep the people shut off from information from the outside world. This state of affairs hardly constitutes a firm foundation for the rapid take-off that Kim Jong-Il has promised his people.

Articles in the press fail to offer suggestions about how people are supposed to acquire the new technology. An article in the government paper *Minju Choson* simply repeats the old local responsibility line: "To modernize local industry plants with up-to-date technology is a major requirement that each local organ of power has to meet to fulfill its duty as the householder responsible for local economic development and improvement in the residents' living standards."[45] One can only imagine what the average North Korean, who has trouble getting food and water and electricity and heat, thinks of Kim's call for everyone to study the

---

43. "Century of Science," KCBN, April 22, 2001.

44. Chin Kyong-Ho, "The North's IT Is in the Toddling Stage; Enthusiasm Alone Is High," *Taehan Maeil*, Internet version at www.seoul.co.kr, May 10, 2001.

45. Song Kun-Cho, "Modernizing Local Industry Plants with Up-to-Date Technology Is a Major Task Facing the Local Organs of Power," *Minju Choson*, June 10, 2001, p. 2.

latest international trends in information and technology and learn how to use a computer.

The North will need to depend heavily on S&T donations from the international community. This possibility, directly contradicting the *Juche* doctrine of self-reliance, has already been prepared for in the context of the new thinking, as *Juche* undergoes reinterpretation. Consider this recent statement from Kim Jong-Il: "We should have a correct understanding of self-reliance. The nature of self-reliance we referred to in the past is qualitatively different from the one we refer to now."[46] Self-reliance is now defined as the pursuit of efficiency and technology. Of course it is the prerogative of a totalitarian dictatorship to define language in any way it pleases. The people are unlikely to object; perhaps they do not even notice.

North Korea's new thinking is a milestone in its economic development, not because the prescriptions about pragmatism and practicality and new technology are likely to be put in place by the Kim regime, but because the campaign marks the point at which the North Korean leaders publicly admit that the old economy is not working. It remains for Kim Jong-Il to admit that the reason it is not working is because of his socialist teachings.

In 1998 at least 91 North Koreans were sent abroad to study capitalism and foreign technology, a dramatic increase over the 15 known cases in 1997. The number of economic travelers increased to 109 in 1999 (then fell back slightly to 90 in 2000), and 90 in 2000, including at least 1 economic delegation visiting the United States (in secrecy).[47] The South Korean government estimates that North Korean economic officials have made approximately 400 such visits since 1998.[48] In 1997 lectures on capitalism were delivered at Kim Il-Sung University; a training center for capitalist practices and trade was opened in 1998; and a research institute on capitalism was opened in 2000.[49] At the same time, the Kim regime still clings to the Marxist myth that socialism is sure to triumph and capitalism is doomed. In a typical tirade against capitalism, *Minju*

46. Yi Yong-Hwa, "Important Conditions for Promoting Self-Reliance," *Minju Choson*, May 16, 2001.

47. Chu Yong-Song, "DPRK Sent 90 Trainees Overseas Last Year," Yonhap News Agency, Internet version at www.yonhapnews.co.kr, March 9, 2001.

48. Yonhap News Agency, Internet version at www.yonhapnews.co.kr, June 4, 2001.

49. Yonhap News Agency, June 1, 2001.

Choson in June 2001 alleged that capitalism "paralyzes people's sound mind and turns them into mentally handicapped, encourages the stronger-prey-upon-the-weaker way of life, and causes such social ills as immorality, murder, and rape to dominate society."[50]

A New Turn in Foreign Relations

Diplomacy in a Hurry

Ever since Kim Jong-Il's public debut in 1998, North Korea has achieved a series of highly visible foreign-policy firsts that signal a turn from ideology to pragmatism. Certainly the most notable was Pyongyang's cordial hosting of President Kim Dae-Jung at the inter-Korean summit of June 2000, although the promised reciprocal visit of Chairman Kim Jong-Il to Seoul has yet to materialize. Relations with the United States were improved by the visit of North Korea's top general, Cho Myong-Rok, to Washington in October 2000, and the visit of Secretary of State Madeleine Albright to Pyongyang two weeks later. Kim Jong-Il's visits to China in May 2000 and January 2001 reflected better relations with his communist neighbor; Chinese president Jiang Zemin paid a September 2001 visit to Pyongyang in his capacity as CCP chairman. Relations with Russia were furthered by President Putin's visit to Pyongyang in July 2000 and Kim Jong-Il's marathon three-week train trip to Russia in July and August of 2001. In 2000 and 2001 Pyongyang completed its diplomatic normalization with all but two members of the EU (France and Ireland were the exceptions), in addition to other Western nations such as Australia and New Zealand.

Diplomatic Hurtles

For all its foreign-policy accomplishments, North Korea has failed to establish normal relations with the United States, the de facto gatekeeper to the international community, and Japan, the largest potential bankroller of North Korean economic recovery. As part of the 1994 Agreed Framework, Pyongyang was invited to establish a political liaison office in Washington (simultaneously with the establishment of a U.S. office in Pyongyang), but has declined to do so. North Korea and Japan

---

50. Kim Myong-Chol, "Socialist Way of Life," *Minju Choson*, May 18, 2001, p. 4.

began talks on normalizing relations in 1991, but after eleven rounds of talks through 2000, the two governments remained far apart in their views.

Why has it been so easy for North Korean officials to sweep through Europe but so difficult to make headway with the United States and Japan? The United States considers itself to be ultimately responsible for preventing the spread of weapons of mass destruction and for promoting democracy and human rights around the globe, and has made North Korean nuclear and missile nonproliferation a precondition for better relations. Culturally, the Americans harbor a legacy of hatred and suspicion against the North Korean government that can be traced back to the Korean War. Japan and North Korea are also culturally divided by years of hostility, and Japan's foreign policy tends to follow Washington's. Japan is also well aware of its vulnerability to North Korean missiles, nuclear or conventional, and North Korea frequently reminds the Japanese of this vulnerability.

In negotiations, the North Koreans guard against being taken advantage of by never showing the slightest sign of weakness or haste. They try keep the other side off balance by using stop-and-go tactics and surprise moves. They put little stock in developing trust or goodwill, and remain suspicious of everyone, communists as well as capitalists. Largely shielded from their country's economic problems, Kim Jong-Il and his associates can afford to wait patiently for improved relations with the United States and Japan, for they would personally gain little from closer relations, and might well incur increased risks in terms of holding on to power.

Diplomatic Moves

North Korea waited almost ten years after the collapse of the Soviet Union before making a concerted effort to gain political recognition from the Western powers. In his 1994 New Year's address, Kim Il-Sung announced that "we will make positive efforts to unite with socialist countries and non-aligned countries and develop good-neighborly relations also with capitalist countries which respect the sovereignty of our country."[51] But in the throes of its struggle with the United States over nuclear issues, and then during the three-year mourning and political

---

51. For the 1994 speech, see "New Year Address of President Kim Il-Sung," *The People's Korea*, no. 1633 (January 15, 1994), pp. 2–3; quote from p. 3.

consolidation period following the senior Kim's death in 1994, North Korea took few political initiatives, although, beginning in 1996, it appealed to the foreign community for economic aid. Even its relations with China and Russia were at low ebb throughout much of the 1990s.

A new push to establish diplomatic relations with the West was signaled by the attendance of Foreign Minister Paek Nam-Sun at the UN General Assembly in September 1999, the first UN appearance of a North Korean foreign minister in seven years. Relations with the United States improved somewhat in September 1999 with North Korea's agreement at the Berlin talks to suspend long-range missile tests in return for continued dialogue on compensation for a missile freeze and a relaxation of the U.S. trade embargo. In July 2000, North Korea was accepted as a member of the ASEAN Regional Forum, the closest thing Asia has to a security forum.

In January 2000, Italy became the first of the major market economies to recognize North Korea. The move was largely symbolic, given the negligible economic and personal contacts between the two countries. A Milan newspaper dubbed the diplomatic relationship a deserved but expendable "luxury" that cost Italy no more than the price of a foreign consulate.[52] Western governments one after the other normalized relations with Pyongyang: Australia, the Philippines, and the United Kingdom in 2000; Canada, Spain, Germany, Brazil, Greece, and New Zealand in the first half of 2001 (to name the larger countries in the order of their diplomatic initiatives). In May 2001 the EU, at the moment under the leadership of Prime Minister Goran Persson of Sweden, collectively normalized relations with North Korea. (Sweden has had diplomatic relations with North Korea for many years.)

Whereas North Korea had long desired to broaden its foreign relations, Western nations showed little interest in North Korea, which offered few economic or political inducements and was seen as a problem for the United States and South Korea to handle. The fruition of the normalization process was the result of North Korea's taking the time to cultivate foreign governments, and of these governments' following each other's lead, which provided a cover for establishing relations with the world's last Stalinist regime. The inter-Korean summit undoubtedly provided a strong argument that North Korea had abandoned its hostile

---

52. Sergio Romano, "A Role from Algiers to Pyongyang: A Good PR Operation," *Corriere della Sera*, January 5, 2000, p. 12.

intentions toward South Korea, thereby making the Kim regime more respectable. Most of the Western governments justified their diplomatic recognition by citing their desire to support Korean reconciliation and to preserve peace in Northeast Asia.

In recognition of the fact that North Korea would play a very small role in their international affairs, most Western governments gave to their ambassador in Beijing the additional role of providing representation in Pyongyang. Germany held out for permission to allow its diplomats and aid workers to travel freely throughout North Korea, although it appears that this provision is not being honored. A scheduled April 2001 visit by a Bundestag delegation was canceled when the North Koreans refused to let the delegation travel directly from Seoul to Pyongyang, rather than by the usual roundabout route through Beijing.

For North Korea, an enlarged circle of diplomatic partners offers more opportunity to gain aid and investment. The North Koreans may also hope that increased recognition will pressure Washington and Tokyo to establish relations with Pyongyang as well. A broader goal of normalization with the international community may well be to provide North Korea with alternatives to establishing closer relations with South Korea. If this is the case, not a few of these foreign governments may come to regret their diplomatic initiatives.

Limits on Foreign Relations

If a distinction is made between "high" foreign relations between governments (such as treaties and diplomatic recognition) and "low" foreign relations between peoples (including economic and social exchanges), it is clear that the Kim Jong-Il government desires the first but cannot afford the second.[53] The North Korean government, whose legitimacy rests on a large corpus of lies, must prevent its people from discovering the truth from outside sources.

Kim Jong-Il has framed the national security threat to North Korea in the following terms: "We have a short coastal borderline. Furthermore, the entire coastline is dotted with military fortresses. . . . In this case,

---

53. To quote from our recent book on North Korea, "Liberal democracies need little in the way of policy to guide people-to-people contact. . . . Totalitarian regimes, however, must institute strict controls over international contact to maintain total control of society." Kongdan Oh and Ralph C. Hassig, *North Korea through the Looking Glass* (Washington, D.C.: Brookings Institution Press, 2000), p. 176.

opening up is no different from the withdrawal of a country's troops, is it not?"[54] Yet North Korea's exposed geopolitical position is not the greatest threat to Kim Jong-Il and his associates. More important to their personal security are threats to their authority from the people. North Korean propaganda is full of calls to reject capitalism and foreign culture and to defend the leader at all costs. The North Korean leaders must set limits to opening, either selectively, by deploying "mosquito nets" on open windows, or by keeping the windows tightly shut. Because mosquito nets are not as reliable as closed windows, with every foreign-policy initiative Kim is taking a chance on weakening his regime. He needs to obtain foreign aid, investment, and political recognition without letting foreigners and their culture into his country. It would be especially damaging to open the North's borders to the economically successful South Koreans, who would provide an example to the North Korean people that would shame their own government.

In each agreement on the opening of diplomatic relations, the North Koreans stipulate that the two countries must recognize the sovereignty of each other's governments and not interfere in each other's domestic affairs. These provisions constitute a clear warning of the obstacles that North Korea's diplomatic partners will face in using diplomatic recognition to change North Korea.

Prospects for Foreign Relations

Optimists hope that dialogue and diplomatic recognition will activate a process of opening and reform in North Korean society. Pessimists predict that the newly engaged nations will quickly become disappointed in North Korea, and that North Korea will ignore them except to ask for aid and support. The danger that greater diplomatic recognition, to say nothing of foreign aid and investment, will strengthen and prolong the life of the Kim regime without appreciably softening it cannot be overlooked. The human rights issue, largely dormant because North Korea has remained closed to prying foreign eyes, may become more important if North Korea opens its borders. The Kim regime's stipulation of

---

54. Kap-Che Cho, "Recorded Tape of Kim Chong-Il's Live Voice—60 Minutes of Astonishing Confessions Similar to That of a Reactionary," *Wolgan Choson*, October 1995, pp. 104–28; translated by the Foreign Broadcast Information Service (FBIS-EAS-95-213) on November 3, 1995, and entitled "Transcript of Kim Chong-Il 'Secret' Tape Viewed," pp. 40–52, quote from p. 47.

noninterference in its deplorable domestic affairs flies in the face of a growing acceptance of international intervention in the cause of human rights. Twenty years after its opening and the beginnings of economic reform, China is still parrying criticisms of its human rights record, and by all accounts Chinese domestic repression never reached the level found in North Korea today.

But human rights has not yet become a central issue for South Korea and the major powers dealing with North Korea. Neither China nor Russia is likely to voice any objections to North Korea's human rights abuses, given their own records and their continuing authoritarian governing style. South Koreans want peace above anything. Japan is preoccupied with deterring North Korean threats. Policy makers in Washington are more concerned about containing or eliminating North Korea's weapons of mass destruction than addressing its human rights problems. American foreign-policy makers may swallow hard and agree to support the Kim regime in the service of their own national interests, much as the United States supported many authoritarian regimes during the cold war so long as they were anticommunist. These interests and attitudes may allow the Kim regime to garner foreign recognition and aid without having to open North Korea to foreign social and cultural influences.

Down Which Path?

The last two years of the twentieth century have seen some remarkable changes in North Korea. For South Koreans, these changes have raised hopes of reconciliation and reunification; for other nations, the changes offer hope of continued peace in Northeast Asia. But how substantial are these changes? It is a foregone conclusion that North Korea is sorely in need of change. The old North Korea was bad for its people, bad for its neighbors, and bad for the international community—despite the insistence of North Korean propagandists that North Korea is a shining beacon of socialism, that Kim Il-Sung was the sun of the twentieth century, and that Kim Jong-Il will be the sun of the twenty-first century.

In politics it appears that Kim Jong-Il has consolidated his power within the National Defense Commission, where he rules with the consent and support of the top generals. Through a few judiciously staged meetings, Kim has also heightened his stature in South Korea and the international community. But the politics of North Korea are unchanged. Kim and the party are still in firm control of all North Korean institutions. The only predicable political event of any consequence is Kim's choice of a successor: surely one of his sons is even now being positioned to continue the Kim dynasty for another generation.

North Korea's economy lacks sufficient resources to pull itself out of the deep depression that has become the normal style of life for its citizens. Despite the North's diplomatic outreach to South Korea and the West, foreign investors remain wary of entering the tightly controlled North Korean market. Food, fuel, fertilizer, along with cash from the Mount Kumgang concession and foreign arms sales, barely keep the economy afloat. Somewhat better harvests in 1998 and 1999 have marginally improved the people's living conditions, but widespread hunger persists. In response to economic problems across the board, the Kim regime has proposed rebuilding the entire economy with the latest technology.

Kim Jong-Il has looked abroad for aid and recognition to help sustain the failed North Korean system. North Korea has gained diplomatic recognition from some thirty governments in the last few years. But diplomatic recognition has not been accompanied by foreign investment and social exchange. Any further opening of North Korea's borders threatens to disturb the domestic equilibrium and shine a harsh light on the Kim government's abominable human rights policies. The big diplomatic prizes for North Korean diplomacy—the United States and Japan—remain beyond reach. Kim Jong-Il has not yet achieved his goal of gaining international acceptance of his modern-day dictatorial regime.

South Korea's president Kim Dae-Jung has been relentlessly optimistic about the consequences of engaging North Korea, although he frankly predicts that reunification lies twenty years in the future. Whatever its shortcomings in terms of changing North Korea in the direction of a more democratic and open society, engagement does have the important virtue of preserving peace on the Korean peninsula. But one year after the inter-Korean summit, the South Korean people had become increasingly frustrated with North Korea's failure to open its society in return. In fact, by March 2001 Pyongyang had severed virtually all its official contacts with Seoul. A skeptical American attitude toward unverifiable agreements with North Korea has further weakened President Kim's engagement policy, and may partially account for North Korea's boycott in 2001 of South Korea. The restricted nature of change in North Korea raises the question of whether the two Koreas are indeed walking down a path toward reconciliation and reunification, or whether aid to North Korea may simply strengthen the dynastic Kim regime. After three years of an engagement policy that can boast of some notable successes (although it cannot be known what successes might have been achieved from some alternative policy), some people advocate continued engagement while others believe enough is enough.

The engagement process raises two important questions. First, by what standard should North Korean change be measured? Second, how can the current trend of engagement be extrapolated to predict the future of inter-Korean reconciliation? Standards of change take on a practical significance in making decisions about whether engagement with North Korea should continue, and if continued, what the rules of engagement should be. Is the Kim government a worthy recipient of aid? Is the aid reaching the people? Is it furthering or hindering needed change? Is it simply a payoff for peace?

In evaluating the magnitude of change, should the new North Korea be compared with the old one, or with a "normal" twenty-first century state?[55] In projecting trends, should one assume a linear trend in which North Korea slowly but steadily opens up (presumably more slowly than China, which has far to go after its first twenty years of reform)? Or should one expect accelerating change, or a stop-and-go series of openings and retrenchments? Of the many factors involved in influencing change and its trajectory, arguably the most important is the logic of regime survival. Because North Korea is governed by the will and whim of Kim Jong-Il (who presumably takes into account the interests of the generals), the costs and benefits of change should be viewed from Kim's perspective. This is the one constant and knowable factor in North Korean affairs. Those who predict substantial change in North Korea must explain how that change will benefit Kim and the elite in Pyongyang. If maintaining their power depends upon keeping the rest of the North Korean people under their thumb, prospects for an opening of North Korean society are dim. This is not a new or surprising conclusion: it has been accepted wisdom for the last fifty years. But recently the logic

---

55. In a recent paper we have looked at engagement standards from another perspective: the costs and benefits of correctly inferring change or no change, compared to the costs and benefits of incorrectly inferring change or no change. See Kongdan Oh and Ralph C. Hassig, "Guessing Right and Guessing Wrong about Engagement," *Journal of East Asian Affairs*, vol. XV, no. 1 (Spring/Summer 2001), pp. 15–41.

has been ignored by some North Korea observers who focus on what's good for the North Korean people and their economy and forget to consider what's best for their leaders.

As Kim Jong-Il sees it, whatever the people receive comes as a "gift" from their benevolent leader. In fact, Kim seems to think that the leaders of other countries view their people in the same way. One indication of this viewpoint is the North Korean telephone message on the first anniversary of the summit talks, which says, "By upholding the intentions of the leaders of the North and the South to unite the strength of our nation in resolving the reunification issue. . . ."[56] This statement is mild compared to the treatment inter-Korean relations receive in the North Korean press, which boasts that the summit talks and the Joint Declaration "marked a great milestone for national reunification and provided thanks to the broad patriotic magnanimity and outstanding political ability of leader Kim Jong-Il."[57] For their part, many South Koreans complain that their own president has been behaving autocratically by pursuing his engagement policy without the advice and consent of the electorate and its chosen representatives.

In the final analysis, only the North Korean people can change their fate, and so far they have been neither permitted nor prepared to tackle this formidable challenge. The goal of the engagement policies of South Korea and other countries is to open North Korea with aid, investment, and contact, thereby giving the North Korean people scope to exercise their self-will. But Kim Jong-Il may be able to keep enough of North Korea closed to preserve his control. The North Korean people have a long way to go, and their predicament remains serious. At the current pace of change, millions will never live to experience freedom and reunification. The human condition in North Korea is accurately described by a Kim Il-Sung University professor in a radio address purporting to describe the plight of citizens in capitalist countries: "If a social being does not know politics and cannot achieve any political demand, the life is not different from animal's life. Only eating and living without knowing anything about the state and politics is not human life."[58]

---

56. Chu Yong-Cong, "Full Text of Telephone Messages between the North and the South to Mark the 15 June Joint Declaration," Yonhap News Agency, Internet version at www.yonhapnews.co.kr, June 15, 2001.

57. KCNA, June 14, 2001.

58. Yi Song-Chol, "The *Juche* Idea Is a Great Idea That Has Scientifically Explained the Contradiction and Inevitable Destruction of Capitalist Society," KCBN, May 25, 2001.

China, Japan, and Russia in Inter-Korean Relations

Samuel S. Kim

*The geographical position of a nation is the principal
factor conditioning its foreign policy—the principal reason
why it must have a foreign policy at all.*

—Jules Cambon (1935)[1]

The Old/New Geopolitical Environment

At the dawn of the new millennium there is something very old and very
new in the regional security complex surrounding the Korean peninsula.
At one level of generalization, to quote the well-known French expression, *plus ça change, plus c'est la même chose*—the more things change,
the more they stay the same. What remains unchanged and unchangeable
is the geographical location of the Korean peninsula. Geography is important in the shaping of any state's foreign policy, to be sure, but it is
especially so for the foreign policies of the two Koreas and the neighboring powers. The Korean peninsula, divided or united, shares land and
maritime borders with China, Russia, and Japan. Surrounded by all three
Northeast Asian giants, Korea's unique place in the geopolitics of Northeast Asia is at once a blessing, a curse, and a litmus test. The Korean
peninsula has long been a highly contested strategic crossroads, the site
of great-power rivalry and sanguinary wars that have involved, to vary-

---

1. Jules Cambon, "The Foreign Policy of France," in Council on Foreign Relations, ed.,
The Foreign Policy of the Powers (New York: Harper & Brothers, 1935), pp. 3–24, cited in
Robert Pastor, "The Great Powers in the Twentieth Century: From Dawn to Dusk," in Robert
A. Pastor, ed., *A Century's Journey: How the Great Powers Shape the World* (New York:
Basic Books, 1999), p. 27.

ing degrees, czarist Russia, the Soviet Union, Qing China, the Republic of China, the People's Republic of China, Japan, and the United States.

Even today, almost a half-century after the Korean War was "ended" with an armistice, the so-called demilitarized zone (DMZ) remains the most heavily fortified area of conflict in the post-cold-war world, where more than 1.8 million military personnel, armed to the teeth with the latest weapons systems, confront each other. In the latter half of the 1990s, the volcano of potential implosion or explosion in North Korea seemed to have become more active than ever before. An unstable or collapsing North Korea with inordinate asymmetrical military capabilities has extraordinary refractory ramifications for great-power politics in Northeast Asia and beyond. Each of the Big Four—China, Japan, Russia, and the United States—regards the Korean peninsula as falling within its own geostrategic ambit. Koreans, for their part, have long recognized their own security predicament, likening Korea to a "shrimp among whales."

Thus, the Korean peninsula is still seen by many as the pivot of Northeast Asian security, just as Northeast Asia, where the Big Four uneasily meet and interact, is the most important strategic nexus of the Asia-Pacific. The world's heaviest concentration of military and economic capabilities is in Northeast Asia, including the world's three largest nuclear weapons states, three threshold nuclear weapons states (North Korea, South Korea, and Japan) and the world's three largest economies.[2] That the United States, China, and Russia hold permanent membership in the UN Security Council substantially blurs the divide between Northeast Asian regional and global politics.

Neither has the external environment of states in Northeast Asia been stagnant in the post-cold-war era. The momentous changes in the late 1980s and 1990s have been unprecedented in their nature, scope, and rapidity. The common view of the ongoing Korean security predicament—that Korea is a weak country in a region where so many countries are strong—is no longer a reliable guide to the peace process on the Korean peninsula. For the first time in many years, the Korean peninsula is no longer a site of traditional confrontational great-

---

2. According to the purchasing power parity (PPP) estimates of the World Bank (which are not unproblematic), China, with a 1994 gross domestic product (GDP) just under $3 trillion, has become the second-largest economy in the world after the United States. See *The Economist* (London), January 27, 1996, p. 102; World Bank, *World Development Report, 1996* (New York: Oxford University Press, 1996), p. 188.

power rivalry. All four major external powers now have expressed their interest in seeking peace and stability on the Korean peninsula. Indeed, the two Koreas may now be experiencing greater security sovereignty than they have had at any time since the opening of the "hermit kingdom" in the 1870s.

There are at least three sets of momentous forces reshaping the international relations of Northeast Asia. First, the normalization of Moscow-Seoul relations in 1990 and Beijing-Seoul relations in 1992 has knocked out one of the cold war alliance systems in the region. Second, with a rising China and a declining post-Soviet Russia, and a rising South Korea and declining North Korea, the greatest shifts in power—defined and measured in conventional terms—in the last two decades have taken place in this region.[3] Third, the forces of globalization in the 1990s have transformed both the context and the conditions under which Northeast Asian regional geopolitics can be played out. Contrary to Thomas Friedman's claims, however, globalization has not yet become the new international system replacing the cold-war system, at least not in Northeast Asia.[4] Instead, globalization as a worldwide, multidimensional revolutionary process has greatly accelerated interconnectedness in all aspects of human relations and transactions—economic, social, cultural, environmental, political, diplomatic, and security-related. Northeast Asian states now must worry not only about their military power but also about the economic, cultural, and knowledge power needed to survive and prosper in a world that is becoming increasingly globalized and competitive.[5] In post-cold-war Northeast Asian international relations, geopolitics is no longer the only game in town; it coexists and even competes with geoeconomics and geogovernance.

In addition, the clarity, simplicity, and apparent durability of East-West conflict have been replaced by the multiple complexities and un-

---

3. Viktor N. Pavliatenko, "Russian Security in the Pacific Asian Region: The Dangers of Isolation," in Gilbert Rozman, Mikhail G. Nosov, and Koji Watanabe, eds., *Russia and East Asia: The Twenty-first Century Security Environment* (Armonk, NY: M. E. Sharpe, 1999), pp. 20–21; Pastor, "The Great Powers in the Twentieth Century," Robert Legvold, "The Three Russias: Decline, Revolution, and Reconstruction," in Pastor, *A Century's Journey.*

4. Thomas Friedman, *The Lexus and the Olive Tree* (New York: Farrar, Straus and Giroux, 1999), pp. 7–8.

5. For further discussion in the context of South Korea and East Asia, see Samuel S. Kim, ed., *Korea's Globalization* (New York: Cambridge University Press, 2000) and *East Asia and Globalization* (Lanham, MD: Rowman & Littlefield Publishers, 2000).

certainties of an emerging Northeast Asian regional order of indeterminate shape and content. The end of global bipolarity and the U.S.-China-USSR strategic triangle have not brought a new global and regional order. Although great-power conflict and rivalries in traditional form have dissipated, uncertainties abound about the shape of the post-cold-war Northeast Asian regional order to come.

Consider also the continuing, if somewhat dilapidated, cold-war alliance systems linking the two Koreas, Japan, China, and the United States in the bilateralized regional security complex, and the festering fratricidal politics of divided but assertively nationalist nations. The Sino-Japanese relationship is another crucial yet uncertain factor in the shaping of a Northeast Asian regional order. China's ambivalent Asian identity largely mirrors Japan's no less awkward and problematic Asian identity.

As a result, the shape of Northeast Asian international life to come is closely keyed to the state of Sino-American relations, which will in turn impact upon and shape the future of Sino-Japanese relations. And yet, in the absence of the East-West conflict, the relations between the world's lone superpower, with its creeping unilateralism, and the world's most populous country, with its rooted exceptionalism, have become the single greatest source of uncertainty in the shaping of the post-cold-war East Asian regional order. There also seems little doubt that North Korea's position as East Asia's most dangerous crisis-in-waiting intersects with the shaping of the future of Sino-American relations, as well as with the future geopolitics of Northeast Asia.

Differences in internal constructions and resulting domestic politics have a substantial impact on how states define threats and vulnerabilities, and therefore on the whole security problematique.[6] With the recent changes of political leadership in 2000–2001—the more Realpolitik Putin in Moscow, the more hard-line Bush administration in Washington, and the more nationalistic Koizumi government in Tokyo—the foreign policies of Northeast Asian states and the United States have become increasingly reflective of highly charged, nationalistic domestic politics. By any reckoning, all the countries involved in the management of the emerging engagement process on the divided Korean peninsula are experiencing, albeit to varying degrees,

---

6. Barry Buzan, "Security, the State, the 'New World Order,' and Beyond," in Ronnie D. Lipschutz, ed., *On Security* (New York: Columbia University Press, 1998), chap. 7.

corresponding disorientation and readjustment of their Korea policies and international roles.

Indeed, it is this unique, combustible cocktail of sui generis regional characteristics—high capability; abiding animus; deep, albeit differentiated, entanglement of the Big Four in Korean affairs; North Korea's recent emergence as a loose cannon; the absence of multilateral security institutions, and the resulting uncertainties and unpredictability in the international politics of Northeast Asia—that challenge scholars and policy makers alike to divine the shape of things to come in the emerging regional order. In short, Northeast Asia conflates in one place all the new-world-order challenges that pivot around two central concerns: the source of possible threats to the region's stability and the feasible and desirable conflict-management models needed to establish peace and stability in the region.

The Summit: A Year of High Hopes and Low Returns

Of all the major events of the past two years (from August 1999 to mid-2001), it was the three-day summit meeting in Pyongyang between President Kim Dae-Jung and Chairman Kim Jong-Il (June 13–15, 2000), with the resulting North-South Joint Declaration (June 15), that easily stands out as the single greatest, with potentially enormous repercussions for the region and beyond. The Pyongyang summit, the first of its kind in the half-century history of the politics of competitive legitimation and delegitimation on the divided peninsula, has generated opportunities and risks for all the neighboring powers, even as they step back and reassess the likely future of inter-Korean affairs and its implications for their own national interests. The dramatic summit has also led to some paradoxical expectations and consequences for both Koreas and the neighboring powers. As such, the Pyongyang summit provides a point of departure for examining the shifting roles of China, Japan, and Russia in Korean affairs.

Historically, the Pyongyang summit is most remarkable because it was initiated and executed by Koreans themselves with no external shock or great-power sponsorship. The previous inter-Korean accords were responses to major structural changes external to the Korean peninsula. The South-North Joint Communique of July 4, 1972, was a product of the panicked reaction of both Koreas to the "Nixon-in-China" shock. The Basic Agreement—officially the Agreement on Reconciliation, Nonaggression, Exchanges and Cooperation, which took effect on February 19, 1992—was Pyongyang's grudging response to Seoul's *Nordpolitik*. It followed a rapid succession of external shocks in 1990–91: Moscow-Seoul normalization, German reunification, and the collapse of the Soviet Union. Even the scheduled inter-Korean summit that had to be aborted because of the sudden death of Kim Il-Sung in July 1994 was a stepchild of Jimmy Carter's personal diplomacy. There is no mistaking the fact that the chief catalyst for the Pyongyang summit was President Kim Dae-Jung's consistent and single-minded pursuit of his pro-engagement "Sunshine Policy." In a policy speech dubbed the Berlin Declaration, which was delivered at the Free University of Berlin on March 9, 2000, he made a major offer that Kim Jong-Il would be hard pressed to decline:

> The Government of the Republic of Korea is ready to help North Korea tide over its economic difficulties. . . . However, to realize meaningful economic collaboration, the social infrastructure, including highways, harbors, railroads and electric and communications facilities, must be expanded. . . . The Government of the Republic of Korea is ready to respond positively to *any North Korean request in this regard.*[7]

More than anything else, the offer of substantial if unspecified *governmental* aid to refurbish North Korea's decrepit infrastructure was the main causal force behind Kim Jong-Il's decision to agree to an inter-Korean summit, setting the stage for a highly asymmetrical "engagement" process. Until the Berlin Declaration, Pyongyang had taken a two-handed approach, attacking the Sunshine Policy as a "sunburn policy" on ideological grounds while simultaneously pursuing mendicant diplomacy to extract maximum economic concession. The fact that before its official unveiling in Berlin, an advance text had already been delivered by Seoul to Pyongyang, as well as to Beijing, Moscow, Tokyo, and Washington, through various diplomatic channels, is evidence that the Big Four had little to do with the initiation of the summit and that the offer had stretched the outer limits of the Sunshine Policy.

The timing of the April 10 announcement, coming only three days before the South Korean National Assembly elections in which Kim Dae-Jung's party was trailing in the polls, raised questions about the

---

7. For a full English text, see Yonhap, March 9, 2000; emphasis added.

kind of deal struck in the secret negotiations in Shanghai and Beijing. One thing remained clear: Pyongyang quickly appropriated the politics of the inter-Korean summit for its game of brinksmanship as one-upmanship, taking the upper hand and the advantage of holding the meeting on home turf to control the atmospherics, agenda, pace, and direction of the emergent inter-Korean summit process. All the same, the North Korean official announcement of the summit made clear who was the supplicant: "At the *request* of President Kim Dae-Jung, he will visit Pyongyang from June 12 to 14, 2000."[8]

Kim Jong-Il also seized on inter-Korean summit diplomacy to showcase his leadership in North Korea. It seems safe to assume that he would neither have been willing nor able to embark upon such a historical journey without a prior consolidation of power. He apparently saw in the inter-Korean summit a great opportunity to kill several birds with one stone and to produce multiple normative, diplomatic, and material benefits without seriously threatening the North Korean system.

According to North Korean diplomats in Russia, romancing the inter-Korean summit accomplished at least three things. First, Kim Jong-Il reportedly boosted his prestige among the power elite by kindling expectations that the summit would empower the DPRK to improve its economic fortunes and to acquire more food, clothing, and medicine for its people. Second, he apparently pulled off a public relations coup, a wholesale image transformation in South Korea. In the process he added fuel to the politics of fragmentation and anti-Americanism in the South. The Pyongyang summit would help demonstrate the superiority of the DPRK in the eyes of all Koreans living in the South and abroad by forcing the morally weaker party, to kowtow before the real and only leader of all Koreans. And third, the summit enhanced the prestige of the DPRK and Kim Jong-Il throughout the world and attracted more countries to cooperate with Pyongyang, particularly the United States. Because the summit was viewed and projected as a major concession to the United States, the United States was therefore expected to make major economic and strategic concessions. Pyongyang also did its best to exploit the new connection with Seoul to speed up normalization talks with the United

---

8. Korean Central News Agency (KCNA), April 20, 2000.

States and in the process gain access to bilateral and multilateral aid and foreign direct investment.[9]

Suddenly, at least from June to November, the capital city of Pyongyang—the city of darkness—became a city of diplomatic light and a primary arena for diplomatic influence and competition among the Big Four. Within the short span of a few months, the infamously reclusive Kim had no less than three summit meetings—with Chinese president Jiang Zemin in a secret visit to Beijing in late May, with South Korean president Kim Dae-Jung in June, and with Russian president Vladimir Putin in July—and received a flurry of first-ever diplomatic missions to Pyongyang, including those of U.S. Secretary of State Madeleine Albright and Chinese defense minister Chi Haotian in October and a European Union delegation in November. The notion that the Pyongyang summit had improved prospects for melting the remaining portion of the cold-war glacier on the Korean peninsula seemed to have intensified the needs and efforts of the four major powers to readjust their respective Korea policies to reflect rapidly changing realities on the ground.

A year later, however, the initial euphoria in the South has turned into sobering realism about the many fault lines running through the emergent rapprochement process. Pyongyang controls all the levers to extract maximum aid for minimal concession, the select and controlled opening of its doors. Although the fundamentals of the North Korean system, including its military-first politics, remain intact, financially, Seoul will be bled dry in its quest for peace at any price.

Despite all the South's unification pomp surrounding the historic inter-Korean summit and the Joint Declaration, and despite the official claim in the North that these are "the greatest successes in the reunification movement since the country was divided into two parts over half a century back,"[10] North Korean leader Kim Jong-Il and South Korean president Kim Dae-Jung embraced each other before global television audiences, signaling in

9. For analysis by Russia's Korea experts based on their discussion with North Korean representatives, see *DPRK Report*, no. 24 (May–June 2000) and *DPRK Report*, no. 26 (September-October 2000) at the Nautilus Institute home page on the World Wide Web at www.nautilus.org/pub/ftp/napsnet/russiadprk. Interestingly enough, Han Sik Park of the University of Georgia, who has extensive connections and who regularly visits North Korea, argues that the Pyongyang summit is a continuation of "legitimacy war" by other means, not the end of it. See Han S. Park, "The Nature and Evolution of the Inter-Korean Legitimacy War," in Kyung-Ae Park and Dalchoong Kim, eds., *Korean Security Dynamics in Transition* (New York: Palgrave, 2001), pp. 3–17.

10. KCNA, November 18, 2000.

a symbolically powerful way for a few clicking photo-opportunistic minutes their acceptance of each other's legitimacy. The summit seemed to
have brought the two Koreas down from their respective hegemonic-unifi-
cation dreamlands to a peaceful coexistence of the two separate states.

Indeed, the Joint Declaration glossed over the ineluctable fact that
there is no common formula for reunification, broadly stating that the
"North and the South agreed to solve the question of the country's reunification independently" (Article 1) and, recognizing common elements in each side's unification formula, "agreed to work for the
reunification in this direction in the future" (Article 2). While Pyongyang
paid mandatory lip service to the supreme task of building "one nation,
one state with two governments and two systems" without delay under
the "federation system" (formerly "confederation system"), in the wake
of the summit it proclaimed publicly for the first time that "the issue of
unifying the differing systems in the north and the south as one may be
left to posterity to settle slowly in the future."[11] Throughout, Kim Dae-
Jung repeated his now familiar line that he does not expect Korean reunification on his watch and in his lifetime.

Equally revealing is the fact that the Joint Declaration has nothing to
say about military and security matters, not even in general terms about
working together for tension-reduction and confidence-building measures. The summit has hardly made a dent in the military power of South
and North Korea, and the potential for renewed hostilities on the Korean peninsula remains. It is clear that Pyongyang wants to discuss security issues last, if at all, and then only with the United States. In contrast,
the Basic Agreement stipulates that "the two sides shall endeavor together to transform the present state of armistice into a solid state of
peace between the South and the North and shall abide by the present
Military Armistice Agreement (of July 27, 1953) until such a state of
peace has been realized" (Article 5). The Joint Declaration of the De-
nuclearization of the Korean Peninsula, which became effective as of
February 19, 1992, also stipulates in peremptory language that "the South
and the North shall not test, manufacture, produce, receive, possess,
store, deploy or use nuclear weapons."

That Pyongyang backtracked on its pledge to this joint denucleariza-
tion declaration, let alone sign the Comprehensive Test Ban Treaty
(CTBT), requires no elaboration here. What is not widely known or

---

11. *Rodong Shinmun*, June 25, 2000, p. 6; emphasis added.

remembered is that the DPRK also breached its pledge to abide by the Korean Military Armistice Agreement (MAC) by taking several provocative unilateral actions between April and September 1994 in the course of exercising its coercive leverage diplomacy with the United States. It withdrew its MAC members, prevented Chinese "People's Volunteers" staff officers from attending a UNC staff meeting, forced the Polish delegation to withdraw from the Neutral Nations Supervisory Commission (NNSC), and succeeded in forcing China to withdraw its delegation from the MAC for good.[12]

By the first anniversary of the summit in mid-2001, Kim Dae-Jung's Sunshine Policy was in deep domestic trouble. In the glow of the summit a year earlier, four out of five South Koreans (81.9 percent) were ready to give the benefit of the doubt to his pro-engagement Sunshine Policy and its offers of aid for North Korea in hopes of a genuine reciprocal process of comprehensive engagement. A year of many disappointments later, barely one in five supports it.[13]

Tellingly, Pyongyang has held the new hard-line administration in Washington hostage to the resumption of inter-Korean dialogue and engagement, breaching not only the letter and the spirit of the North-South Joint Declaration (Article 1) but also its own longstanding party line that Korean affairs should be handled without foreign intervention or interference. Viewed from Pyongyang's own Realpolitik perspective, however, Kim Jong-Il met Kim Dae-Jung's request for summitry as a kind of a quid pro quo concession to the United States and as another way of accelerating the DPRK-U.S. normalization process. Herein lies the logic of Pyongyang's refusal to resume the inter-Korean engagement process, including Kim Jong-Il's "promised" visit to Seoul for a second inter-Korean summit. Against the backdrop of a looming economic crisis, Kim Dae-Jung as much as admitted in a major policy speech in Singapore in late November 2000 that without parallel improvements in North Korea's ties with the United States, the emerging inter-Korean ties would be inadequate to take the peace process forward.[14] In the course of the fourth ministerial talks in Pyongyang in mid-December 2000, ROK Unifica-

---

12. For a more detailed discussion of this incident and its deliberation in the UN Security Council, see Samuel S. Kim, "North Korea and the United Nations," *International Journal of Korean Studies*, vol. 1, no. 1 (Spring 1997): 78–105.

13. *Chungang Ilbo*, August 13, 2000, and *The Economist*, June 16, 2001, p. 11.

14. Agence France Presse (AFP), November 27, 2000, on the World Wide Web at afp.com/english/home.

tion Minister Park Jae-Kyu told his North Korean counterpart that "due to looming economic difficulties, South Korea may not be able to give much economic aid to the North,"[15] only to provoke a new demand for energy aid. Both Kims thus reintroduced the role of the United States as part of the Korean problem and as part of the Korean solution.

That said, however, the ineluctable reality has become progressively clear—Kim Dae-Jung's Sunshine Policy will not work and cannot be sustained for several reasons. First of all, he is now widely perceived as an ineffective, lame duck president. With growing economic troubles compounded by searing labor-management disputes and strikes, nothing seems to fail like a failure in the politics of everyday life in a newly democratizing South Korea. Paradoxically, Kim Dae-Jung finds himself in danger of being remembered as the man who brought the two Koreas together only to be sunk by the politics of fragmentation in the South: His popularity was at an all-time high abroad but at an all-time low at home. Endless pleading for reciprocal engagement will not work if Kim Jong-Il continues to wiggle out of promises and then asks for more aid.

In the South, central to the reality of the growing signs of a rift in North-South relations is the issue of leadership credibility on two points: the presence of U.S. troops and Kim Jong-Il's visit to Seoul. What was the basis for President Kim Dae-Jung's public declaration on several occasions that Kim Jong-Il had made a surprising concession by agreeing that U.S. troops must stay even after the two Koreas are unified for the sake of peace and security in Northeast Asia? If indeed Kim Jong-Il made such a promise, why has Pyongyang resumed its clarion call for the troops' removal in recent months with greater vigor than before? To many, such a promise from North Korea seems like raising a white flag in the legitimacy war. In any event, the alleged concession on the U.S. troops issue creates a nagging credibility problem for both Kim Jong-Il and Kim Dae-Jung.

Kim Dae-Jung's repeated, almost nonstop prodding for Kim Jong-Il's reciprocal state visit to Seoul is no less vexing. In May 2001 alone, President Kim Dae-Jung is reported to have requested on five separate occasions that Chairman Kim Jong-Il fulfill his "promise" of a return visit, thus providing a field day for South Korean conservative pundits and the opposition party. Whether he intended or not, Kim Dae-Jung

---

15. *Korea Herald*, December 13, 2000, on the World Wide Web at www.koreaherald.co.kr.

has succeeded in projecting the image of a desperate supplicant begging for Kim Jong-Il's favor, and many pundits, not all of them hawkish conservatives, criticize his behavior as "unbecoming of the leader of our country." In advancing the claims that Kim Jong-Il should carry out the "promise" of his return visit, Kim Dae-Jung does not stand on solid ground, for this was treated as a peripheral issue and not as one of the five articles in the Joint Declaration, which merely states that Chairman Kim would visit Seoul "at an appropriate time." In other words, Kim Jong-Il will decide what constitutes "an appropriate time" without violating the letter, if not the spirit, of the joint declaration. Moreover, there are no means by which the president of democratic South Korea can guarantee the kind of manufactured public welcome witnessed in the streets of Pyongyang on June 13, 2000, let alone a formal acceptance of the South-North peace agreement Kim Dae-Jung has been touting. A second summit gone awry would be worse than no summit at all for all parties concerned.

Kim Jong-Il's potential southern visit aside, the realities of inter-Korean relations at the midpoint of 2001 do not augur well. Not content with punishing Kim Dae-Jung for his "see no evil, hear no evil" Sunshine Policy and for the Bush administration's hard-line policy by suspending all inter-Korean dialogue and exchange, Kim Jong-Il resumed coercive leverage diplomacy in June 2001. Pyongyang's cargo ships violated South Korean territorial waters by taking shortcuts through the channel between Cheju island and the peninsula and then the Northern Limit Line (NLL), prompting an outcry from the opposition and the mass media. Even in the functional domain of economic exchange and cooperation, and despite the ex cathedra pronouncement of "a new ideological viewpoint" for building kangsong taeguk (a powerful and prosperous state),[16] the first half of 2001 saw the inter-Korean relations bus hardly moving.

China: Multitasking Realpolitik

To understand China's role in inter-Korean affairs, it is important to recognize that there is an uneasy, shifting balance of competing forces and identities—both conflictive and cooperative—in Beijing's post-cold-

16. "Motun munche rul saeroun kwanchom kwa nopi eso poko pulo nakacha" [Let Us View and Solve All Problems from a New Idea and a New Height], Rodong Shinmun, editorial, January 9, 2001, p. 1.

war foreign policy. China's normalization decision in 1992 was the culmination of a gradual process of balancing and adjusting post-Mao foreign policy to the logic of the changing domestic, regional, and global situations. In implementing the two-Koreas decision in the postnormalization period, Chinese policy-makers were confronted by contradictory historical, ideological, strategic, and economic forces. Necessarily, Beijing pursues multiple mutually competitive goals on multiple fronts. These goals include: maintaining peace and stability on the Korean peninsula; promoting economic exchange and cooperation with South Korea; supporting North Korea's regime survival through aid and trade; preventing dominance of Korea by any external power; halting the flow of North Korean refugees and South Korean Christian missionaries into Jilin Province; stopping the rise of ethnonationalism among ethnic Chinese-Koreans; and preventing the formation of any anti-China coalition in East Asia.[17]

With the demise of the Washington-Beijing-Moscow strategic triangle there emerged in its place a more complex economic and strategic triangle involving three sets of asymmetrical mutual interests and perceptions: Beijing-Seoul, Beijing-Pyongyang, and Seoul-Pyongyang. Beijing has pursued a multitasking Realpolitik strategy of seeking different but complementary interests—strategic, economic, and antihegemonic—on all three sides of the Beijing-Pyongyang-Seoul triangle. On the first and second sides of the triangle Beijing sought to maintain its strategic ties— if not "lips-and-teeth" organic links—with North Korea even as it promoted new economic ties with South Korea. On the third side of the triangle, Beijing tried hard to keep out of harm's way by following an indeterminate equidistance policy. As a way of maximizing its influence over Korean affairs, China often becomes all things to all parties, leaving many anxious about its real intentions and final decision. China has seldom put itself in the front line of the Korean conflict as either a mediator or a peacemaker for fear that it might get burned if something goes wrong.

Beijing's role in Korean affairs is also closely keyed to Sino-American relations, and it shadows the rise of any U.S.-DPRK warming-up

---

17. For a detailed discussion, see Samuel S. Kim, "The Making of China's Korea Policy in the Era of Reform," in David M. Lampton, ed., *The Making of Chinese Foreign and Security Policy in the Era of Reform, 1978–2000* (Stanford: Stanford University Press, 2001), pp. 371–408.

process with a sharp Realpolitik eye. To the extent possible, China will continue to invest the necessary minimum of political and economic capital in its relationships with the two Koreas in order to enhance its leverage in inter-Korean affairs. That said, however, China's multitasking two-Koreas strategy is more reactive than proactive, and concentrated on the short-term challenge of maximizing short-term gains and minimizing or avoiding short-term constraints. It does not, however, appear to include a long-term strategic vision for the Korean peninsula, other than to keep it a buffer zone and to slow down the Korean reunification process as much as possible to maintain the two-Koreas status quo.

Of the three neighboring powers, China has managed to maintain a relatively more stable two-Koreas policy than any other neighboring power over the past two years. The most notable accomplishment of the two-year period under review was a reconfirmation of Sino-DPRK geopolitical ties in 1999. In the wake of the NATO air war against Yugoslavia, NATO/U.S. bombing of the Chinese embassy in Belgrade and the rapid deterioration of Sino-American relations, China made a subtle but significant readjustment in its Korea policy. Beijing's displeasure with its unruly socialist ally in the strategic buffer zone was largely put aside as the Chinese leadership began to see the United States as the main threat to its political and economic interests in the region.

Against this backdrop, starting from mid-1999, Beijing's relations with North Korea began to be "renormalized" through the exchange of high-powered delegations. In early June 1999, a fifty-member North Korean delegation led by Supreme People's Assembly (SPA) President Kim Yong-Nam made a high-profile state visit to China. The visit was remarkable for at least three reasons: (1) It was the first high-level state visit since President Kim Il-Sung's visit in late 1991 (compared to a myriad of summit meetings between South Korean and Chinese leaders in 1992–98); (2) it was a "military-first delegation" headed by SPA President Kim Yong-Nam (a former foreign minister who functions as a de facto head of state for ceremonial functions) but consisting almost exclusively of military generals and including not a single economic official; (3) Kim Yong Nam made an elliptical remark to Premier Zhu Rongji that Chinese economic reforms "suited China's national conditions." For Pyongyang, the visit was a success not only for signaling a turning point in the Sino–North Korean strategic partnership, but also for obtaining China's promise of an additional 150,000 tons of grain and 400,000 tons of coal.[18] In October, on the fiftieth anniversary of the establishment of diplomatic relations, Chinese foreign minister Tang Jiaxuan traveled to Pyongyang to discuss ways of expanding bilateral ties.

Kim Jong-Il's choice of Beijing for his first-ever unofficial state visit on May 29–31, 2000, spotlights China's place in Pyongyang's diplomatic outreach. The secrecy of the state visit also speaks volumes about his reputation as the world's most reclusive leader as well as about the hypersensitivity of Sino-DPRK relations.[19] By all indications, the China trip was catalyzed by and concerned with the proper handling of the upcoming Pyongyang summit, with Beijing playing the supporting role of a socialist elder brother and tutor. Without prior Chinese encouragement and tutoring, and without an advance trial run at being and becoming a smiling public persona, Kim Jong-Il would not have dared to take several bold image-remaking steps during the televised inter-Korean summit process.

Unlike Kim Yong-Nam's state visit a year earlier, Kim Jong-Il's China trip led Pyongyang to sing publicly sweet music for the emergent Sino-DPRK renormalization process. By achieving a "consensus of views on all the matters discussed," we were told, the Beijing summit advanced the cause of socialism and further consolidated the DPRK-China friendship—a relationship sealed in the blood of the Korean War—at a time when the international situation was becoming increasingly complicated.[20] For the first time in the post-cold-war era, *Rodong Shinmun*, the official organ of the Korean Workers' Party (KWP), declared that the two leaders expressed their solidarity and support for each other's unification policy and construction of socialism during the Kim-Jiang summit in Beijing, that there had been significant achievements in China's socialist modernization, and that these achievements were possible only under the leadership of the Chinese Communist Party (CCP).[21]

More than any other major power, China, at least in the short run, has

---

18. Economist Intelligence Unit, *Country Report: South Korea, North Korea,* Third quarter, 1999, pp. 42–43.

19. Senior Chinese diplomats informed Russian counterparts that in the four years since Kim Jong-Il assumed supreme power in the DPRK, he has refused to hold a summit with PRC leaders. As Pyongyang has explained it, KJI is too preoccupied with internal affairs (DPRK Report, no. 15 November-December 1998).

20. KCNA, June 1, 2000.

21. *Rodong Shinmun,* June 3, 2000.

the most to gain from the inter-Korean rapprochement process that the Pyongyang summit has reflected and effected. As Kim Jong-Il's visit to Beijing a couple of weeks before the summit underscores, Beijing was back on the center stage of peninsular affairs playing the role of facilitator and cheerleader, if not honest broker. Yet the rapid pace of postsummit events and developments revealed Beijing's geopolitical opportunity and danger, a crisis (*weiji*) in the Chinese usage of the term, indicating not only danger (*weixian*) but also an opportunity (*jihui*) to be seized. Beijing welcomed the summit as a first giant step in the inter-Korean peace process while simultaneously worrying about the adverse consequences of a rapid improvement of U.S.-DPRK relations.

As if determined to showcase its multitasking balancing act, in October 2000 Beijing dispatched a high-powered military delegation headed by Defense Minister Chi Haotian to Pyongyang to reaffirm Sino-DPRK military ties, and a high-powered civilian delegation headed by Prime Minister Zhu Rongji to Seoul to elevate Sino-ROK relations from a "cooperative partnership" to a "full-scale cooperative partnership," pushing the United States and Japan to the sidelines. China's proactive balancing strategy may have contributed to the uncharacteristically hasty move by the Clinton administration to accelerate its normalization talks with the DPRK, which stemmed from its worries about losing control over the rapidly moving Korean target and about China's expanding role in the region. Yet Beijing was greatly surprised and even unnerved by the extent to which Secretary of State Madeleine Albright's quasi-summit meeting with Kim Jong-Il overshadowed Chi Haotian's presence in the city. Such a reaction is hardly surprising, considering the rapid pace of unprecedented diplomatic events, especially the U.S.-DPRK normalization talks, for the emerging inter-Korean peace process in the latter half of 2000 immediately put into play several plausible future scenarios for the reshaping of the regional security architecture in Northeast Asia. One possible scenario was that if the United States were to take command of the emerging reconciliation process, it would redound to the disadvantage of China's influence on peninsular affairs. Even some of the harshest critics of the "rise of China" thesis admit that the Korean peninsula is the one and only place where Chinese power matters, where China is more than a "middle power."[22]

---

22. Gerald Segal, "Does China Matter?" *Foreign Affairs*, vol. 78, no. 5 (1999): 24–36, especially p. 32.

Kim Jong-Il's second "secret" visit to China (Shanghai and Beijing) in less than eight months during January 15–20, 2001, was designed as a more extensive personal inspection of "capitalism with Shanghai characteristics." During the widely publicized "secret" trip, Kim Jong-Il was reported to have visited the Shanghai stock market and economic export zones in and around Shanghai accompanied by tutoring Premier Zhu Rongji, underscoring the need for "new thinking" that had been emphasized by the North Korean media in preceding weeks. Is this not evidence enough of *Juche* being Shanghaied? However, a simple reality check suggests that post–Kim Il-Sung North Korea is no post-Mao China and that the initial conditions of post-Mao China do not apply to and are not readily reproducible in post–Kim Il-Sung North Korea.

Nonetheless, thanks to the renormalization process, Sino-DPRK trade registered a 32-percent increase in 2000 ($488 million) and a whopping 127.7-percent increase in the first quarter of 2001 ($154 million) after two consecutive years of decreases. A highly asymmetrical Beijing-Pyongyang-Seoul triangular trade relationship has emerged with Sino-DPRK trade representing 25 percent of the total North Korean trade volume in 2000, but only 1.6 percent of the Sino-ROK trade volume ($31.3 billion) and less than one-half of 1 percent of the total Chinese volume (down from about 4 percent in the 1960s). More revealing, South Korea's trade with China in 2000 generated a huge trade surplus of $5.7 billion, while North Korea's trade with China generated a trade deficit of $414 million.

By providing more aid in a wider variety of forms—direct government-to-government aid, subsidized cross-border trade, and private barter transactions—Beijing also became more deeply involved, playing a more active role in the politics of regime survival in the North. Although the exact amount and terms of China's aid to North Korea remain unclear, it is generally estimated at one-quarter to one-third of China's overall foreign aid. Nonetheless, Beijing's multitasking strategy is made palpably evident in "humanitarian aid," which is designed to lessen flows of refugees to China, to delay a possible North Korean collapse, and to enhance China's own leverage in Pyongyang and Seoul.[23]

Pyongyang's growing dependence on Beijing for its economic and political survival, coupled with Beijing's growing frustration, has bred

---

23. See Scott Snyder, "The Rise of U.S.-China Rivalry and Its Implications for the Korean Peninsula," in Park and Kim, *Korean Security Dynamics in Transition*, p. 121.

mutual distrust and resentment. Pyongyang has taken a sleight-of-hand approach by privately asking for more and more aid to avoid getting less and less, even as North Korean diplomats habitually deny that they have ever asked for or received any Chinese aid.[24] "The most frightening prospect," according to Hwang Jang-Yop, "is not that North Korea will collapse. What I fear most is that Kim Jong-Il will bow down to China to get the help he needs, and North Korea will slip into the Chinese orbit."[25] In every high-level meeting between the two governments, according to one Chinese scholar, the North Korean request for economic aid dominates the agenda.[26] Despite the renormalization process there remain structural asymmetries between Pyongyang's needs and expectations and Beijing's multitasking Realpolitik priorities.

There can be no doubt that Kim Dae-Jung's Sunshine Policy, especially the pledge not to undermine or absorb North Korea, played like a violin to Chinese geostrategic ears.[27] Powered by the Sunshine Policy, Sino-ROK relations continued to expand unabated. Sino-ROK trade dropped from $23.7 billion in 1997 to $18.4 billion in 1998 (a 22-percent decrease) due to the 1997 Asian financial crisis but rose to $22.6 billion in 1999 (a 22-percent increase) and to $31.3 billion in 2000 (a 39-percent increase), which has upgraded each as the other's third-largest trade partner. Put in comparative terms, the annual value of Sino-DPRK trade is less than the weekly value of Sino-ROK trade.[28] By mid-2001, China had surpassed Japan as the second-largest importer of South Korean goods. South Korea's foreign investment in China reached over $29.3 billion in 2000, and by mid-2001 China had surpassed the United States as the ROK's largest foreign investment destination. With

---

24. In a closed executive session in New York in late May 1998 involving two high-ranking North Korean ambassadors and a dozen U.S. scholars, including this author, ambassadors categorically denied any Chinese aid, saying: "If we wanted Chinese aid, we could get one million tons of grain from China tomorrow but it would come with an unacceptably heavy price of 'dependence.'"

25. Hwang's statement in an interview granted to U.S. journalist Selig Harrison. See Selig Harrison, "North Korea from the Inside Out," *Washington Post,* June 21, 1998, p. Co1.

26. You Ji, "China and North Korea: A Fragile Relationship of Strategic Convenience," *Journal of Contemporary China,* vol. 10, no. 28 (August 2001), pp. 390–91.

27. For further discussion see Samuel S. Kim, "Will Seoul's Sunshine Policy Also Rise in Beijing? A Chinese Perspective," in Chung-in Moon and David I. Steinberg, eds., *Kim Dae-jung Government and Sunshine Policy: Promises and Challenges* (Seoul: Yonsei University Press, 1999), pp. 199–230.

28. See KOTRA Web site for the latest Sino-Korean trade data.

Beijing's imminent entry into the World Trade Organization and its hosting of the 2008 Olympics, Seoul is now mapping out more aggressive strategies for the Chinese market, even as Beijing has stepped up filing of antidumping suits and other retaliations against perceived unfair trade practices. It is worth noting that out of the nine such antidumping investigations launched by China since 1997, seven were related to South Korean products.

Premier Zhu Rongi's state visit to Seoul on October 17–18, 2000, marked another turning point in the steady and progressive development of Sino-ROK relations. In a quasi-summit meeting in Seoul, both leaders agreed to elevate the "cooperative partnership" established during President Kim Dae-Jung's November 1998 state visit to Beijing to a "full-scale cooperative partnership." The change in terminology was intended to signal the advancement of Sino-ROK cooperation beyond the economic domain to include political and social issues. China's concessions were largely economic, allowing South Korean telecommunications firms promoting CDMA (code division multiple access) to participate in the Chinese market, since China had finally decided to allow the CDMA standard to be developed in tandem with the current GSM (global service for multiple communication) system in order to meet its wireless telecommunications needs. South Korea's quid pro quo concessions were largely political and social, including Kim Dae-Jung's rejection of the Dalai Lama's scheduled and long-awaited visit to Seoul. In addition, the two countries signed a criminal extradition treaty, followed by a Sino-ROK fisheries agreement eight months later. Despite the flare-up of trade disputes from time to time—over garlic and poisoned seafood, to mention two—the politics of complex economic interdependence is now in the driver's seat and moving Sino-ROK relations into a new phase of cooperation and competition.

The rapid growth of Sino-Korean interactions at all levels involving political, economic, educational, religious, and humanitarian (human rights) actors has created a mixed bag of emerging challenges for identity politics in the complex triangle of asymmetrical interdependence. There has already emerged a Pyongyang-Beijing-Seoul triangle of human movements and frictions involving flows of some 100,000–300,000 refugees and defectors from North Korea to northeast China, flows of more than 400,000 Chinese middle-class tourists and about 135,000 Chinese-Korean (*chosenjok*) illegal migrant workers from China to South Korea, and almost a million South Korean tourists to China in 2000.

Against this backdrop, the plight of seven members of a North Korean family (referred to as NK-7–I hereafter), ranging in age from thirteen to thirty, captured the public imagination and prime-time media coverage in Seoul. The tragic odyssey started when the NK-7–I risked their lives by crossing the Tumen River into China and then entered Russia only to be arrested by Russian border guards on November 10, 1999. Thanks to the mass-media frenzy and a major global NGO conference in Seoul, the office of the UN High Commissioner for Refugees (UNHCR) intervened and declared them to be bona fide refugees. At the same time, the hapless NK-7–I told a Russian television crew that they would be killed if repatriated to their homeland and that they preferred to remain in Russia even if it meant going to prison. The case of the NK-7–I became an instant cause célèbre. Seoul was forced to launch a flurry of diplomatic activities on their behalf, though largely for show, all to no avail. On December 30, Moscow decided to disengage itself from the NK-7–I imbroglio by sending them back to China as illegal immigrants rather than accepting them as refugees. Beijing in turn acted decisively in forcibly repatriating them to North Korea on January 11, 2000.

The plight of the NK-7–I underscores with particular clarity the variegated responses of all the involved parties. For Beijing, a "red line" of state sovereignty was crossed and China had to repatriate them as illegal immigrants in accordance with the 1960 Sino-DPRK Criminal Extradition Treaty. The bottom line seemed clear enough: To grant refugee status to North Korean escapees was to open a Pandora's box of a potentially massive refugee exodus. Meanwhile, UN High Commissioner Sakako Ogata sent a letter to the Chinese government on January 12, 2000, protesting its violation of the 1951 Refugee Convention (of which both China and Russia are signatories) and urging China to refrain from additional deportations of North Korean refugees in the future.[29] The response of Tokyo and Washington has been one of total silence, suggesting that there is no contest between Realpolitik and Idealpolitik.

On June 26, 2001, another North Korean refugee bomb exploded right in the middle of Beijing when a family of seven North Korean refugees/

---

29. Article 1 of the 1951 Refugee Convention defines a "refugee" as anyone who is outside of his/her own country and unable or unwilling to return home due to a well-founded fear of persecution for reasons of race, religion, nationality, membership in a particular social group, or political opinion.

defectors (referred to as NK-7–II hereafter) managed to sneak into the Beijing office of the UNHCR and requested political asylum. Once again Beijing was forced to perform a delicate, balancing diplomatic act, but unlike previous cases, including the Hwang Jang-Yop affair in the spring of 1997, it took less than four days of negotiations between Chinese authorities and UNHCR officials to resolve the crisis by permitting the North Korean asylum seekers to leave Beijing on June 29, 2001, on "humanitarian medical grounds." By letting them leave for Seoul via Singapore and Manila as "patients" ostensibly in need of medical care, Beijing managed to avoid taking a stand on the central question the incident raised. At the outset, a total of fifteen family members reportedly had fled North Korea and five of them had already been sent back, two to a concentration camp for their crimes against the state. North Korean security agents have also been looking for the rest of this family in China. From the beginning, Beijing had no "rational choice" decision but to quickly settle the case in a humanitarian-cum-Realpolitik way. Consider the multiple pressures confronting the Chinese leadership: (1) The global media spotlight and coverage; (2) an on-the-fly task force established and dispatched by the Kim Dae-Jung government on June 27, 2001; (3) a petition submitted in May 2001 to the Seoul office of the UNHCR signed by some 11.8 million South Koreans asking that so-called defectors from North Korea be granted refugee status and allowed to come to South Korea if they wished; and (4) perhaps most important, Beijing's all-out bid for the 2008 Summer Olympic Games with the final decision due on July 13, 2001. What kind of message would reach China's Yanbian area, the largest Korean diaspora in the world, where as many as 300,000 North Koreans are hiding out after fleeing their famine-stricken homeland?

The North Korean refugee question, hitherto much ignored but a potential time bomb for both Koreas, has brought into sharp focus how easily and quickly such unplanned incidents could throw China's delicate two-Koreas policy into a tailspin. Even before the eruption of the second North Korean refugee incident in late June 2001, China's "Strike Hard" campaign had already been launched at the end of May 2001, resulting in a dramatic increase in the number of humanitarian aid workers arrested and fined and North Korean refugees repatriated.

Indeed, central to Beijing's two-Koreas Realpolitik is growing concern about the possibility of Korean reunification by southern absorption. There is far more than meets the public eye in Beijing's status quo—and antiunification—policy. Apart from maximizing its leverage as a balancer in Northeast Asian politics, China genuinely fears that North Korea could come to feel cornered and see no choice but to fight back, triggering a regional war at the least. Beijing does not doubt that Pyongyang would fight rather than succumb to German-style hegemonic unification. Even if the system in the North were to simply collapse, such an event is more likely to trigger a bloody civil war than immediate absorption by the South.

An alternative scenario in which the North Korean economy declines apace, leading to another collapsing socialist regime on China's northern borders, could hardly be more comforting. Fearing both the ideological and strategic consequences of a united Korea, Beijing might intervene to rescue the post–Kim Il-Sung system from political or economic collapse as a way of maintaining a strategic shield in the northern half of the Korean peninsula or as a way of arresting a massive exodus of refugees into China's northeastern provinces.

With the world's second- or sixth-largest economy and a strong sense of nationalism, a unified Korea could become a "regional power" in Northeast Asia—an unwelcome scenario reflected in China's Realpolitik perspective toward the peninsula. In short, China sees far more dangers than opportunities in Korean reunification. A unified Korea would remove the DPRK as China's critical buffer zone and would deprive Beijing of the use of the Korean issue to advance its own national interests across the board, including in its dealings with the United States. Korean unification would also diminish Beijing's leverage in Korean and world affairs, would mean a more lonely, anti-socialist world with one less socialist regime, would spew more refugees into China's northeastern provinces, and could trigger Japanese rearmament if the U.S. troops were to withdraw from Korea.

Japan: Rising-Sun Nationalism and Diminishing Dividends

Of the three neighboring powers involved in Korean affairs by virture of their geography and history, Japan made the least progress in the now-on, now-off normalization talks with North Korea in 1999–2001. In the first half of 2001, the long shadow of Japan's imperial past and a seemingly endless series of historical controversies (the right-wing revisionism of history textbooks, visits to the Yasukuni Shrine) returned with a vengeance, rubbing more Japanese colonial salt into Chinese and Korean nationalistic wounds. On top of this, a fishing controversy in June 2001 badly shook up Tokyo-Seoul relations.

For most of its modern history, Japan has been *in* Asia but not *of* Asia. Even during the cold war, when Tokyo and Seoul were geographically, culturally, and strategically close because of the United States, they were far apart in many other ways. Situated at the junction of Chinese, Korean, and Russian historical enmities but protected by American hegemony in East Asia during the cold war, Japan sought comfort and safety in a relatively low-profile, quiescent role in international affairs, giving rise to its postwar identity as a pacifist and reactive state.

In the past several years, however, Japan's assertive rising-sun nationalism has been growing apace, reviving its problematic "Asian identity." In a move that spoke of strong nationalist sentiment among Japan's politicians, on August 9, 1999, the upper house of Diet voted resoundingly—166 to 71—to officially designate the rising-sun flag and longtime unofficial anthem as legal symbols of the nation.[30] Far from a simple matter of symbols, the debate turned into a contest among politicians and intellectuals over Japan's national identity and its international role a half-century after its defeat in World War II. This cause has long been dear to right-wing hypernationalists but has been at odds with the country's postwar efforts to project a pacifist identity.

All the same it is a lightening rod issue for Northeast Asian countries, especially for Korea and China, because it is organically linked with Japan's imperial aggression and atrocities. Note for comparison that Germany discarded its "Deutschland Uber Alles" anthem and the swastika flag after the war. Of course such right-wing nationalism in Japan can only beget right-wing and left-wing nationalism in Seoul, Beijing, and Moscow, let alone in Pyongyang. Tokyo's official acceptance signals a shift toward a more hawkish stance that is emerging across a broad range of political opinions and is likely to rattle regional rivals in Northeast Asia. Growing popular support for changing the constitution makes evident that not only right-wing hypernationalists are involved in this imperial/national identity legislation. More than 60 percent of the public now supports such a constitutional change and a whopping

---

30. Howard W. French, "Japan Now Officially Hails the Emperor and a Rising Sun," *New York Times*, August 10, 1999, p. A3.

90 percent of Diet members under fifty years of age want such a constitutional revision.[31] In Northeast Asia, especially in Seoul and Beijing,
Prime Minister Junichiro Koizumi is widely perceived to be a right-
wing nationalist; his popularity among young politicians and people does
not augur well for the future of cooperative Northeast Asian international relations.

Viewed in this light, the launching of the Taepodong-I missile over
Japan on August 31, 1998, was at once a strategic surprise, a crisis, and
perhaps even a blessing in disguise in terms of the legitimation of the
born-again, rising-sun nationalism. Indeed, no single event is said to
have impacted and reshaped Japanese public opinion as much as the
North Korean Taepodong-I missile launch. The widely expected test
launch in late August 1999 of a new long-range missile, Taepodong-II,
is also said to have supplied the necessary justification for the passage
of the rising-sun flag and anthem legislation. The launch of Taepodong-
I was a complete surprise to the international community, initially sum-
moning anything but a united response from Tokyo, which was shocked;
Seoul, which gave no response; and Washington, which gave a delayed
and mixed response.

By contrast, Taepodong-II was the most anticipated missile launch of
the 1990s, concentrating American and Japanese minds on the question
of how to cope with another impending crisis. Taepodong brinkmanship
once again brought Pyongyang and Washington to direct bilateral talks
in Berlin. The Berlin Agreement of September 12, 1999—the outcome
of the Berlin talks between the United States and the DPRK—provided
relief as both parties agreed in principle that Washington would lift its
sanctions on North Korea in exchange for Pyongyang's suspension of
the Taepodong-II firing, while at the same time the two countries would
accelerate normalization talks.

After a hiatus of seven years, Japan-DPRK normalization talks started
gaining momentum in the wake of the Berlin Agreement and the easing
of U.S. sanctions. Prodded by Seoul and Washington and always anxious not to lag too far behind the United States, the Japanese government lifted the ban on charter flights in November, sent a multiparty
delegation led by former Japanese prime minister Tomiichi Murayama
in early December to Pyongyang, where the Japanese delegation agreed

31. Michael Green, "Why Tokyo Will Be a Larger Player in Asia," Nautilus's Northeast
Asia Peace and Security Network, Special Report, July 31, 2000.

to resume negotiations to restore bilateral ties, and lifted the remaining sanctions on North Korea on December 14. As a result, North Korean and Japanese Red Cross delegations held bilateral talks in Beijing from December 19 to 21 to settle "humanitarian issues of mutual concern," reaching an agreement in the form of a joint statement on December 21. The next day foreign ministry officials of the two countries met to discuss details for full-fledged normalization talks.

Despite three rounds of normalization talks in 2000—the ninth round in Pyongyang from April 4 to 8, the tenth round in Tokyo from August 21 to 25, and the eleventh round in Beijing from October 30 to 31—and Tokyo's aid offer of 500,000 tons of rice (worth nearly $1 billion) from domestic reserves, little progress was made on this front, leaving the respective positions and priorities of the parties as wide apart as before. The eleventh round of normalization talks in Beijing effectively collapsed, with both parties failing to set a date for the next round of normalization talks. Japan's officially chosen course toward North Korea is "to make efforts to redress abnormal postwar relations with North Korea in close coordination with the United States and the ROK, in a manner that can contribute to the peace and stability of the Northeast Asian region; and to strike a balance between dialogue and deterrence in the execution of these policies."[32] This official policy pronouncement glosses over two nagging issues: settlement of the colonial past and the alleged abductions of ten Japanese nationals by North Korean security agents in the 1970s and 1980s.

At first glance the abduction issue seems the easiest to settle. In actuality, it is the more intractable problem as it excites national-identity politics in both countries in a zero-sum, winner-take-all way. At the tenth round of normalization talks in Tokyo, for example, Japan's chief delegate, Takano Kojiro, underscored the importance of finding a satisfactory solution to the abduction issue by explaining its links to Japan's domestic politics. Any normalization treaty that may come of the talks, he argued, must receive the approval of the Diet. He went on to point out that Diet approval would not be forthcoming without public support, which in turn would hinge on whether the abduction issue had been resolved. With a surge of new publicity, the abduction issue has become a political hot potato in Japanese domestic politics. A citizens' group that has long campaigned for the disappeared people recently

---

32. See *Diplomatic Bluebook 2000* at www.mofa.go.jp/policy/other/bluebook/2000/ 1–b.html, accessed June 12, 2001.

stepped up a petition drive for stronger government action that had already collected 1.3 million signatures. A recent public opinion survey showed that some 80 percent of Japanese want their government to resolve bilateral disputes first before establishing full diplomatic relations with North Korea.[33] The Japanese government is caught in a dilemma as it tries to keep pace with Seoul and Washington in dealing with Pyongyang, while at the same time encountering a mounting public outcry at home for being too soft on North Korea.

But in Japan as elsewhere, all politics are local. For Pyongyang to yield on the abduction issue is to admit it is a terrorist state, a self-delegitimating act of a high order. A quick fix for this problem outside the global media spotlight seems no longer possible. That Pyongyang went ballistic on the eve of the tenth round of normalization talks in mid-2000—savaging Tokyo for calling it "North Korea" instead of using the official name "Democratic People's Republic of Korea," which is claimed to be "the sacred name of the sovereign country recognized by the world"[34]—only underscores the continuation of the Tokyo-Pyongyang legitimation war.

On the question of settling the past, there were a few developments of a potentially positive nature. Japan is reported to have advanced for the first time at the tenth round of normalization talks a proposal to apply the same formula it had used in normalizing relations with South Korea in 1965—that is, "economic cooperation" aid in lieu of "compensation," consisting of a grant of $300 million and a loan of $200 million. North Korea also made a concession of sorts by no longer insisting on "reparations" from Japan, settling instead for "compensation." It was against this seemingly hopeful backdrop and in advance of the eleventh round of normalization talks in Beijing that the Japanese government announced on October 6, 2000, its decision to donate 500,000 tons of rice to North Korea via the World Food Program (WFP), a five-fold increase over past contributions, in order, "from a broader perspective, to improve relations with North Korea and to maintain peace and stability in the region, given the historic new developments in the Korean Peninsula."[35] Moreover, Tokyo decided to donate from its own re-

---

33. Frank Ching, "Japan's Korean Dilemma," *Far Eastern Economic Review* (November 16, 2000) (Internet version).

34. KCNA, July 25, 2000, at www.kcna.co.jp/item/200007/news07/25.htm.

35. For the official announcement of this aid decision, see www.mofa.go.jp/announce/announce/2000/10/1006-4html, accessed February 3, 2001.

serves Japanese rice, which is twelve times more expensive than Thai or Chinese rice, with the total cost amounting to 120 billion yen (more than $1 billion).

Nonetheless, the eleventh round of normalization talks in Beijing lasted only two days, ending without any agreement on the next round of talks. What is most notable about the eleventh round is that Japanese negotiators put forth a proposal for a $9-billion "economic aid" package (60 percent in grant aid and 40 percent in loans) as quid pro quo for North Korea's moderation of the missile threat and satisfactory resolution of the abduction issue. Contrary to Japanese expectations, Pyongyang responded that such attempts to short-circuit an admission of colonial repentance and compensation were unacceptable. The eleventh round of normalization talks thus collapsed with each side saying in effect that the ball was in the other's court.

Apart from the continued asymmetry between the two sides' demands, Pyongyang was apparently betting on the fully established Washington connection, which would inevitably force Tokyo to accommodate its "just demands" for a Japanese apology for past wrongs and both economic aid and compensation for the colonial period. Put differently, Pyongyang was banking on the "Clinton in Pyongyang" shock to bring Tokyo back into negotiations. On the other hand, Tokyo is increasingly pressured by domestic politics, and public opinion is in favor of not rushing toward normalization, especially when it is viewed as cost-ineffective, too little in return on a large investment. "We're not really afraid of missing the bus, because we are one of the drivers," said a Japanese Foreign Ministry source.[36]

The Pyongyang summit seems to have generated no discernable positive impact on Japan-DPRK normalization talks. While Tokyo supports the engagement policy bilaterally, trilaterally (via the Trilateral Coordination and Oversight Group, or TCOG), and multilaterally (via the Korean Peninsula Energy Development Organization, or KEDO), rising-sun nationalists warn of the danger of being trapped in a position in which the inter-Korean rapprochement process could come about at the expense of Japan's security interests.

For Japanese security planners the intermediate-range Nodong missiles are far more threatening than the long-range Taepodong missiles.

---

36. Quoted in Doug Struck, "Talks with Japan Key to North Korea's Revival," *Washington Post*, October 31, 2000, p. A20.

While the Taepodong missile program is still in the development and testing stage and still subject to the 1999 Berlin Agreement and self-imposed moratorium, North Korea has successfully tested and deployed Nodong missiles in substantial numbers at various sites inland and along its northern borders. In 1999 alone it is estimated that Pyongyang produced between 75 and 150 Nodong missiles, of which one-third were sold to foreign countries. With an estimated range of 1,000–1,300 kilometers and payloads of 700–1,000 kilograms, more than half of Japan is within the Nodong missile's range. The possibility that North Korea might develop the capability to load its weapons of mass destruction (WMD)—chemical, biological, and nuclear—on its intermediate-range ballistic missiles makes the Nodong a greater threat than the Taepodong. Moreover, the Nodong is among the North's most developed asymmetrical military capabilities (a credible terror weapon against large cities in western Japan)—an ace in the hole for system maintenance and survival—and North Korea is not likely to give it up. The strategic threat that Japan confronts from the Nodong missiles, not to mention recent Chinese missile advances, is perceived as real.[37]

As if the collapse of normalization talks with North Korea was insufficient to project Japan's born-again, rising-sun nationalism, in the first half of 2001 Tokyo brought history back in to fuel national-identity clashes in Japan-ROK relations. Once again the old historical controversies plaguing Japanese-Korean relations—the prime minister's official visit to the Yasukuni Shrine to worship the Japanese war dead (including fourteen class A war criminals and Hideki Tojo, who was sentenced to death by the Far East International Military Tribunal after World War II), the Ministry of Education's approval of sanitized history textbooks that gloss over Japan's past aggression and atrocities in the 1930s and early 1940s, and the so-called comfort women (mostly Korean) who were abducted and sent to Japanese military "comfort stations" (brothels) in occupied China and Southeast Asia during World War II—have ignited storms of anti-Japanese condemnation and protest in Seoul.

---

37. See Kent E. Calder, "The New Face of Northeast Asia," *Foreign Affairs*, vol. 80, no. 1 (January/February 2001): 115; Victor Cha, "The Ultimate Oxymoron: Japan's Engagement with North Korea," *North Korea's Engagement: Perspectives, Outlook, and Implications*, Conference Report (National Intelligence Council, Washington, D.C., CR 2001–01, May 2001), 73–85; B. C. Koh, "U.S.-Japan Security Cooperation and the Two Koreas," in Park and Kim, *Korean Security Dynamics in Transition*, pp. 139–41.

In some respects, this latest round is worse than the previous ones. The most controversial issue in the latest bout of historical revisionism is the participation by the right-wing Society to Make a New History Textbook—the group that has repeatedly sought to justify and legitimatize Japanese colonialism as a move to liberate Asia from Western imperialists. The 1997 textbooks described comfort women as "sex slaves" but the forthcoming texts in 2001 use euphemisms like "comfort facilities" and "many Korean women were sent to factories," and replace "invasion of" with "advance into" other Asian countries. During a similar row in 1982 a history publisher agreed to delete the controversial "advance" and replace it with "invasion." But this time around, nationalists who view Japan's textbooks as "masochistic" are proving less accommodating. As of mid-2001, Tokyo's unyielding stand and the ensuing war over national identity threatened to pass the point of no return in the "partnership for the twenty-first century" between Tokyo and Seoul that was forged during Kim Dae-Jung's state visit to Japan in October 1998.

As if this were not trouble enough, a fishing dispute flared up between Japan and the ROK when Tokyo announced on June 19, 2001, that it would ban South Korean fishing vessels from waters near the Russia-held Kurile Islands off northern Japan. According to Tokyo, the area is in Japan's EEZ. Seoul, however, argued that its vessels were allowed to fish around the Kuriles under a fisheries accord reached with Moscow in December 2000. In protest, Tokyo also declared a ban on South Korean fishing in the waters off the coast of Sinriku in the Pacific Ocean until the Korean government promised not to send its fishing boats into the waters off the Kuriles. Behind the Japanese government's hard-line stance is its scheme to gain the upper hand in its ongoing territorial dispute with Russia over the Kuriles at the expense of Korean fishermen. Not surprisingly, Seoul was considering various reprisals, including suspending permission for Japanese fishing boats to operate in South Korea's EEZs. One thing is for sure: South Korea is no longer a shrimp between the Russian and Japanese whales.

Given the many difficulties of peacefully achieving the kind of united Korea that they favor, Japanese policy makers seem to have quietly concluded that their wisest course is not to hasten unification but rather to maintain the status quo as long as possible. For Japan, Korean reunification poses a catch-22 dilemma of another kind. On the one hand, a strong, united, and nationalistic Korea could pose a formidable challenge to

Japan. On the other hand, however, the continuation of a divided Korea with an unpredictable rogue state in the North is no less threatening to Japan's security.[38] The challenge, therefore, is how to navigate between the Scylla of a unified Korea with all its uncertainties, potential instability, and new challenges, and the Charybdis of a divided Korea with the continuing danger of implosion or explosion in the North.

Russia: Loud Thunder But Little Rain?

At first glance Russian president Vladimir Putin seems to have brought Moscow back onto center stage of inter-Korean affairs by becoming not only the first Kremlin leader ever to visit the neighboring communist country, but also the first among the Big Four to make an official state visit to North Korea. On the eve of the historic inter-Korean summit, Moscow announced on June 8, 2000, that Putin's official state visit to Pyongyang for his first Korean summit meeting with Chairman Kim Jong-Il would take place on July 19–20. Two weeks later on June 20, Putin also accepted an invitation to visit Seoul for his second Korean summit meeting with President Kim Dae-Jung (February 26–27, 2001). And yet, one may ask if this is not a case, as an old Chinese saying has it, of *leisheng da, yudian xiao* ("loud thunder but little rain").

What is most striking about Moscow's relations with Pyongyang is not that there had been abrupt vicissitudes and fluctuations throughout the 1990s—for indeed there were many—but that the downward spiral of Russia-DPRK relations that had resulted from a series of domestic and external shocks has been reversed and put back on the renormalization track in the past two years. In 2000 the renormalization process gained momentum when the newly elected president's vigorous pursuit of Realpolitik intersected with Kim Jong-Il's new diplomatic opening to the outside world. Indeed, the precipitous and traumatic decline of Russia from great-power status to that of a poor and powerless state—and the lack of a widely accepted "national" identity—explains the turbulence of Russia's Korea policy in the 1990s.

Moscow's tilted two-Koreas policy started with a bang in 1990 but

---

38. See Michael H. Armacost and Kenneth B. Pyle, "Japan and the Unification of Korea: Challenges for U.S. Policy Coordination," in Nicholas Eberstadt and Richard J. Ellings, eds., *Korea's Future and the Great Powers* (Seattle, WA: University of Washington Press, 2001), p. 128.

ended with a whimper. Ironically, if Moscow was the chief catalyst for transforming the political and strategic landscape of Northeast Asia, including the initiation of cross-recognition and the two Koreas' entry into the United Nations, Beijing became the major beneficiary, occupying the pivotal position from which it could exert greater influence over Seoul and Pyongyang. As if to emulate Beijing's much-touted equidistance policy, Moscow has retreated significantly from its tilted policy towards a more balanced policy since mid-1994 as a way of reassuring (and thus enhancing its leverage in) Pyongyang and resuming its great-power role in the politics of divided Korea. Moscow was unhappy with Seoul because it reaped so few economic and political rewards for its diplomatic and strategic contributions to Seoul's Nordpolitik. Moscow was miffed especially about the partial implementation of the $3 billion in aid and about being sidelined from the $4.6-billion nuclear reactor deal.

Accordingly, Moscow has made strategic reassessments of the situation in North Korea, concluding that the North Korean system will not collapse in the immediate future, as was predicted in the early 1990s, and that should such a collapse occur, it might cause even greater risks. All the same, Russia's domestic politics have become more nationalist by the day. From Moscow's Realpolitik perspective, the Korean peninsula is an important region where during the last one hundred and more years it fought several wars—the Russo-Japanese wars of 1904–1905 and 1945, and the Korean War in 1950–53—to protect its great-power interests. Nevertheless, in the post-cold-war setting post-Soviet Russia found itself pushed off the Korean peninsula both politically and economically. The primary challenges of Russia's Northeast Asia policy are said to have three components: to ensure a peaceful and stable external environment for domestic reforms, to establish stable partnerships with the region's leading economic powers (Japan, China, and South Korea), and to get back into the games the great powers play on multiple chessboards in Northeast Asia.

Against this backdrop, upon assuming office as president of Russia on May 8, 2000, Putin reaffirmed his pledge to restore Russia as a great power. His state visit to Pyongyang on July 20–21, 2000, also coincides with the completion and ratification of three national-security and foreign-policy blueprint documents in 2000, a new national-security concept (January 10), a new military doctrine (April 21), and a new foreign-policy concept (July 10). Together, these blueprints put inordinate stress on safeguarding Russia's "national" interests, defined in terms of Russian exceptionalism, great power prerogatives, and economic interests. The 1998–99 period was a turning point in Moscow's painful reappraisal of the rapidly changing and threatening international environment and the reconstruction of its ruling coalition. The liberal-statist balance of political elite interests was shattered by the August 1998 financial crisis, and even more significantly, by the NATO/U.S. war in Kosovo.[39] Both the new national security concept and the new military doctrine lower Russia's threshold for using nuclear weapons when attacked with conventional weapons, thus negating its declared policy of not being the first to use nuclear weapons under any circumstances. The new military doctrine, like the 1993 doctrine, extends Russia's nuclear umbrella to its allies (for example, Belarus and other members of CIS that have entered into alliance agreements with Russia).

Russian exceptionalism is said to stem from the ineluctable geographical fact that even post-Soviet Russia has the largest territory in the post-cold-war world and from Russia's status as the only truly Eurasian continental power. That is, even in an era of globalization, size matters in the mobilization and projection of Russia's identity as a great power. It also expresses Moscow's inability and unwillingness to define its identity as anything but a great power, and "great powers seldom operate under the same rules and constraints as lesser powers."[40] The new foreign policy concept gives pride of place to "balance" as a distinctive quality of Russia's foreign policy: "This quality [of balance] derives from Russia's geopolitical position as the largest Eurasian power, a position which necessitates an optimal combination of its efforts on all fronts. This approach imposes a responsibility on Russia for maintaining world security on both global and regional levels, and it presupposes that it pursue complementary foreign policy activities in bilateral and multilateral frameworks."[41]

39. Celeste Wallander, "Wary of the West: Russian Security Policy at the Millennium," *Arms Control Today*, vol. 30, no. 2 (March 2000): 7–12; "Russia's New Security Concept," *Arms Control Today* 30:1 (January/February 2000): 15–20; and Philipp C. Bleak, "Put Signs New Military Doctrine, Fleshing Out New Security Concept," *Arms Control Today*, vol. 30, no. 4 (May 2000): 42.

40. Ronald Grigor, "Provisional Stabilities: The Politics of Identities in Post-Soviet Eurasia," *International Security*, vol. 24, no. 3 (Winter 1999–2000): 149.

41. Quoted in Seung-Ho Joo, "Russia and Korea: The Summit and After," a paper presented at the Forty-second Annual Convention of the International Studies Association, Chicago, February 20–23, 2001, p. 3.

The new foreign policy concept also makes a reference to the Korean peninsula, expressing Russia's desire to play an important role in the inter-Korean peace process and to seek balanced relations with the two Koreas: "The situation on the Korean peninsula gives rise to the greatest concern. Russia's efforts will be concentrated on ensuring our country's full and equal participation in efforts to settle the Korean problem and on maintaining balanced relations with both Korean states."[42] Stripped to the core, power-balancing, interest-maximizing, result-oriented Realpolitik has come back with a vengeance.

What were the specific measures taken to enhance Russia's great-power role in inter-Korean affairs? In February 2000 Russian Foreign Minister Igor Ivanov traveled to Pyongyang to sign a new treaty—the DPRK-Russia Treaty on Friendship, Good Neighborliness and Cooperation—as a "fresh start" to replace the 1961 security pact that was scrapped in 1996. The new treaty, which took effect in late October with an exchange of certificates of ratification, was hailed as providing political and legal guarantees to boost cooperation and exchange in all aspects of the DPRK-Russia relationship. The automatic military intervention clause of the 1961 treaty (Article 1) was replaced in the new treaty by a more ambiguous "immediate contact" clause in case of a security crisis (Article 2): "In the event of the emergence of the danger of an aggression against one of the countries or a situation jeopardizing peace and security, and in the event there is a necessity for consultations and cooperation, the [two] sides enter into contact with each other immediately."[43]

Putin's personal diplomacy in 2000–2001 is a dramatic step toward bringing Moscow back into the rapidly changing Korean peninsular equation in order to reassert Russia's identity as the greatest Eurasian power. That the United States looms large in the Putin-Kim summit—some of Putin's and Kim Jong-Il's statements have had more to do with their opposition to the U.S. National Missile Defense (NMD) and Theater Missile Defense (TMD) plans than with the Russia-DPRK relationship—is evident not only in the itinerary of Putin's personal shuttle diplomacy (from Beijing to the G-8 summit meeting in Okinawa with a twenty-four-hour stopover in Pyongyang) but also in the eleven-point joint declaration that the two leaders signed. The joint declaration is far more

---

42. Ibid., p. 4.
43. Ibid., p. 12.

muscular and provocative than the South-North Joint Declaration, and includes trenchant attacks against infringement on state sovereignty under the pretext of humanitarianism, and against the United States' TMD and NMD programs. The Russian–North Korean summit captured global prime time and headlines when Putin revealed that the North Korean leader had pledged to eliminate his country's Taepodong missile pro-gram—a key rationale for NMD—if Western countries (read: the United States) provided access to rocket boosters for peaceful space research. Putin also managed to put Kim Jong-Il's "satellites for missiles" gift horse on the agenda of the G-8 summit meeting in Japan.

Moreover, Putin's personal diplomacy to gain Kim Dae-Jung's agree-ment to oppose NMD at their February 2001 summit meeting in Seoul and the resulting joint communique were greatly successful in creating a rift in the U.S.-ROK alliance. After several awkward attempts to dis-pel any notion of disagreement between Seoul and Washington and a disastrous summit meeting with George W. Bush in Washington, Kim Dae-Jung resolved the crisis in the old-fashioned (Kim Young-Sam) way—a major shake-up of his cabinet, replacing key officials including the foreign minister and the unification minister.

Kim Jong-Il's gift horse turned out to be no less Machiavellian than Putin's. In a three hour interview with a fifty-six-member delegation of South Korean media executives on August 12, 2000, Kim Jong-Il for the first time confirmed DPRK missile sales to Iran and Syria while at the same time dismissing the satellites-for-missiles offer as a "joke." But he went on to say: "It [the joke] must be a headache for the United States. It is reluctant to give us money, but it has to stop our scientific development. It must be a big headache."[44]

Although Pyongyang is increasingly active in economic contacts with Russia, economic cooperation between the two financially troubled coun-tries flounders. Putin's new foreign policy doctrine, with its unprec-edented stress on safeguarding Russia's economic interests, and Pyongyang's damage-compensation mendicant diplomacy were often out of sync with each other. Pyongyang still feels that it has been mate-rially "betrayed and damaged" by its former mentor and asks for Rus-sian assistance in repairing and modernizing all the industrial facilities

---

44. For a full English text of the interview, see Foreign Broadcast Information Service (FBIS), *Daily Report/East Asia (DR/EA)*, August 13, 2000, on the World Wide Web at wnc.fedworld.gov, accessed August 30, 2000.

and enterprises built in North Korea by the former Soviet Union in the 1950s and 1960s. Pyongyang has been insisting on barter deals and low-interest credits that would be impossible to implement in a market economy and to which Moscow cannot agree. Russia-DPRK trade dropped from $2.57 billion in 1990 to $50.1 million in 1999, which amounts to only 2.2 percent of Russia-ROK trade in 1999 and only one-tenth of Sino-ROK trade in 1999. One possible solution, according to Russia's Koreanists, is to have South Korean banks and firms provide credit to the DPRK in exchange for Russian technical assistance[45]—wishful thinking given the looming economic crisis in the South, where one *chaebol* after another is going belly up.

Still, Moscow seems excited about the geoeconomic opportunities resulting from increasing inter-Korean economic cooperation, particularly about the prospect of rail links across the DMZ, which would create a new trans-Siberian freight route linking South Korea to Europe via North Korea and the Russian Far East. The difficulty is in leveling the playing field of the highly asymmetrical Moscow-Pyongyang-Seoul economic interdependence by triangulating Russia's technical know-how and natural resources, North Korea's labor, and South Korea's capital—as well as Russia's debt to Seoul ($1.8 billion) and Pyongyang's debt to Moscow in a mutually complementary way. In order to have this Iron Silk Road dream come true the Russian way, however, Moscow would have to overcome some major obstacles, including the huge cost ($9 billion), Russia's economic weakness, China's comparative and competitive advantage in connecting its railway to the inter-Korean Seoul-Sinuiju line, which would make it the gateway for cargo travel from Asia to Europe, North Korea's ongoing economic crisis and unpredictable behavior, and the ideological and regional fragmentation in South Korea. Fearing that the new rail projects would diminish the role of local ports that depend on trade with South Korea, some Primorskii Krai officials are opposed to the development of a new Russian-Korean rail corridor."[46]

Regional relations provide a short-term basis for economic relations, especially through contracts for North Korean guest workers, but the expanded North Korean presence in the Russian Far East has raised new

---

45. *DPRK Report*, no. 26.
46. Irina Drobysheva, "Primorskii Krai Concerned about Russian-Korean Rail Link," *Russian Regional Investor*, vol. 3, no. 10 (May 23, 2001).

concerns about Pyongyang's involvement in nuclear smuggling, the heroin trade, and counterfeiting activities in Russia. Russian–North Korean regional cooperation will accelerate as major regional development projects such as the Tumen River project, the Kovyktinskoe gas pipeline, and the inter-Korean railway move forward, but progress will depend on the ability to attract considerable outside investment, especially from Japan but also from South Korea and China.[47]

In April 2001, North Korean defense minister Kim Il-Chol made the first official state visit to Moscow since the collapse of the Soviet Union in 1991. During this visit, the two governments signed on April 27 two "military technological cooperation" agreements that Moscow would modernize North Korea's aging Soviet-era weapons systems, provide regular security consultations, and train North Korean military personnel to upgrade and refurbish North Korean military facilities.

Kim Jong-Il's scheduled state visit to Moscow in April 2001 concerned rough sailing over the issue of arms sales-cum-aid as North Korea demanded such arms-delivery agreements as a precondition for Kim's official state visit for a second Kim-Putin summit. Apparently, the April 27, 2001, accords met the precondition sufficiently for Kim Jong-Il to make an official state visit to Moscow. Moscow and Pyongyang also agreed in principle to settle the pestering debt issue through a labor-for-debt swap deal, whereby North Korea would cover $5.5 billion in Soviet-era debt over the next thirty years by supplying workers who will toil unpaid in Russian labor camps across Siberia. About 90 percent of Pyongyang's debts to Moscow was covered in such a manner in 2000 to the tune of $50.4 million.[48] At this rate it would take 109 years to pay off Pyongyang's debts to Moscow!

Against this backdrop, Kim Jong-Il began his nine-day, 6,000-mile-plus trek by a twenty-one-car armored (Japanese-made) train with darkened windows and gun-toting guards across Russia's vast expanse for a two-day summit in Moscow. Apparently, he relished the dubious distinction of being the one and only state leader in the jet age who would spend no less than three weeks on a train ride for a two-day summit, and of being the only visiting state leader who has demanded and received an honor guard that had been removed from the Lenin Mausoleum in Red Square after the collapse of the Soviet Union in 1991.

---

47. See Elizabeth Wishnick, "A New Era in Russian–North Korean Relations?" in Samuel S. Kim, ed., *North Korea and Northeast Asia* (Lanham, MD: Rowman & Littlefield Publishers, forthcoming).

48. AFP, August 4, 2001.

In an eight-point DPRK-Russia Moscow Declaration of August 4, 2001, full of Soviet-style lingo,[49] both parties addressed both international (read: the United States) and bilateral issues. In fact, four of the eight points seem to have been designed to send a strong message to the United States: (1) "a just new world order" (point one); (2) the 1972 ABM Treaty as a cornerstone of global strategic stability (point two); (3) Korean reunification process by independent means and without foreign interference (point seven); and (4) the pullout of the U.S. forces from South Korea as a "pressing issue" to which Putin expressed his "understanding" (point eight). The remaining points have to do with the promotion of bilateral political and economic cooperation, especially "the plan for building railways linking the north and the south of the Korean peninsula, Russia and Europe on the principle of the mutual interests recognized in the worldwide practice" (point six).

Moscow's decision to help North Korea has had rather more to do with enhancing Russia's geopolitical trump cards than with money-making considerations, because Pyongyang already owes Moscow some $5.5 billion for Soviet-era military and nonmilitary deliveries and does not intend to repay that money. There is no guarantee whatsoever that this same story will not be repeated with the latest arms agreements. Perhaps the most revealing part of the Moscow Declaration is embodied in point five: "In order to carry out a series of bilateral plans, the Russian side confirmed its intention to use the method of *drawing financial resources from outsiders* on the basis of understanding of the Korean side."[50] In other words, Moscow and Pyongyang are now looking to Seoul, Washington, and Tokyo to foot the bill.

Russia's Koreanists are always quick to point out that only Russia among the Big Four is an unequivocal supporter of Korean reunification since the status quo gives a rising China more influence in the politics of divided Korea than would a strong, nationalist, and reunified Korea, especially one friendly to the United States.[51] "One of the obstacles to the Korean peace and unification process is doubts and concerns among major powers surrounding the peninsula about the potential of a united Korea

---

49. For an English text of the Moscow Declaration, see KCNA, August 4, 2001, at www.kcna.co.jp/contents/05.htm.

50. Ibid.; emphasis added.

51. See Vadim Tkachenko, "Russian-Korean Cooperation to Maintain the Peace on the Korean Peninsula," *Far Eastern Affairs*, no. 3 (1999): 45.

being a political and economic power," said Dmitri Rogozin, chairman of the Foreign Affairs Committee of State Duma (the Russian parliament).[52] The bottom-line logic seems simple enough: Russia would reap a huge economic reward from a successful unification which could link transport networks from Korea's Pacific ports to Russia and Europe while opening the Korean market for new Russian natural gas fields (and also enabling a unified Korea to repay North Korea's huge debt to Russia).

Concluding Remarks

For good or bad, Northeast Asia has spawned all kinds of strategic triangles over the years but there has been no virtuous cooperative triangulation of Beijing, Moscow, and Tokyo on any regional or global issues. There emerged in the post-cold-war Northeast Asia a few regional multilateral institutions—also known as "bi-multilateral" or "mini-multilateral" institutions—with varying degrees of institutionalization to deal with regional security and economic issues. And yet, with the exception of the ASEAN Regional Forum (ARF), which is more Southeast Asian than Northeast Asian in structure and orientation, none of the five remaining minilateral institutions has all three Northeast Asian powers in membership. Japan and Russia are excluded from the currently stalled Four-Party Peace Talks. China and Russia are excluded from the Trilateral Coordination and Oversight Group (TCOG) and KEDO. Russia has yet to be admitted to the APEC. Japan and the United States are not members of the Tumen River Area Development Programme (TRADP).

Indeed, one of the most striking features of the great-power politics on the highly uneven field of the Korean game is that none of the three neighboring powers has its military presence on the peninsula. The United States as the lone superpower still maintains some 37,000 troops on South Korean soil. With the Pacific Ocean becoming an "American Lake"[53] and Korea "the fuse on the nuclear power keg in the Pacific,"[54] the United

---

52. Cited in *Korea Herald*, November 30, 2000 (Internet version).

53. Peter Hayes, Lyuba Zarsky, and Walden Bello, *American Lake: Nuclear Peril in the Pacific* (New York: Penguin, 1986).

54. Peter Hayes, *Pacific Powderkeg: American Nuclear Dilemmas in Korea* (Lexington, MA: Lexington Books, 1991); quote at p. xiv.

States remains a de facto "neighboring" power by dint of its involvement in peninsular affairs. In the post-cold-war era the United States has come to play the rather unusual role of the "honest broker" in the resolution of the Korean conflict without first dismantling its cold-war U.S.-ROK alliance system or removing or reducing its troops in South Korea and without first having normalized its relations with North Korea.

Thus the security challenge of this rough neighborhood in the post-cold-war era is being met, however imperfectly, not by a multilateral security dialogue but by shifting and unstable bilateral strategic relations. Despite the vaunted Beijing-Moscow strategic partnership, the Korea issue is notable for its lack of Sino-Russian cooperation. To the contrary, China and Russia are facing off as competitors especially in the making of the Iron Silk Road. China has been pursuing a separate agenda on Korean issues, and has not provided needed space for Russia's inclusion in expanded peace talks. While the Sino-Russian strategic partnership works in arms trade—giving the Russian military-industrial complex 90 percent of the substantial and growing Chinese arms market —Russia's new president is reshaping his foreign policy in a remarkably Realpolitik way, which may not be welcomed by his Chinese counterparts. Nevertheless, despite Putin's high-profile Realpolitik debut, post-Soviet Russia remains for all practical purposes a minor force concerned largely with domestic and "near abroad" threats.

A stable and cooperative Sino-Japanese relationship is all the more necessary, yet all the more problematic. Recent Chinese naval activities in the disputed areas of the East China Sea, the strengthening of U.S.-Japan defense guidelines, and the Agreement on Cross-Services and Acquisition in 1996 have greatly accelerated the deterioration of Sino-Japanese relations. Despite being the economic superpower of Asia, according to one sharp but sympathetic Japan watcher, "the most unfortunate victim of the new geopolitics is undoubtedly Japan."[55] The combination of China's steadily rising military expenditures, its naval activities in the disputed areas of the East China Sea, its rising trade surplus with Japan, Japan's growing nationalism, and Japan's aid fatigue (some $23 billion during the past twenty years) could easily undermine a long-standing pillar of interdependence (China as Japan's largest aid recipient). All the same, Tokyo will not receive any of the direct economic benefits from the emerging inter-Korean economic co-

---

55. Calder, "The New Face of Northeast Asia," p. 109.

operation that its continental neighbors anticipate. Instead, Japan could easily be saddled with the huge costs.[56]

Japan's relations with Russia remain as stagnant as Japan's economy. With the rise of assertive nationalism in Moscow and Tokyo, the prospect of settling the Northern Territories issue and finally signing a peace agreement seem as remote as ever before. Japan's deteriorating relations with China compound its problems with the other Northeast Asian neighbors (Russia and North and South Korea).

Although the three powers share common interests in maintaining the peace and stability of the region, a high degree of distrust—born of both historical and contemporary concerns and issues—stands in the way of restructuring this trilateral relationship on a stable post-cold-war footing. With the demise of the shared Soviet threat, long-standing differences regarding questions of past aggression, territorial and commercial disputes, human rights, and competing "cost-effective" foreign-policy goals have been exposed and exacerbated by the rise of unstable domestic politics in Moscow, Tokyo, and Beijing. There is little that binds the Chinese, Japanese, and Russian states and societies together, but much that divides them.

In closing, there is as yet no Northeast Asian regional order nor the basis for the creation of one, owing to the absence of rules, norms, and governing procedures around which state actors' expectations converge. Instead, uncertainties over the nature and viability of U.S. security commitments, the future of Sino-Japanese and Sino-American relations, Russia's reemergence as a great regional power, and above all, the future of North Korea itself, whether it will survive or collapse, abound.

---

56. Ibid.

U.S. Policy Toward the Inter-Korean Dialogue

Edward A. Olsen

U.S. policy toward the two states within the divided Korean nation has been shaped by many factors over the years since the Korean peninsula became enmeshed in cold-war tensions. Although Koreans have sound reasons to prefer that American policy makers with regard to Korea would guide their decisions primarily in response to circumstances and events on the peninsula, the United States is frequently motivated by pursuit of its own national interests vis-à-vis Korea, which are also determined by Korea's regional setting and by U.S. domestic affairs. The period from mid-1999 to mid-2001—the focus of all the chapters in this volume—offers vivid examples of the multifaceted factors that shape U.S. perceptions of, and reactions to, inter-Korean relations. Though the United States clearly has been attentive to the inter-Korean dynamic, it also has been responsive to Chinese, Japanese, and Russian interactions with both Koreas, and has been strongly guided by its own domestic politics in an election cycle and a change of administrations in Washington.

Historical Context

Although there were unique developments within the two-year period being addressed here (they shall be analyzed in detail), it is important to note, prior to dealing with these specifics, that they are part of an evolving pattern of U.S. strategic, political, and economic policies with regard to Korea's division and to the prospects for rectifying that problem that predate the emergence of that issue. This essay is not the place to engage in a detailed historical assessment of the United States' role in Korean affairs,[1] but it is still worthwhile to briefly lay out the context that spawned the events of the last two years.

---

1. For insightful historical overviews of modern Korea, and its interactions with the United States, see historian Bruce Cumings, *Korea's Place in the Sun: A Modern History*, New York: W.W. Norton, 1997; and journalist Don Oberdorfer, *The Two Koreas: A Contemporary History*, Reading, MA: Addison-Wesley, 1997.

U.S. policy has long exhibited a split personality with regard to Korea's division and its resolution of that division. This is attributable to an American sense of responsibility for—and guilt over— the Korean nation's fate following World War Two. Several issues loom large; the U.S. commitment to Korean self-determination, through the wartime Cairo Declaration, remains unmet. The United States' early postwar policies toward Korea were poorly thought through. So, too, were U.S. policies toward Korea as part of the emerging cold war. Although the United States' rescue of its protégé, the Republic of Korea (ROK), during the Korean War was a major humanitarian act, the necessity of the United States, the ROK, and other UN countries accepting a truce created a stalemate that entrenched the division of Korea as a quasi-permanent facet of the cold war. Although the Korean War greatly elevated the United States' appreciation for its South Korean ally, and forged an alliance profoundly strengthened by the memories of both allies' casualties, it also solidified the United States' opposition to the alliance's shared Korean adversary—the Democratic People's Republic of Korea (DPRK). A major consequence of this sequence of events was to enmesh the United States in the inter-Korean struggle, but also to foster a set of U.S. interests in its Korean ally that resulted in reinforcement of a divided Korea.

In the wake of the Korean War, U.S. policies became far more sophisticated as they dealt with two maturing Korean states in an inter-Korean context. This was particularly true of the diplomatic, economic, and military dimensions of U.S.-ROK relations under a succession of military-backed governments—under Presidents Park, Chun, and Rho. The United States had to deal with the ROK's growing international stature and consequent reduction in bilateral client-state overtones, Seoul's more innovative foreign policies and domestic democratic evolution, and South Korea's dualist roles as a trade partner and competitor for the United States. In contrast to this complexity, U.S. policy toward North Korea witnessed few positive changes as the DPRK's adversarial role became increasingly ingrained.

As much as U.S. policies toward the Korean peninsula evolved throughout the cold-war years and the still fledgling post-cold-war era, on one front relatively little change occurred—namely the ways in which the United States dealt with the question of Korean unification. No other aspect of U.S. policy toward the Korean nation displays such an obvious split personality; this was true of the decades prior to the period being addressed here, as well as during the 1999–2001 time frame. The United States has been a consistent supporter of South Korea's quest for national reconciliation with North Korea, and American officials have been steadfast in that regard. U.S. support for South Korea's inter-Korean agenda has been a key ingredient in the U.S.-ROK alliance, helping to legitimize it for South Korean domestic consumption. While that alliance was part of a worldwide network of U.S. relationships designed to meet U.S. national interests, that alliance also was supposed to serve South Korean goals of national stability, reconciliation, and reunification.

The "split-personality" label is warranted here, because there is a contradictory quality within U.S. support for South Korea's past political, economic, diplomatic, and strategic overtures toward inter-Korean normalization. Until recent years, the United States did relatively little with regard to balancing its support for South Korea's position by facilitating change in North Korea that was conducive to reunification. To be sure, some efforts were made in the name of "smile diplomacy" during the Reagan-Bush years and through the nuclear nonproliferation-related diplomacy of the early Clinton years, but overall there was little genuine balance within U.S. policy toward the two Koreas. Washington clearly favored its South Korean ally against its North Korean adversary in ways that hardened Korea's national division. In that context the United States' overt support for the ROK's evolving stance toward unification could not actually mean very much if the United States was convinced that unification was highly unlikely, and could be perceived as undesirable in terms of the realpolitik of U.S. strategy in the Asia-Pacific region. There has long been a de facto catch-22 quality in U.S. policy toward Korean unification, for overt American support for such a goal is assumed by many Americans and South Koreans to be unreachable because of built-in mutually unacceptable hurdles. This raises profound questions about the sincerity of that supportive atmosphere.[2] The fact that similar doubts can be raised about the past (and present) sincerity of Japanese, Chinese, and Russian expressions of support for Korean reconciliation

---

2. The author first raised this analytical point in an op-ed piece that was too blunt for many tastes in South Korea and the United States: "The Catch-22s of Korean Unification," *Asian Wall Street Journal*, June 1–2, 1984, editorial page.

does not mitigate any criticism of the United States. It is important to note here that none of these countries have demonstrated highly principled policy positions.

U.S. policy toward Korean reconciliation in the formative stages of the post-cold-war era just prior to the two-year framework also was influenced by several other external factors. Concern about North Korea's nuclear ambitions looms large as a reference point in U.S. policy toward Korea, but it also is important in that it is a major example of a reversal of long-term trends toward U.S. reliance on Korean expertise within American society. One of the ways U.S. policy in the early postwar period can be criticized is due to a paucity of Korea experts to draw upon to shape U.S. policy, with results that displayed either ignorance of—or indifference to—issues that mattered most to Korea. Standing in sharp contrast to Soviet policy, this situation was rectified by cultivating and using American specialists in Korean affairs to help shape U.S. policy. However, with the end of the cold war and the disappearance of the Soviet Union as the focus of U.S. nuclear policy, two concurrent trends emerged: (1) The United States began to focus on new nuclear threats, and; (2) U.S. nuclear experts applied their credentials to these threats. North Korea's nuclear program fit this bill, leading to the ascendancy of non-Korea specialists from the counter-proliferation camp in shaping U.S. policies toward Korea. North Korea's "rogue-state" characteristics led to an intensification of the U.S. focus on coping with North Korea as an enemy that had to be simultaneously coped with in military terms and engaged diplomatically in an effort to deal with its potentials preemptively. The entirety of this effort led to U.S. policy toward Korea becoming once more part of a larger global policy framework, where Korea expertise was either extraneous or secondary. For better or worse (and examples of both are evident), the need to deal with Korean issues in a non-Korean context exacerbated the ambiguity of U.S. policy toward a divided Korea's efforts to reconcile.

Two other external priorities also were interjected periodically during this period, namely American concerns about U.S.-PRC and U.S.-Japan relations, which influenced U.S. positions vis-à-vis Korea. Despite the legacy of the 1989 Tiananmen Square incident, U.S.-PRC relations generally improved in the early to mid-1990s, as the United States engaged with China as an emerging strategic partner and a burgeoning economic colleague, while maintaining mutual ambiguity regarding Taiwan's role in a divided China. U.S.-Japan relations were tangentially hurt by the levels of U.S. attention paid to China and by Japan's less than stellar economic performance, but the relationship remained basically on track as the United States' most important bilateral relationship in Asia—helped by post–Gulf War strategic reassessments, including the Nye Initiative and resultant new Defense Guidelines that elevated Japan's stature.[3] The juxtaposition of the United States placing high levels of concurrent importance on its ties to both China and Japan was, simultaneously, both positive and negative for U.S. policy toward Korea. Positive in that it made clear the high priority Americans assigned to the Korean region. However, it was negative in the sense that the two Korean states—despite the range of issues they could point to warranting intense U.S. attention—remained overshadowed by their neighbors' larger spectrum of issues. As a result of this disparity, U.S. policy toward Korea remained disproportionately skewed due to the context created by China and Japan, and subjected to influence with regard to each nation's views of a divided Korea and its prospects for reconciliation.

The PRC, as the main portion of a functionally divided nation, has had manifest sensitivity to Korea's division and how it may be resolved. There is every reason to assume that China expects to play a significant facilitator's role in aiding its traditional younger brother Koreans in their task. In those terms South Korean *Nordpolitik* policies of the late 1980s opened the diplomatic door for China, enabling Beijing (unlike Washington) to cultivate official political, economic, and security ties to both Koreas. Although the PRC became a participant in the four-party talks regarding inter-Korean reconciliation (the ROK, DPRK, PRC, and the United States), and enjoys nominal parity with the United States, China's position vis-à-vis the two Koreas is marked by its bilateral rivalry with the United States and its reservations about the United States' presence in South Korea and U.S. intentions toward a future unified Korea. Beijing's posture on Korean issues consequently is important in U.S.-PRC relations, and China loomed large over U.S. policy toward Korea in the formative phase of the post-cold-war era. Nonetheless, China's role has been relatively benign.

Japan, on the other hand, has been a far more complicated player in

---

3. For background on the these factors, see Michael J. Green and Patrick M. Cronin, Editors, *The U.S.-Japan Alliance: Past, Present, and Future,* New York: Council on Foreign Relations Press, 1999.

U.S.-Korean affairs. Though Tokyo was a constructive player in the Korean Peninsula Energy Development Organization (KEDO) process, and consulted bilaterally with both Seoul and Washington about how to deal with North Korea, other facets of Japanese policy have been more problematical for U.S.-Korean relations. Although Japan, like the United States, refrained from official diplomatic ties with the DPRK, unofficially Japanese society helped to bankroll North Korea's separate survival through repatriated funds from the pro–North Korea community in Japan. This is an indicator of Japan's preference for the status quo of a quasi-stable, divided Korea. Though Japan clearly wants to avoid another war in Korea, it almost as clearly is content to keep the two Koreas at odds with each other because of Japan's interest of keeping U.S. forces deployed in Korea as a form of deterrence against both war and unification. A single Korean state could pose a threat to Japan, might tilt toward China, and might not perpetuate the ROK's security ties with the United States, thereby enabling that alliance to serve as a buffer for Japan.

Tokyo's interests in the future of Korea have an even more profound level of influence on U.S. policy toward Korea than those of Beijing. Moreover, Japan's ability to make use of its interests has been more skillful than China's. Consequently, some aspects of U.S. policy toward Korea have long borne a partial "made-in-Japan" imprint. While that imprint has diminished over the years as Korea's intrinsic importance to the United States has grown in ways that is reflected in U.S. national interests, in certain areas Japan's influence over American views remains strong. One of those areas is the issue of inter-Korean reconciliation and unification.

Contemporary Relations

Against the background of an evolution in U.S. appreciation for the significance of the inter-Korean relationships' importance to U.S. national interests, melded with U.S. recognition of global and regional factors in the balance of power surrounding the Korean peninsula, the mid-1999 to mid-2001 period unfolded. This era emerged in a somewhat unusual atmosphere in that, unlike the 1980s and early 1990s when South Korea's economic "Miracle on the Han" was receiving widespread praise in contrast to North Korea's faltering performance, these years witnessed a degree of shared vulnerability. South Korea was still far better off than North Korea, but the ROK was struggling with its post-1997 IMF-rescue recovery. As a consequence of this level of shared vulnerability, the two Koreas were poised to explore opportunities that could be mutually beneficial. Seoul's desire for such cooperative engagement was embodied by President Kim Dae-Jung's overtures of humanitarian assistance to famine-wracked North Korea that were carried out after his February 1998 inauguration, coupled with his "Sunshine Policy," which added a political desire, modeled on one of Aesop's fables, to "warm North Koreans with some sunshine, . . . and the North will warm back to us."[4]

Clearly, in retrospect, the year 2000 proved to be a momentous year for that policy; its advocates had envisioned symbolizing a transition appropriate to a new century and a new millennium. The previous year, 1999, was not entirely auspicious. Though North Korea in February proposed a late-1999, high-level North-South meeting, which Seoul welcomed, that proposal had unpromising themes—including the withdrawal of U.S. forces from South Korea. This tended to reinforce U.S. suspicions about the nature of ROK-DPRK interactions. Nonetheless, that same month President Kim Dae-Jung expanded the meeting's parameters by urging a "package deal" that would incorporate nuclear weapons and missile-development issues, inter-Korean economic cooperation, and security assurances for North Korea, as well as South Korean affirmation of the desirability of U.S.–North Korean diplomatic recognition. By May 1999, President Kim pressed this "package deal" by coordinating its inclusion into the effort being made by former U.S. Secretary of Defense William Perry's visit to Pyongyang that month. During a pre-Pyongyang visit to Seoul, Perry stressed the ways the United States supported President Kim's brand of engagement with the North, despite domestic critics—especially from conservatives in the Congress—who urged less appeasement in the Clinton administration's stance. President Kim also emphasized the importance of North Korea being flexible as it responds to the ROK and the United States. To help this budding process along South Korea and the United States joined with Japan in April to institutionalize their consultations by forming the Trilateral Coordination and Oversight Group (TCOG).

---

4. President Kim's comment was made during his campaign and is quoted in Shim Jaehoon, "Spring Thaw?" *Far Eastern Economic Review*, June 11, 1998, p. 30. For the metaphor's origins, see: Michael Keirnan, "Kim's Sunshine Policy Only Way to Go," *Korea Herald*, June 18, 1998, p. 2.

The Perry delegation's trip to Pyongyang at the end of May offered several commercial, energy, and diplomatic "carrots," while keeping the implied "sticks" discreetly off the table. Though U.S. policy toward North Korea was being carefully coordinated with South Korea, and Seoul remained very proactive in its policy, there was no way to control how the North would respond. Pyongyang's positive responses tilted more toward the United States than South Korea, partly because of long-standing North Korean hopes to drive a wedge between the United States and the ROK, but also because the United States was taking the diplomatic lead more than Seoul, and the U.S. economy was a far larger magnet than the still recovering South Korean economy. This predisposition was accentuated by yet another armed skirmish between North and South Korea, in mid-June 1999, near the South Korean–controlled West Sea island of Yonpyong, offshore North Korea close to the maritime Northern Limit Line. Though this episode was one of the most serious naval clashes since the Korean War truce, fortunately Seoul and Washington were able to handle it in a way that did not undermine their engagement policies toward North Korea. However, this proved easier for the United States than for South Korea. In contrast to the post-Perry-visit expectations regarding U.S.-DPRK contacts, and to South Korea's early July agreement to back a $3.2-billion loan through KEDO for constructing two North Korean light-water reactors, overall ROK-DPRK diplomatic efforts in Beijing had stalled by early summer. This was a by-product of the naval clash that led to Pyongyang's demanding an apology (it was rejected) and an incident in which North Korea detained a South Korean tourist who had allegedly made provocative statements while visiting North Korea's Kumgang mountain, supposedly enticing a North Korean guide to defect; this tourist was released only after signing a confession under duress.

South Korea also had differences with North Korea stemming from each other's responses to the controversy surrounding the DPRK's testing of a missile near Japan in August 1998. By the summer of 1999 the United States was simultaneously coping with efforts to engage North Korea about missile limitations, accommodating to Japan's rethinking of its strategic options regarding Korea, including the possibility that Tokyo would join a U.S.-led Theater Missile Defense (TMD) system, and coping with South Korea's desires to expand the ROK's missile capabilities beyond an existing 300-kilometer range in order to enhance South Korea's deterrence with 500-kilometer short-range missiles capable of reaching major sites in North Korea. All the while the Clinton administration was finessing a very limited form of U.S. national antimissile defense-development program and deflecting conservative criticism that such a program was inadequate to deal with "rogue states" such as North Korea. It is uncertain whether any of this was calculated to present a "good cop / bad cop" pairing to North Korea's practitioners of brinkmanship, but ROK-U.S. interactions had that effect on North Korea.

September 1999 proved to be a significant month for U.S.-DPRK relations that helped to modify the stage for inter-Korean policies. In quick succession in mid-September a series of promising events occurred. North Korea agreed not to test any more missiles of the sort that alarmed Japan, stirred up American missile-defense hopes, and nudged South Korea toward compensatory missiles. In response the United States eased a significant number of economic sanctions against North Korea, thereby opening the door to greater bilateral engagement. The North Korea Policy Coordinator, Secretary Perry, also submitted his report to Congress on September 15 that supported such initiatives and reinforced South Korea's Sunshine Policy.[5] Cumulatively this augured well for Perry's advocacy of U.S.-DPRK diplomatic normalization, which would strengthen the inter-Korean peace process and provide the United States with the same level of access as China and Russia had to both Koreas as a consequence of South Korea's former *Nordpolitik* policy.

Because the stage for U.S. overtures toward North Korea had been well prepared by American consultations with South Korea, it was no surprise that President Kim responded affirmatively and sought to use the progress made on that front as a catalyst for ROK-DPRK expanded dialogue. That level of coordination was made fairly explicit during Secretary Perry's follow-up visit to Seoul later in September. In the following month, October, President Kim reinforced the United States' overtures toward the North by calling upon the DPRK to see these moves and the ROK's Sunshine Policy as totally sincere and well intentioned. Later in October, President Kim built upon the economic portion of the U.S. overtures by first raising the concept of a combined North-South

---

5. For an unclassified public version of that report, see: Dr. William J. Perry, Special Advisor to the President and the Secretary of State, *Review of United States Policy Toward North Korea: Findings and Recommendations*, Washington, D.C.: Office of the North Korea Policy Coordinator, U.S. Department of State, October 12, 1999.

economic entity, which he developed further in 2000. Given the ongoing strength of U.S.-ROK economic ties and the potentials for U.S. assistance enabling North Korea to both avoid economic disaster and become a more compatible partner for the ROK, it became clear as 1999 unfolded that South Korea's aspirations regarding inter-Korean economic affairs were being facilitated by Washington.

This is not to slight South Korea's unilateral efforts. In the wake of the Perry overtures, Seoul expanded its governmental economic aid to the North and reinforced Hyundai Corporation's major efforts to be a private-sector trailblazer for commercial cooperation with North Korea, despite the formidable nature of that task. Seoul also used the post–Perry Report aura of optimism in the remainder of 1999 to cultivate broader systemic support in various ways, such as supplementing ROK policies toward the DPRK with efforts to work more closely with Beijing on China's policy toward North Korean defectors and with Tokyo to encourage Japanese counterparts to the Perry initiative, aimed at normalizing DPRK-Japan ties. Seoul also sent signals to North Korea and the world at large by using the Internet to publicize North Korean culture, reducing the barriers to North Korean-TV broadcasts to South Koreans, and reemphasizing inter-Korean sports cooperation.

Though these efforts in retrospect can be seen as stepping-stones to events that unfolded in 2000, at the time they were overshadowed by U.S.-DPRK momentum, because the latter was breaking new ground. Even though North Korea's intentions to drive a wedge between the United States and South Korea were ill concealed—the United States went out of its way to reassure Seoul during the November Security Consultative Meeting (SCM) where Secretary of Defense Cohen and ROK Defense Minister Cho affirmed that the alliance was "unshakable"—the United States' leading role versus North Korea was a cause of some concern. This was illustrated by the leadership role played in the negotiations that led to a KEDO contract, signed in mid-December, in which South Korea's Korea Electric Power Corporation (KEPCO) was to build two nuclear power plants in North Korea. Even though South Korea was to do the "heavy lifting" on this project, the United States' role appeared to be central. In a lighter vein, the United States also enjoyed high visibility thanks to President Clinton's brother, who, along with some South Korean entertainers, gave a concert in Pyongyang the same month.

Although 1999 was significant in the ways that the Perry Report helped to facilitate an expanded inter-Korean dialogue, the year soon paled in comparison to the developments during 2000, marking it with all the hallmarks of a watershed year in inter-Korean relations. President Kim's New Year's address, "New Millennium, New Hope," included a major proposal to form a "North-South Korean Economic Community." With its overtones of Europe's "EC," the predecessor to today's European Union, this was a propitious concept with sound timing. It also was well positioned for U.S. support, albeit with some reservations stemming from North Korea's limited appeal to American investors in the free market, which could detract from U.S.-ROK harmony.[6] South Korea's private sector, through the Federation of Korean Industries (FKI), followed up on Seoul's initiative in April by creating guidelines for inter-Korean economic cooperation which would facilitate interaction with third parties, obviously including the United States as South Korea's main economic partner. This was precipitated on March 9 by President Kim's famed "Berlin Declaration" that called for high-level North-South governmental talks, which included economic issues. President Kim underscored that offer by using the Seoul meeting of the Asia-Pacific Economic Cooperation (APEC) group on March 31 to invite North Korea to become a guest member of APEC. These developments, in turn, led to North Korea's groundbreaking invitation on April 10 for a Kim Dae-Jung/Kim Jong-Il summit to be held in Pyongyang, June 12–14. When South Korea tried to reinforce these positive developments by encouraging North Korea's membership in the Asian Development Bank (ADB) on May 7, during its annual meeting in Chiang Mai, Thailand, the United States (and Japan) opposed the move because of Washington's labeling of the DPRK as a "terrorist state" unworthy of membership. Offsetting that rejection somewhat, North Korea in mid-May—the period preceding the inter-Korean summit—applied for membership in the ASEAN Regional Forum (ARF) and established diplomatic relations with a visible U.S. ally in the region, Australia.

Among the various impacts of the North-South Korean summit, ana-

---

6. For background on the proposal, see: "Building the South-North Economic Community" in *Korean Unification Bulletin*, January 2000, pp. 2–3. The author evaluated U.S. options regarding the proposed community in his "The Role of the United States in the Construction of a North-South Korean Economic Community," in *International Journal of Korean Unification Studies*, Vol. 9, No. 1, 2000, pp. 97–115.

lyzed elsewhere in this volume,[7] the massive amount of media coverage the summit received shifted public attention to a focus on what is crucial for reconciling the differences between the two Koreas and away from any sense that improving U.S.-DPRK relations was a priority. Although the summit was most notable for its symbolic qualities and atmospherics, commitments were also made to establish more concrete agendas and to hold a reciprocal summit in Seoul at an "appropriate time," which was widely interpreted to be by mid-2001. Understandably the participants avoided use of the infamous phrase "in due course." As much as the focus was on the two Koreas' interactions as the basis for what could become a new peninsular paradigm, the United States, for logical reasons, loomed large offstage. The foremost reason for this de facto diplomatic presence is the existence of approximately 37,000 U.S. armed forces in South Korea and the myriad interpretations analysts ascribe to that geopolitical reality.

One of the most intriguing outcomes of the summit was the attention given in the media, and, undoubtedly, in all salient government circles, to the message reportedly conveyed to President Kim from Chairman Kim that North Korea recognizes the utility of U.S. forces in Korea as a stabilizing element for Korea and its East Asian neighborhood. President Kim stressed this point several times in the months after the summit, but skeptics wondered why North Korea never explicitly confirmed that Chairman Kim held these views. Although Pyongyang's apparent acceptance of this strategic reality certainly was reluctant, and marked by overtones of double containment vis-à-vis U.S. restraints on South Korea and Japan, plus ambiguous signals about Sino-U.S. influences over the Korean peninsula's context, it was—nonetheless—a positive development. It permitted the United States to put an even more positive spin on the results of the Korean summit's meaning for U.S. interests in Korea and to proceed with American policies that supported President Kim's Sunshine Policy. A significant part of that effort was Washington's decision to implement the recommendation of the Perry Report to lift a

---

7. For Seoul's initial official spin on the summit, see: *Korean Unification Bulletin*, June 2000; and *Together As One*, Seoul: Ministry of Unification, July 2000. For Seoul's in-depth presentation on the overall consequences of the inter-Korean summit through the end of the year 2000, see: *Peace and Cooperation; White Paper on Korean Unification 2001*, Seoul: Ministry of Unification, April 2001. When evaluating the content of this White Paper, it is important to note that it was finalized and published a month after the controversial Kim-Bush summit.

larger array of economic sanctions against North Korea, which was announced in the wake of the summit.

North Korea's evident position on the value of a U.S. military presence in Korea also constituted a signal to Washington that the DPRK was being responsive to U.S. overtures. Whether such a signal was sufficient for the United States was, and is, a debatable issue. At the time, however, it was perceived positively, helping to make a series of ROK-DPRK post-summit high-level meetings far more palatable for the United States than they would have been if North Korea had not acknowledged some value in a U.S. armed presence in Korea. In mid-August President Kim announced there would be a North-South meeting of defense ministers that was held on Cheju island in late September. He also began, in mid-August, the process of revising South Korea's controversial National Security Law that imposed harsh restrictions on most South Koreans' ability to deal with North Korea, and which had been criticized on human rights grounds by the U.S. State Department. In keeping with these developments, in late August the United States and South Korea decided to scale back some joint military exercises as yet another message to Pyongyang that times were changing. All of this contributed to an evolving series of inter-Korean ministerial- and working-level talks on various confidence-building cooperative themes.

The overall tone of summer and fall of 2000 was decidedly upbeat on the inter-Korean front. This quality received another major boost in mid-September when a combined ROK-DPRK contingent marched together in a show of unity under one flag bearing a map of the Korean peninsula at the opening ceremony of the Sydney Olympics. For much of the world, which pays scant attention to Korea's efforts to reunify, certainly including a large proportion of the American public that is more attuned to sports than to arcane aspects of U.S. foreign policy, that parade garnered fairly widespread attention. Despite such interest, including Americans, among others, who rarely follow the ins and outs of inter-Korean affairs, the United States' approach contained elements of ambiguity. As the State Department's policies cultivated proactive engagement of North Korea, the Pentagon and U.S. military authorities in Korea emphasized reports publicized in September that the threat posed by North Korea remained undiminished and might be worsening. Such assessments aside, the United States diplomatically remained supportive of Seoul's initiatives, and kept Japan on board in the name of solidarity. Even though the post-summit core of inter-Korean cooperation endured, as it should have, other events began to attract more attention during October. Kim Dae-Jung was named on October 13 as the winner of the Nobel Peace Prize, which he received in Oslo on December 10; this simultaneously shifted the spotlight away from the post-summit developments as it focused on President Kim's broader achievements, putting the media glare on Korea's situation. Though this was highly positive for the moral ethos of the Korean-peace process—subtle pressures were exerted on all the other participants, so that the post-summit opportunity would not slip away or be dashed by counterproductive policies—it also proved to be a distraction from the main inter-Korean issues.

During the same period, U.S. policies aimed at bolstering U.S. support for South Korea's initiatives in the afterglow of President Kim's Nobel Prize had an unintended consequence of attracting a great deal of media attention back to the U.S.-DPRK budding relationship and to U.S. domestic political questions about the wisdom of encouraging that relationship to "bud" during a presidential campaign year. On the eve of the U.S. elections two visits occurred that would have been deemed so far-fetched as to be laughable had they been raised as a proposal in the not-so-distant past. As a sign of North Korea's readiness to engage with the United States, Pyongyang surprised most observers by announcing on October 12 an invitation to President Clinton to visit North Korea before his term expired. Though the invitation's timing (presumably accidental) led to the North Korean announcement being overshadowed by the Nobel Peace Prize announcement, it also set into motion a flurry of activities. First, North Korea dispatched its second-ranking official, Vice Marshall Jo Myong-Rok to Washington as an emissary from Kim Jong-Il. He was graciously received at the White House and the Pentagon by an array of top U.S. officials, as well as President Clinton. Shortly thereafter, in late October, Secretary of State Albright made an exchange visit as the highest ranking U.S. official to go to North Korea (Dr. Perry was a former secretary of state when he visited). She held widely publicized formal meetings in Pyongyang, including with Kim Jong-Il. Although Secretary Albright's visit achieved its goal of accentuating the positive potentials of U.S.-DPRK contacts, her participation in a ninety-minute propaganda spectacle with 100,000 performers at a Pyongyang stadium stirred animosity toward Clinton administration policies among U.S. conservatives.

Against the backdrop of the inter-Korean summit and both Koreas' follow-up cooperation, President Kim's Nobel Peace Prize, which he magnanimously shared the credit for with his North Korean counterpart, and a remarkable series of steps toward U.S.-DPRK engagement, the year 2000 seemed poised to usher in precisely the kind of new era that President Kim aspired to. However, as noted, it also was an election year for the United States, and the November results unleashed an unprecedented episode of political uncertainty and rancor. Well into what would normally be an inter-administration transition period, it was not clear whether a President Al Gore or a President George W. Bush would succeed President Clinton. This situation, coupled with President Clinton's far greater and longer term commitment to the Middle East peace process, which would affect his legacy in American history, led to his putting off a possible visit to Pyongyang for so long that by the end of December the White House announced he would not be going and attempted to set the stage for his successor to carry forward the engagement processes intensified during his term in office. Without question, Clinton had reason to believe that would be done during a Gore administration put in place by Gore's popular-vote victory. However, the U.S. Constitution and the federal role of state elections through the electoral college prevented that expectation from being realized. But none of this became clear until the final days of 2000; so, for the most part, the year can be declared remarkably successful in terms of the inter-Korean peace process and in terms of U.S. support for that evolving process.

Bush Policies

The year 2001 took a rather different course than the one shaped by the much touted initiatives of 2000. High expectations were genuine, albeit tinged with unrealistic overtones. Had the final electoral college count in the United States at the end of 2000 been nudged in Vice President Gore's favor by enough enigmatic Floridian "chads," it is entirely possible that the new U.S. administration would have stayed entirely on track in Clintonian policy toward the two Koreas, brushing aside charges of appeasement and not pursuing parallel policies in the Asian region that would impede U.S. engagement with North Korea. That was not in the political cards, however, and president-elect Bush by New Year's was ensconced in the wings of power in Texas, with his Washington transition team poised to assume office.

The political facets of this looming U.S. transition raised some generic concerns pertaining to Korean issues. Although ROK president

Kim had benefited from past Republican interventions in Seoul on his behalf while he was an endangered opposition figure, there was no doubt that his progressive politics within South Korea and his political connections within the United States were enmeshed with the U.S. Democratic party. Overall, U.S. Republicanism was more supportive of Kim's opponents politically. Similarly, on the foreign- and defense-policy fronts, mainstream American conservative views were more harmonious with President Kim's conservative opponents. These generic indicators did not auger well for ideological harmony between a progressive South Korean leader and a conservative U.S. leader. Despite such background factors, basic U.S.-ROK overlapping national interests suggested that core continuity would persist.

Early in the Bush administration ambiguous indications about its approach to North Korea surfaced in the press. The outgoing U.S. ambassador and career diplomat, Stephen Bosworth, stated in Seoul that he was confident that U.S. policy on the inter-Korean dialogue process would not be significantly altered. However, a subtle hint that change was afoot emerged from Richard Armitage (then widely assumed to be deputy secretary of state nominee), who was reported in the Korean and U.S. media to want South Korea to drop the Sunshine Policy label in favor of an improved approach to engagement. Amid such uncertain signals from Washington, President Kim took the initiative by calling President Bush on January 25; this followed up on a mid-December call to congratulate Bush on becoming president-elect. Seoul's intent, evidently, was to broach its issues while the new U.S. administration was in its malleable early phase. It is also possible that echoes of former President Chun Doo-Hwan's successful summit early in the Reagan administration resonated in South Korean memories, inspiring Seoul to replicate such success by getting a new conservative government to anoint the wisdom of ongoing policies. Furthermore, South Korea may well have wanted to be the first Asian country to gain access to the Bush team, thereby conveying a not very subtle point to Japan. That theme was underlined in a somewhat odd manner when a Blue House spokesman told the Korean press that President Bush told President Kim that "South Korea is the region's most important ally of the United States." Undoubtedly, that unorthodox perception was noted in Tokyo.

It's clear that the Kim administration hoped to guide the new Bush administration toward a bipartisan level of support for the type of U.S.-ROK cooperation evinced during the Clinton years. As the presidential summit approached, South Korea persisted with its bilateral military and economic working-group talks with North Korea in January and early February. These dialogues tended to reinforce the sense of momentum spilling over from the year 2000 and to sustain expectations for continuity. So, too, did the tenor of opinion generated by American pundits on Korean affairs who passed through Seoul prior to the U.S.-ROK summit. One measure of President Kim's confidence at that stage was his willingness to utilize Russia's president Putin in early March, virtually on the eve of the summit, as a catalyst for change in North Korea's missile-development program. Though an intrinsically worthwhile notion, the obvious linkages between Russia's opposition to the new Bush administration's missile-defense-system proposals and South Korean reservations about such a system because it would be overtly aimed at North Korea, and, more obliquely, could get the ROK entangled in both a rising Chinese threat and U.S. commitments to Taiwan, made the whole proposition a de facto act of South Korean independence from Washington's emerging security parameters. Whether South Korean leaders understood these ramifications at the time is unclear.

Just prior to the Washington summit Secretary of State Colin Powell affirmed U.S. intentions to continue the essence of the Clinton-era engagement policy. Although this comment was intended to be supportive of Seoul's position, in retrospect it left enough wiggle room for modifications that might not mesh well with South Korea's engagement model. So, too, did an op-ed piece on the eve of the summit in the *Washington Post* by former Secretary of State Henry Kissinger appear to support the ROK's top billing in U.S.-Korea policies by stressing the necessity of inter-Korean dialogue. However, Kissinger asserted: "Pyongyang must be convinced that the road to Washington leads through Seoul and not the other way around."[8] Though well intentioned, this statement undercut one of the core elements of South Korea's policy in that President Kim sought to use U.S.-DPRK bilateral engagement as an instrument of Seoul's international leverage over North Korea, designed to induce evolutionary change, making it a better partner for South Korea en route to reconciliation and eventual reunification.

Despite South Korea's high hopes, the Kim-Bush summit fell short of Seoul's expectations. Positive spin notwithstanding, the summit was

---

8. Henry Kissinger, "A Road Through Seoul," *Washington Post*, March 6, 2001, p. 23.

a setback for South Korea's agenda and made clear that the United States' approach to North Korea would steer clear of anything that could be characterized as appeasement and would stress greater balance in the array of carrots and sticks. Secretary Powell's stated support for continuing President Clinton's brand of enlightened engagement aimed at normalizing U.S.-DPRK relations was bluntly rescinded by President Bush during the meeting with President Kim at the White House, in Secretary Powell's presence, based on the argument that North Korea did not deserve to be trusted and was not ready to change. President Bush made it clear that his administration did not share the level of enthusiasm for engagement with North Korea that Presidents Kim and Clinton did. President Bush's message to President Kim was underlined by Secretary Powell who, outside the Oval Office, explained that the United States would "not be naive about the nature of the [North Korean] threat" and declared "imminent negotiations" would not occur.[9]

Although President Kim, at meetings in the United States after the summit, attempted to make the best of what had happened by emphasizing the need to work closely with the new administration and urging the United States not to lose an invaluable opportunity to help bring about lasting peace in Korea, his efforts seemed forlorn. This state of affairs was reflected in some of the analytical descriptions in the media about what had transpired at the summit: "Bush Rains on Kim's 'Sunshine,'" "The new American president . . . cut out Kim's heart," and "America has thrown cold water over the North-South rapprochement."[10]

American reactions to the questions raised about the intent of a U.S. policy shift injected yet another layer of uncertainty. Had the new Bush administration been in office long enough to fully think through what it desired and adequately staffed the policy issue? Whether the United States had or had not fully intended to launch a revised policy toward North Korea, the questions provoked by the Bush-Kim summit had that effect. At a minimum these developments suggested that President Kim and his advisors misjudged their timing by pressing for a summit so early in

9. Quoted in David E. Sanger, "Bush Tells Seoul Talks with North Won't Resume Now," *New York Times*, March 8, 2001, p. 1.

10. These quotes, respectively, are from: a *Far Eastern Economic Review* editorial, March 22, 2001, p. 6; columnist Tom Plate's "Shadow Falls on Outlook for Koreas," *Honolulu Advertiser*, March 11, 2001, editorial page; and Sejong Institute professor Kim Jong-Won cited in Michael Zielenziger, "Bush Stirs Korea Doubts," Knight Ridder wire service, *Monterey Herald*, March 9, 2001, p. A1.

the Bush administration, despite warnings about going to Washington too soon, thereby risking a premature dialogue and gratuitously denying themselves the opportunity to help shape what the new U.S. administration might be prepared to do about inter-Korean issues.

Seoul's efforts to finesse the changes in U.S. policy, and to help ease the Bush administration back on the former track, were aided by media coverage given to a Council on Foreign Relations–backed "Task Force on Managing Change on the Korean Peninsula"; the council had sent an open letter to President Bush on March 22 that urged basic continuity so as to avoid missing an existing opportunity. The fact that the task force included two former Republican-appointed U.S. ambassadors to South Korea (Donald Gregg and James Lilley) helped make President Kim's point. Other prominent late-March public expressions of support for South Korea's brand of engagement with North Korea included an op-ed piece by Senator John Kerry in the *Washington Post* and a speech by former Clinton Secretary of Defense (and former Republican Senator) William Cohen given at the George Bush School of Government at Texas A&M University.

On the other hand, post-summit statements by CINCPAC, Admiral Dennis Blair, and the U.S. CINC in Korea, General Thomas Schwartz, about their perception of North Korea as the region's primary threat, added to the image of a harder line U.S. policy. These were consistent with larger developments within U.S. national security policy stemming from the new administration's reappraisal of U.S. defense policy options. Although the entire package of eventual revisions will be salient for the United States' Korean ally, a few stand out. Foremost, as of this writing, is the decision to pursue plans to develop and deploy both national and theater missile-defense systems (NMD and TMD). Because North Korea is seen as a rogue state, a terrorist state, and a state deemed a danger because of its potentials for delivering weapons of mass destruction via missiles, it occupies center stage on the Bush administration's spectrum of state-based threat perceptions. In these terms North Korea constitutes a core portion of the justification for most of those who back major NMD and TMD programs for the United States. As such, it has greater utility as an adversary than as a focus of engagement.

This perception of North Korea's utility as an adversary, and the Bush administration's readiness to make use of it in that manner, lent credence to Seoul's manifest anxieties in the spring of 2001 about the possibility that the United States also would seek to make revisions in the

1994 Agreed Framework that has been the foundation for U.S.-DPRK relations dealing with North Korea's nuclear capabilities and ambitions. This, too, tended to raise questions about how far the United States could go in support of President Kim's agenda. For, if engagement of the "Sunshine" variety actually succeeded, the United States might have to face a Northeast Asia that lacked a North Korean threat. Not only would that knock a prop out from under the TMD rationale, it also would exacerbate troublesome questions about why U.S. forces in the ROK, or in a united Korea, should remain where they are doing what they have been doing in the name of regional stability. That probability is reinforced by growing nationalism in the ROK as reunification looms over the horizon. It also is intensified by the United States' pressure on Seoul to pay a larger amount for host-nation support of U.S. forces in Korea at a time when Koreans can visualize reduced defense costs in a post-unification context, where they might not want to subsidize a presence of U.S. forces. Such an eventuality could be extremely awkward for U.S. security relations with its other Northeast Asian ally—Japan.

Making the TMD situation still more tenuous has been Seoul's ambivalence about it for reasons that go far beyond bilateral engagement of North Korea. There were sizable anti-TMD popular protests in South Korea in the wake of the Kim-Bush summit that were partially motivated by Korean sympathies with anti–TMD/NMD views in various other countries based on concerns about undercutting international arms-control paradigms, and by Korean anxieties about too much U.S.-Japan enthusiasm for using North Korea as a rationale and regarding the possibility that the real target of U.S. anti-missile attention will prove to be China— thereby entangling South Korea in an adversarial relationship with the PRC that could totally wreck Seoul's engagement policy toward North Korea. Furthermore, as with the nuclear issue in the early post-cold-war era that imposed a new framework of non-Korea-determined guidelines on U.S. policies toward Korea, so too has TMD/NMD's substantial focus on North Korea's threat tended to override and distort U.S. interests vis-à-vis inter-Korea reconciliation. In short, the American TMD issue is layered with nuances that jeopardize Seoul's inter-Korean agenda. It is no surprise, therefore, that South Korea is conflicted as a U.S. ally, in that it would like to be supportive of the United States' evolving security policies in East Asia, but finds it difficult to do so when such support may well damage the ROK's own security interests.

The United States' shifting security priorities in Asia under the Bush administration have complicated South Korea's policies toward the region in other respects as well. In the wake of the Bush-Kim summit, as Seoul was reevaluating how to respond to the altered situation vis-à-vis an inter-Korean dialogue—and was making domestic adjustments by reshuffling the ROK cabinet in late March in ways that might enhance its persuasive capabilities among American leaders—yet another cloud obscured the sunshine. A pair of April controversies in U.S.-PRC relations caused by a collision between a U.S. Navy reconnaissance plane and a Chinese jet fighter, followed by President Bush's expansion of the U.S. commitment to Taiwan by stating that the United States would do "whatever it took to help Taiwan defend herself," raised the specter of deteriorating U.S.-PRC relations. This was bad news for Seoul in that the ROK, at a minimum, clearly preferred U.S.-PRC harmony as an ingredient in each's role in the intermittent Four-Party Talks on Korea. Moreover, Seoul had no desire to see a new cold war erupt in ways that could see a U.S. containment policy, aimed at deterring the PRC, envision U.S. forces in South Korea as an outpost of encirclement of China. That would be tremendously damaging to hard-won ROK-PRC harmony, wreck Seoul's ability to utilize Beijing's diplomatic good offices that were reaffirmed in late May by Li Peng during a visit to Seoul, and shred the progress made on the inter-Korean diplomatic, economic, and security fronts. Though South Korea obviously wants to remain the United States' ally in the region, Seoul also wants some say in any reshaping of the alliance's purposes. Barring unforeseen circumstances, it is difficult to visualize the logical reasons South Korea would want to join the United States in a China-focused, cold-war-style strategy. Similarly, South Korea has ample reason to be nervous about U.S.-PRC conflict over Taiwan, which might lead Washington to expect its two Northeast Asian allies to rally around the cause.

Amid these growing regional concerns, South Korea's policy differences with the United States in regard to how best to deal with North Korea received a boost from an unexpected quarter. The European Union (EU), in the wake of the Kim-Bush summit, announced in late March that it would take up some of the slack left by the harder line U.S. policy toward North Korea by dispatching its president (Swedish prime minister Goran Persson) to Pyongyang in early May. In keeping with the European states' growing engagement with all of Asia through the Asian European Meeting (ASEM) format, the EU went out of its way to point out that it was supplementing the United States, not replacing or undercutting it. Nevertheless, the EU was sending a not-very-subtle signal that the policy revisions occurring in the Bush administration left much to be desired. More important, the EU's actions and commitment to work on formalizing EU-DPRK diplomatic ties provided an alternative external catalyst for the inter-Korean dialogue. This demonstrated that President Kim's policies were viable, and provided both Koreas and China with another Western voice to compare to that of the United States.

The EU's readiness to speak out on this Korean issue, when combined with the European members of NATO's differences with the Bush administration on other issues—notably pursuing TMD-NMD and backing away from the Kyoto environmental treaty—suggested a willingness to stand up to Washington. In this dual context, the signals sent by the EU's actions in Korea were received in Washington. So, too, were the anxieties displayed by Seoul on broader security- and China-related issues duly noted in Washington. Because some of those anxieties were shared by Japan, this presumably helped get Washington's attention. As a consequence of the post-summit American debate over the soundness of an evolving set of U.S.-policy changes toward Korea, the Bush administration by early May was indicating its intentions to wrap up its policy-review process and resume a U.S. role in the inter-Korean-engagement process. And, by late May, Washington joined Tokyo in urging North Korea to schedule the second Kim-Kim summit, which gave ROK president Kim an opportunity to press for a specific date for the Seoul inter-Korean summit. However, while Washington clearly was building momentum toward restoring some elements that had been cut from the United States' policy toward inter-Korean affairs, the Bush administration did not alter its harder line attitude on avoiding any hint of appeasement. Nor did the United States drop any of the contextual policy parameters that suggest a more conservative and unilateralist approach to Korea's setting.

Despite early-June frictions between Seoul and Pyongyang over North Korean cargo-ship intrusions into South Korean territorial waters, which Seoul feared would give the Bush administration additional reasons to harden its policy line, Washington did not permit those events to disrupt its plans to announce on June 6 that the United States was prepared to resume talks with North Korea. The U.S. move was widely perceived as a reversal of the initial Bush administration decision that significantly undermined President Kim's Sunshine Policy agenda. That perception was partially, but not fully, warranted, because the Bush administration's new "comprehensive reciprocity" approach expanded the proposed scope of U.S.-North Korea talks beyond nuclear weapons and missiles, to include North Korea's massive conventional forces forward deployed near the DMZ. The latter portion of the U. S. proposal constitutes a major change that precludes treating the revised Bush policy as a reversal.

Nonetheless, the post-review-process Bush policy received considerable praise for getting the United States back on track. That praise was underscored by reports that Bush's decision to reengage in talks with North Korea was decisively shaped through intervention by his father. The former President Bush reportedly sent his son a memo drafted by former ambassador to Korea Donald Gregg that urged a more measured position along the lines of Secretary Powell's initial stance and less attuned to a harder line attributed to the Pentagon.[11] The Kim Dae-Jung government welcomed the United States' decision to return to the dialogue process, particularly because the nuclear portion of the talks meant that the Bush administration's actions implied that the 1994 Agreed Framework was not in immediate jeopardy as Seoul had feared. Though these were all positive developments for President Kim, compared to what had seemed to be happening in Washington, Seoul still had to deal with the ways that U.S. policy toward inter-Korean issues had hardened. The United States was reengaging, but it had not abandoned its harder line tone in the form of greater reciprocity. Moreover, the altered context, created by a focus on TMD/NMD and by changes in U.S. policies toward Korea's Chinese and Japanese neighbors, remained intact in ways that influenced the prospects for U.S. policy toward Korea.

The United States kept its word and rejoined the talks with North Korea in mid-June. The timing was important, because the talks came close to the first anniversary of the Kim-Kim summit, thereby enabling Washington to escape some of the blame for damaging the post-summit optimism and for endangering President Kim's Sunshine Policy. North Korea's rejection of the United States' efforts to include North Korean conventional forces in the talks—on the grounds that it amounted to moving the goalposts in mid-game—may have had some merit, but it was unlikely to be persuasive to Americans focused on the North Korean threat or to those South Koreans who felt obligated to support their U.S. ally's logic in order to keep U.S. forces actively engaged in

---

11. Jane Perlez, "Fatherly Advice to the President on North Korea," *New York Times,* June 10, 2001, p. 6.

Korean security. This situation put South Korea in a bind because Seoul clearly wants to retain a U.S. strategic commitment to Korea, but also wants to stress the ways that North Korea accepts the utility of U.S. forces. By injecting North Korean conventional-force levels into the U.S.-DPRK talks, Washington also puts the issue in the inter-Korean context, making it awkward for Seoul to pursue its case about existing U.S. forces in Korea at the same time as the United States seeks to include for discussion North Korea's portion of the peninsular balance of power.

Also making things difficult for President Kim was the degree of attention received by President Bush's fluctuating policies. The initial rebuffing of President Kim's Sunshine Policy was broad-based and high profile—thanks to the Bush-Kim summit—whereas his apparent reversal after a behind-the-scenes policy review was both more narrowly based and much less publicized. Similarly, during a late-July stopover in Seoul, en route to an ASEAN summit in Hanoi and major meetings in Beijing, Secretary Powell sought to reinforce the United States' readiness to talk to North Korea's leaders whenever and wherever they desire. That readiness reinforced Seoul's desires for further U.S. action and addressed Pyongyang's adverse reactions to revisions in U.S. policy. However, Powell's overtures in Seoul tended to be overshadowed by his activities in Hanoi and Beijing. On balance, the U.S. position toward inter-Korean reconciliation and a U.S. dialogue with North Korea remained formally supportive of the ROK, but far more conditional in tone than it had been previously. The United States was exerting greater pressure for tangible proof of results and was not subtle in conveying these pressures to both Seoul and Pyongyang. Furthermore, the ups and downs of U.S. policy in the first half-year of the Bush administration created an aura of ambiguity, underscored by open expressions of American skepticism about Seoul's wisdom and Pyongyang's ability to become trustworthy.

Though the driving force behind initial changes in, and subsequent second thoughts about, U.S. policy toward the two Koreas is overwhelmingly a mixture of the Bush administration's perception of U.S. national interests and its sensitivity to South Korea's needs, one must also factor in the impact of North Korea's often harsh reactions to American rhetoric and actions, as well as the United States' awareness that North Korea can utilize the ways that American changes and inconsistencies put South Korea off balance. This is yet another example of North Koreans using the DPRK's vulnerabilities, and the regime's reputation for irrational recklessness to its own advantage by playing upon the explicit or latent fears of South Koreans and their supporters.

Outlook

Against the backdrop of evolving U.S. policies toward the inter-Korean peace process, and uneven U.S. bilateral relationships with each Korea, the future—as it has been on the peninsula since the 1940s—remains uncertain. Technically the United States remains broadly supportive of the ROK's efforts to achieve reconciliation. However, the United States clearly is prepared to scrutinize Seoul's efforts more closely and to hold them to a more rigid standard than in the recent past. Exerting this degree of American review of Seoul's policies is ironic at best and perverse at worst, because of the overtones of a return to a quasi-client-state form of hierarchicalism. This is inconsistent with long-term trends in which the United States has accepted and welcomed South Korea's economic and political maturation as a major ally in the region. The ROK may not truly warrant the first-ranking stature President Bush reportedly bestowed on it, but it long ago graduated from client-state status. Yet the United States' quest to impose American standards to measure accountability in a South Korean–derived set of engagement policies toward North Korea appears to be embedded at the core of the Bush administration's evolving support of South Korea's inter-Korean agenda.

Several factors contribute to this sort of conditional support. First, the United States cannot afford to be seen as abandoning an ally's long-standing and long-supported quest for Korean national unification. Reinforcing that basic form of support, American leaders have long assumed that unification will probably not occur for decades, hence the goal in the abstract can be safely supported. Strengthening that reinforcement is American recognition that South Korean leaders, despite their enthusiasm and optimism during 2000, do not want to rush the end-game result of unification, because the ROK cannot do for North Korea what former West Germany did for East Germany. Part and parcel of South Korea's agenda is incrementalism, which also suits U.S. interests in the region that center on stabilizing the status quo, thereby preventing the rise of a rival superpower. Were these the only factors shaping U.S. choices, American decisions about engaging in the inter-Korean dialogue would be relatively simple.

The situation is made even more complex by two other factors. The most obvious is the manifest weaknesses of the North Korean economic system, which have led many to theorize about disastrous end-games on an implosion-explosion spectrum and address solutions within a hard-landing-soft-landing range. If nothing is done externally to help North Korea solve its numerous problems, a very rapid unification of a sort that might devastate the ROK and lead to a traumatized ally for the United States could occur, thereby imposing heavy demands for a long-term rescue package. Because this would happen in the midst of an already-shifting Sino-Japanese power balance, this is not something remotely desirable by Seoul or Washington. Consequently, South Korea's incremental unification through engaging North Korea with an array of countries so that North Korean society can be brought closer to the level of South Korean society almost certainly is the most viable way to avoid disaster. This makes it extraordinarily difficult for the United States to press for policies that could exacerbate North Korea's role as an economically weak but militarily threatening state in order to serve larger U.S. national interests.

Adding to the pressures on the United States to not stray too far from the path carved out by Presidents Kim and Clinton is the chance that China might well assume a leading role as a diplomatic middleman for the two Koreas if the United States either abstains or becomes obstructionist. Given other U.S.-PRC contentious issues, there is little reason for the Bush administration, any more than its predecessors, to look favorably upon Chinese assertion of such a role. Fortunately for the United States, Koreans in both the ROK and DPRK have reasons to be wary of such an expanded PRC role because of the historical legacy of heavy-handed Chinese suzerainty. Nonetheless, if the United States chooses not to do what the two Koreas believe is necessary, the door could be open for greater Chinese activism in inter-Korean affairs.

U.S. hesitancy about supporting President Kim's brand of engaging North Korea is made even more awkward because of long-standing U.S. advocacy of democratic institutions for its ally. Now that those institutions are more effective in South Korea today than they have been in the past—and President Kim's election epitomizes that fact, which was underscored globally by his receipt of the Nobel Prize, in part, for his role as an advocate for democracy—it is truly perverse for the United States to question the policy judgments derived as a result of South Korean democratic processes that are, in turn, aimed at creating circumstances conducive to spreading democracy to the entire Korean nation. Now that the South Korean people's elected representatives have arduously crafted a venue for peaceful negotiation of Korean reconciliation and unification predicated on President Kim's Sunshine Policy, it is unseemly for Americans to try to impose revised criteria on the two Koreas.

U.S. caution on the economic front may be more legitimate because of the inherent uncertainties of the outcome in Korea. There is no assurance that a gradual merger of the two Koreas will prove successful. Though South Korea as an ally deserves full U.S. support for attempting to bring about capitalist-oriented reforms in North Korea that will facilitate national assimilation, and Americans should share the hopes of South Koreans that they will prevail, there are formidable obstacles. The free market being—by definition—free, North Koreans may or may not be able to emulate the degree of success enjoyed by PRC economic reformers. If they do, the United States will be able to join South Korea in rejoicing and working toward a Korean common market that will be a cornerstone of reunification. However, if North Korea bungles it, the United States' South Korean ally would likely be burdened for many years with a very unappealing economic twin. In such circumstances the United States would be confronted by pressures for governmental aid that many Americans might perceive as throwing U.S. tax dollars down a Korean rat hole, coupled with little capitalist incentive for American investors to squander their assets in a noncompetitive sector of the global marketplace.

Whether a unified Korean economy would be robustly prosperous or be in a perilously straitened condition also bears on U.S. strategic concerns about Korea's future role. All U.S. administrations since the founding of the ROK, but especially since the Korean War, have been committed to facilitating South Korea's material well-being as a way to bolster its strategic stability. In the last quarter-century Washington has dealt with a South Korean success story that enabled its ally to become far more of a genuine military ally. In this sense, the Bush, Clinton, and Bush administrations over the past decade have had an ally that counted. Moreover, all three have wanted to help assure that the United States would retain a Korean ally in the region. In those terms there is continuity between the Clinton administration and its successor, but the Bush administration's definition of what it takes to assure the retention of its Korean ally differs on some key points cited above and, overall, is a work in progress. This is accentuated by new pressures stemming from U.S. reactions to the September 11, 2001, terrorist attacks in New York City and at the Pentagon. Though U.S. worldwide security priorities under President Bush may be warranted in terms of U.S. national interests and enjoy Seoul's overall support, they do not necessarily mesh very well with the Kim Dae-Jung government's vision for Korea's future security. This partial gap could grow wider—perhaps leading to a significant rupture in U.S.-ROK relationships—if the United States' security posture hardens in ways reminiscent of the cold war. But the gap could also evaporate if the logic of U.S. strategic thinking persuades the Kim government to dump its policies, or, more likely, if the Kim government's inability to get the Bush administration on to virtually the same policy wavelength contributes to the failure of the Sunshine Policy—leading to the election of a far more conservative government in South Korea that would follow the Bush administration's lead in East Asia. A conservative succession may, in fact, occur because of President Kim's relatively inept handling of South Korean domestic issues. It would be unfortunate for South Korean democracy to be nudged in that direction for the wrong external reasons.

Looking to the future of inter-Korean affairs from the vantage point of nine months into the first year of the Bush administration, it is all too easy to be pessimistic. Given the harsh partisanship that prevailed in the United States during the Clinton years, the Bush administration is unlikely to wholeheartedly endorse major policies in Korea that reinforce Clinton's historical legacy. This remains true despite the wave of patriotic bipartisan support for overall U.S. foreign policy in the wake of the terrorist attacks. American preoccupation with the U.S. war on terrorism is likely to detract from the United States' ability to focus on fashioning a creative policy toward Korea, just when President Kim needs it most—in the final phase of his term in office. Moreover, the U.S. midterm elections, concurrent with the end of President Kim's term, may reignite partisan discord over appropriate U.S. policy toward Korea. Despite these peculiar circumstances that may distort U.S. policy, there are sound reasons for the Bush administration to lend its support to proactive engagement with the Kim Dae-Jung administration's inter-Korean agenda.

President Bush and his advisors should remember that Clinton administration policies toward Korea actually have deep roots that go back to the Reagan years. Inducing change in North Korea via subtle economic and diplomatic incentives is a policy rooted in Reagan-Shultz-era "smile diplomacy" that began in early 1983 and by the eve of the 1988 Seoul Olympics had produced an effort by Washington to encourage an inter-Korean dialogue. By early 1989, at the start of the George H. W. Bush administration, this process produced the first U.S.-DPRK talks, held in Beijing, as North Korea tried to cope with the impact of South Korea's *Nordpolitik* success vis-à-vis China and the USSR. The basic notion behind those efforts was to show North Korea that it had positive alternatives within reach and to create opportunities for reform. The goal was to open up North Korea to societal forces that could undermine its quasi-Stalinist ways. Admittedly, not much progress was made in that regard during the Reagan–G.H.W. Bush years, but the basic policy has solid conservative Republican roots.

Initially during the Clinton years the lack of progress remained intact in the face of North Korean intransigence. However, as an inadvertent by-product of Pyongyang's desperate post–cold-war pursuit of a nuclear capability to compensate for its gross vulnerabilities, the United States was drawn into intense bilateral negotiations with the North Korean regime to defuse the heightened danger of renewed warfare. In doing so, the "new Democrat" Clinton administration did not hesitate to coopt the experimental facets of U.S. policy toward North Korea that began in the Reagan years.

Accordingly, the current Bush administration could readily build on the accumulation of U.S. policy aimed at inducing change in North Korea created during the Reagan-Bush-Clinton years, rather than overreacting to accusations of "appeasement." There are several reasons for continuing to pursue this sound policy line. At the core of U.S. interest in Korea's stability there is a genuine need to support an ally's innovative policy toward an adversary, which has yielded authentic North-South progress. In addition, the United States has a major opportunity to fully terminate Asia's cold war by resolving its last remnant. As part of that adjustment process the United States can take advantage of a chance to reorder U.S. strategic priorities in the form of modifying the Asian balance of power and reappraising the nature of Korea's role in the United States' already-changing, worldwide dual-war scenario contingency planning. Along those lines the United States would be better served by peacefully eliminating the North Korean target of a Northeast Asian version of TMD. Doing so would not necessarily alter the Bush administration's plans to develop a NMD system, because the latter is not solely dependent on a North Korean threat. An NMD system's merits can stand on their own against generic threats that are reinforced by a struggle against terrorist threats. Cumulatively these policies also would be worthwhile because they would send positive signals to the PRC about American intentions in China's front yard.

The Bush administration should bear in mind the connotations of Korean usage of a composite Chinese ideograph used in Korean for the word describing a risky situation (*uigi*) that consists of the separate characters meaning "danger" and "opportunity." For Koreans, in the North and South, this implies that in all such potential crises one finds opportunities created by dangers. The Bush administration would be well advised to seize this geopolitical opportunity to ameliorate these dangers by continuing to explore innovative means to reduce tensions and bring about reconciliation and unification. The Bush administration has an opportunity to pursue a "compassionate-conservative" policy toward North Korea, within the context of a reuniting Korea, reminiscent of President Nixon's overtures toward China. Like the Nixon administration, the Bush administration has the conservative credentials to achieve what the Clinton administration was unable to realize despite its best efforts. If President Bush makes the best of this opportunity, U.S. policy toward Korea can fulfill long-standing goals on the peninsula—furthering peace, stability, and self-determination.

Just as it was in the interests of the two Koreas to try to make as much progress as possible during the year 2000, prior to the U.S. elections, so that whoever might become the next U.S. president would inherit the momentum of Korea's success, now that a new phase of U.S.-Korea relations is taking shape other similar pressures exist that Americans should heed. Because President Kim's term in office will end when his successor is chosen in December 2002, both Koreas have incentives to take advantage of opportunities that may cease to exist if South Korea elects a more conservative president at that point, as it may well do. Just as North Korea tried to engage with President Clinton before his term in office expired, that principle should also apply to South Korea's political timetable. North Korea's societal weaknesses and vulnerabilities, which show no signs of near-term recovery, underscore the logic of Pyongyang joining Seoul in a joint effort to achieve tangible success in their negotiations and then concretely implementing the agreements they achieve so as to instill mutual confidence in each other's sincerity and commitment to Korean reconciliation. However, given the time constraints directly imposed by South Korea's political system, it is in the interests of both Koreas to not allow the opportunity Kim Dae-Jung and Kim Jong-Il have created to dissipate through inattention or because of any external factor—including uncertainties about the United States' readiness to commit itself to whatever resolution the two Koreas can devise for themselves. In this sense, the leadership in Seoul and Pyongyang should collectively resolve to heed the admonition in the sage proverb, "strike while the iron is hot" (or its Korean equivalent, "pull out the ox-horn when it is hot" / *sopul do dankyul ae paera*). If the leaders of the two Koreas fail to seize this opportunity in a timely fashion, the window of opportunity could rapidly slip away from their grasp as President Kim is replaced by someone who is less amenable to innovation, and North Korea finds its options far more constrained by worsening circumstances.

Though Korea's leaders would only have themselves to blame if they fail to make the most of a fragile and fleeting opportunity, it also constitutes a circumstance in which Americans who care about U.S.-Korean relations, and would like to see their government be fully supportive of the inter-Korean peace process, have an opportunity to take it upon themselves to encourage Washington to do the right thing by sustaining a bipartisan level of U.S. support for Korean reconciliation and reunification. If the United States extends such support and the two Koreas mismanage their own dialogue, there will be no valid reason to cast blame on the United States. However, if the United States does not do its utmost and the present opportunity is lost, then the United States risks being blamed for yet another cycle of inter-Korean failure. If the two Koreas are to fail, let it be solely because of their own inadequacies—not because of any U.S. machinations, intentional or inadvertent. Consequently, the United States' most prudent course of action is to be concurrently supportive of the inter-Korean peace process and wary of doing anything toward Korea, toward its East Asian context, or with regard to larger U.S. security policies that could influence inter-Korean issues and derail that process.

The Mellowing of North Korean Power: Lessons of Reconciliation and Unification for Korea from Germany

Dieter Dettke

Introduction

There are a great number of similarities in the experiences of Korea and Germany in the past half-century:

— the territorial division of traditionally rather homogeneous societies;
— the cold war and its alliance systems;
— tensions between a communist dictatorship on one side and Western capitalism with liberal political traditions on the other;
— a sense of national identity deeply uprooted by war: national civil war wrapped in a clash of ideological systems in the case of Korea and responsibility for a murderous world war in the case of Germany.

Just as the old Federal Republic of Germany (FRG) and South Korea were children of the cold war whose identities were deeply influenced by the East-West conflict, East Germany and North Korea found their legitimacy in an ideology that was imposed on their society and supported from the outside. However, Germany is a united country again, whereas Korea remains one of the two cold-war divisions that have not been resolved as of today. Of the four "structurally divided"[1] nations resulting from the East-West conflict—China, Korea, Germany, and Vietnam—only Vietnam and Germany have been reunited, each representing a very different type of national unification.

The views expressed in this chapter are personal and do not represent any branch of the U.S. government.

1. See Immanuel Wallerstein, *The Nobel Peace Prize and Korean Reunification*. Comment No. 51, Fernand Braudel Center, Binghamton University, November 1, 2000; available at fbc.binghamton.edu/commentr.htm.

Cold-War Divisions

The reunification of Germany is an example of a peaceful process that came as a serendipity and not as the result of hard-driven national aspirations as it did in Vietnam. Nobody in Germany—or elsewhere—expected German unification to happen so suddenly, so fast, and so overwhelmingly unopposed inside or outside of Germany. Surprisingly, external unification turned out to be easier than internal unification. Whereas internal unification is still not complete and might require another generation in order to create full equality of living standards and conditions in both constituencies, Germany's international role and status are clear and uncontested in spite of initial reservations vis-à-vis a united Germany, for instance, on the part of some countries, such as France, Great Britain, Poland, and some of Germany's other European neighbors. As a fully sovereign nation-state, Germany is now a vital member of the European Union (EU) willing to give up some national sovereignty for participation in multilateral institutions.[2] Germany is also a member of NATO and a strong supporter of both EU and NATO expansion. The successful resolution of all territorial and border issues of the past, Germany's nonnuclear status, and a military smaller than that of cold-war Germany have helped to make unification more acceptable to its neighbors. With NATO and the coming EU expansion, Germany, for the first time in its history, will be surrounded by friends and allies, and the so-called German question might actually be a thing of the past.

The fact that internal unification was much more complicated than originally anticipated was a result of the bitter consequences of the failure and eventual collapse of the communist system, both economically and politically. The need for West Germany to absorb the eastern part of Germany within a very short period of time once the Berlin Wall had fallen, rather than manage a gradual transformation and modernization process for the East, was dictated by a rather narrow political window of opportunity for unification—especially given the dramatic developments in the Soviet Union at the time. An even more influential factor in the rush to unification on exclusively West German terms was the East

---

2. See speech given by Joschka Fischer, "From Confederacy to Federation—Thoughts on the Finality of European Integration" at the Humboldt University in Berlin, May 12, 2000; available at www.auswaertiges-amt.de.

German people. Once people became aware of their own power vis-à-vis an out-of-step communist regime after staging large-scale demonstrations for freedom and democracy, even the East German government had no alternative—other than a brutal use of force—but to push for the most rapid and complete take-over by West German institutions. The East German regime de facto threw in the towel in the face of the democratic opposition and rushed into the arms of West Germany by promising to hold free elections early—on March 18, 1990, only five months after the fall of the wall. Without the backing of the Soviet Union and the Soviet military forces in Germany, which refused to prop up a regime they thought they could no longer afford to support, East Germany ceased to exist. East Germans had no desire whatsoever to try to reform a fundamentally flawed system and simply chose to join West Germany, an already existing functional democracy and a real market economy.

Because there was no language barrier between East and West Germany and since the East German government made no serious effort to block the free flow of information to the East via electronic media, there was no legitimacy left for the East German regime when the Berlin Wall came tumbling down. The result was an almost complete incorporation of East Germany into the West German system. The Westernization of the East did not leave much room for the survival of the so-called achievements of socialism. People preferred a merger through accession to the Federal Republic of Germany as stipulated in Article 23 of the Basic Law, the once provisional German constitution. Even without a formal vote the Basic Law became the popular all-German constitution.

Vietnam is a completely different case of national unification after the cold-war division.[3] Whereas the Germans had to wait until the end of the cold war and the collapse of communism to come together again, Vietnam was united during the cold war. However, the country had to survive a major war of liberation against the United States and the U.S. ally in the south in order to overcome the division. Its struggle for national unity led to the worst case of military confrontation during the entire cold war. Vietnam is an example of unification by force—the result of a decisive communist victory. The United States had to leave Vietnam under the cloud of an agreement with the North that provided little cover for a military defeat. As a result of a peace agreement negotiated between the United States and North Vietnam, unification of the

---

3. Ibid.

two Vietnams took place on North Vietnamese terms and established a communist regime in all of Vietnam, which led to the exodus of thousands of people from the South after the communist takeover. A national dream was achieved, but freedom was one of the victims of national liberation.

The division of China is yet another special case. In Taiwan's separation from the mainland, cold-war political and ideological structures were reinforced by geography, demography, and ethnicity.[4] After Mao Zedong and his communist movement won the civil war in China, the Kuomintang withdrew to the island of Taiwan, claiming to be the legitimate government of China. The island status of Taiwan makes it extremely difficult to resolve the unification problem by military force, especially since the United States has guaranteed Taiwan's security in a bilateral assistance treaty. Another difficulty is the ethnicity of Taiwan's population, who are Han Chinese. The island has always had a strong independence movement and even without the Kuomintang, who are mostly of Han Chinese extraction and who were often refugees from the mainland, Taiwan has been traditionally independent of the mainland. Today, Taiwan has a very successful economy as well as significant military forces, and has regained democratic legitimacy through free elections. It is no surprise then that the separation of Taiwan from China survived the cold war. Unification will take a long time and it will be an involved process. Just as Hong Kong's reintegration into the People's Republic of China after a century of colonial history was a slow and gradual process, China/Taiwan unification will not be a simple takeover by any standard.

Korea's division is the only other case that has survived the cold war. However, almost half a millennium of common history is a strong indicator that the division of the two Koreas is artificial and they should be together. In fact, as was the case with Germany, both sides in Korea assume the inevitability of their reunification.[5] It is the unique character of the regime in North Korea that keeps the country apart even after Soviet communism collapsed as a global force.[6] Swift unification as in

---

4. Ibid.

5. See Ben Kremenak, *Korea's Road to Unification: Potholes, Detours, and Dead Ends,* Center for International and Security Studies Papers 5, Maryland School of Public Affairs, University of Maryland at College Park, May 1997, p. 75.

6. See Kongdan Oh and Ralph C. Hassig, *North Korea through the Looking Glass.* (Washington, D.C.: Brookings Institution Press, 2000), p. 11.

the case of Germany is unlikely. Although there is little difference of opinion about the abject nature of the North Korean regime, it seems to rest upon an authoritarian stability independent of outside support.[7] It might collapse under the weight of its own oppression, its burdensome military expenditures, and a dysfunctional economy, in which case South Korea would have to absorb a poverty- and hunger-stricken people of roughly 23 million in catastrophic social and human conditions as well as widespread political chaos. While breakup should not be excluded as a possible outcome of developments on the Korean peninsula,[8] it should definitely not be the aim of a South Korean strategy of unification to bring about or even accelerate the collapse of the North. Rather, as in the case of German *Ostpolitik* (relations with Eastern European countries and Russia), the aim of the current Sunshine Policy[9] should be to keep the flame of unity burning on a little fire while at the same time creating all the necessary circumstances to make unification possible, or at least to prevent further polarization.

Containment, Détente, and Policies to Overcome Cold-War Structures

In order to use the appropriate reconciliation and unification lessons, it is perhaps useful to go back for a moment to the original post–World War II strategy of the West designed by George Kennan. More often than not containment policy during the cold war was reduced to a military strategy of the West that included the creation of military alliances around the globe. Korea became part of this military alliance system under U.S. leadership. However, it took an act of war to convince the United States that South Korea was part of the cold-war system and thus a recipient of the military protection the United States was willing to provide. For George Kennan the core of containment was not necessarily a military strategy but rather a political design "to increase . . . the strains under which Soviet policy must operate, to force upon the Kremlin a far greater degree of moderation and circumspection than it has

---

7. Ibid., p. 15ff.

8. See for instance Nicholas Eberstadt, *The End of North Korea* (Washington, D.C.: The AEI Press, 1999), p. 47ff, particularly, p. 50.

9. An excellent source for the foundations of the Sunshine Policy is Kim Dae-Jung's article, "The Once and Future Korea," in *Foreign Policy*, no. 86 (Spring 1992), pp. 40–55.

had to observe in recent years."[10] Kennan's ultimate objective was "to promote tendencies which must eventually find their outlet in either the *break-up* or the *gradual mellowing of Soviet power* [emphasis added by author]."[11] In Kennan's thinking "break-up" was not necessarily the result of outside military pressure but rather the outcome of a process of self-destruction. Likewise, the "gradual mellowing of power" can be the consequence of self-correction or self-inducement of adjustment to a more civilized behavior as the result of appropriate Western strategies of enticement and rewards.

German *Ostpolitik* and even more pronounced West German *Deutschlandpolitik* (internal German relations) clearly used economic rewards and benefits to steer the East German regime into a more benign behavior vis-à-vis its own population, knowing that East Germany would be willing to do a lot for international recognition and participation in economic exchange.[12] One particularly controversial policy instrument was the West German "prisoner buy-out policy." Political opposition in the German Democratic Republic (GDR) was often met with draconian punishment. Long prison sentences for political opponents of the regime were customary. West Germany tried to ease the situation of these dissidents by paying for their freedom to leave the GDR. This was done with utmost secrecy on both sides in order to avoid jeopardizing a humanitarian program.

West German *Ostpolitik* and Western détente policy in the late 1960s and early 1970s are the finest examples of policies to prompt the "gradual mellowing" of Soviet power. Today, under different circumstances, the Sunshine Policy follows the model of German *Ostpolitik* and détente in order to help bring about a lasting peace based initially on the status quo

---

10. See George Kennan, *The Sources of Soviet Conduct.* Originally published as an anonymous article in *Foreign Affairs* (July 1947). Available at www.cnn.com/SPECIALS/cold.war/episodes/04/documents/x.html.

11. Ibid.

12. Three publications in particular highlight *Ostpolitik, Deutschlandpolitik* and the East German economic interests and privileged position in the context of Korean-unification efforts: Thomas H. Henriksen, and Kyongsoo Lho, eds., *One Korea?: Challenges and Prospects for Reunification* (Stanford, CA: Hoover Institution Press, 1994); Kang Myoung-Kyu and Helmut Wagner, eds., *Germany and Korea: Lessons in Unification* (Seoul: Seoul National University Press, 1995); and Jung Ku-Hyun, Dalchoong Kim, Werner Gumpel, and Gottfried-Karl Kindermann eds., *German Unification and Its Lessons for Korea* (Seoul: Institute of East and West Studies, Yonsei University, 1996).

and eventual unification. The gradual mellowing of North Korean power will be an essential prerequisite of Korean unity and therefore, humanitarian improvements will have to come first, before a process of democratization can be initiated—as was the case in Nicaragua and Serbia after long years of communist dictatorship and in South Africa after apartheid. In a divided country, however, peaceful transformation is difficult. Under the conditions of territorial division and political and ideological tension it is hard to find unequivocal international support for peaceful transformation strategies. Transformation can easily be denounced as submission to the demands of the other side. It takes an extraordinary amount of circumspection both domestically and internationally to move a peaceful transformation agenda forward.

When German *Ostpolitik* and *Deutschlandpolitik* were first conceptualized as policies of "change through rapprochement"[13] by Willy Brandt and Egon Bahr, they met bitter and massive resistance by their opponents in government. The fact that *Ostpolitik* and *Deutschlandpolitik* were political strategies of the Social Democratic (SPD) opposition caused the Christian Democratic (CDU) government at the time to launch a particularly fierce battle of resistance to the proposed changes in the official West German position vis-à-vis East Germany. It took years to build the necessary domestic political consensus for *Ostpolitik* to make it election-proof.

In the beginning, *Ostpolitik* had a rather modest goal. The issue was simply to improve the living conditions of people in the GDR. Humanitarian improvements, not the end of the division, were the stated objective of *Ostpolitik*. Crucial mega-issues such as national unity, the final borders of a united Germany, the diplomatic recognition of both Germanys in the international arena, membership in the United Nations, and the legal quality of intra-German relations were left open. It was precisely the openness of the outcome of the cooperation process initiated with *Ostpolitik* that enabled East Germany as the weaker partner to engage in a more cooperative relationship—very often simply for the purpose of material gain. Open acceptance of the territorial status quo by both sides—as well as tacit acceptance of the political and military status quo—while at the same time maintaining unity as the ultimate,

---

13. See for instance Manfred Görtemaker, "Security in the Post Cold War Era: The Role of Germany and New Lessons for Korea," in Kang and Wagner, *Germany and Korea*, op. cit., pp. 311–63.

but in all likelihood rather distant, goal, enabled both sides to engage in dialogue and find solutions for many practical and humanitarian issues. Visitation rights for families that were separated during the cold war was a crucial issue on the agenda for intra-German talks. It is no coincidence that these "little steps"—as they were called by Chancellor Willy Brandt when he was still governing mayor of the divided city of Berlin—started in Berlin. It cannot be emphasized enough how important these human contacts are in a divided nation. South Korea, thanks to its new Sunshine Policy, is just at the beginning of a process that promises great benefits if it can be broadened so that more and more divided families and finally more and more Koreans without family ties will have the opportunity to see each other and communicate with one another.

A good start has been made since the initiation of the Sunshine Policy. From February 1998 until November 2000, more than 15,000 South Koreans had visited the North. Separated family members met in third countries and postal exchanges increased. Humanitarian aid is on the rise both from the South Korean government and from the private sector. There is a military hotline and further military confidence-building measures are being initiated by the defense ministries of both sides.[14] Recognition of the existing political realities and the facts that create the division of a country is an essential precondition for progress in a relationship characterized by stalemate.[15] And this includes the acceptance of an unpleasant but inevitable consequence, namely the fact that people—even as part of a single nation—will have to live apart at least temporarily.

The rather modest goal of *Ostpolitik* was the normalization of relations: first a modus vivendi between the two German states and second between Germany and its eastern neighbors. The intra-German aspect of normalization is an excellent example for the two Koreas. To break up the almost total self-imposed isolation of the Democratic People's Republic of Korea through human contact, economic exchange, and communication with the outside world would be an important step forward and an improvement of the living conditions of the people in the

---

14. See text of a presentation by Ambassador Sung-Chul Yang at the National Press Club in Washington D.C., February 23, 2001.

15. See for instance Hans J. Giessmann, *German "Ostpolitik" and Korean Unification: Parallels, Contrasts, Lessons,* a paper presented at the conference "South Korea's Sunshine Policy and West Germany's *Ostpolitik* for Peace and Stability," May 17, 2001.

North, particularly since we appear to be witnessing one of the most dangerous hunger catastrophes in modern times.[16]

When unification occurred in Germany after the fall of the Berlin Wall on November 9, 1989, a number of political, economic, social, cultural, and humanitarian contacts already existed. As East-West tensions eased in the mid- and late 1980s, economic, trade, and personal contacts increased dramatically. North Korea never had a chance to benefit from the easing of tensions between East and West. Obviously, there is great concern and reluctance in the North to open its borders and risk a higher degree of exposure of its population to Western ideas, values, and economic achievements. However, the pressure of migration is mounting. More and more North Koreans are willing to risk their lives for greater opportunities elsewhere. The border between China and North Korea is beginning to be porous. Many North Koreans risk illegal immigration to China, although China is obliged to send refugees from North Korea back to their country of origin.[17] In 2000 some 50,000–70,000 North Koreans crossed the border to China. Obviously, if China were to open its borders for North Korean refugees, the North Korean government could be seriously destabilized, just as the former East German regime was undermined by an ever-growing stream of refugees to Hungary. Hungary had finally opened its border to Austria and with that the road for refugees to the West was open.[18]

The German Unification Model

If the key issue for Korea is how to manage unification successfully, the German unification treaty can hardly be the script for South Korea and the unification process of the Korean peninsula. German unification was

---

16. See for instance Eberstadt, *The End of North Korea*. op. cit., p. 9 and the report "Diary of a Mad Place" by Dr. Norbert Vollersten, who as a member of a German medical group, Cap Anamur, was stationed in North Korea for eighteen months and witnessed the unfolding humanitarian catastrophe in the North. See *Time Asia*, January 22, 2001, vol. 157, no. 3, and at www.time.com/time/asia/magazine/2001/0122/korea.doctor.pop.htm.

17. See recent newspaper reports about the situation at the border, including Rosenthal, Elisabeth. "China and U.N. Meet on North Korea Immigrants," *New York Times*, June 28, 2001.

18. See John Burton, "Protest against China's Stance on N. Koreans," *Financial Times*, July 2, 2001.

the result of a unique configuration of external and internal circumstances. The long period of preparation that paved the way to unity through *Ost-* and *Deutschlandpolitik* is a more useful model. Once the Berlin Wall fell and the East German government agreed to free elections at an early stage, there was not much room for anything other than the full and complete takeover by West German institutions, de facto the Westernization of East Germany, beginning with the creation of an economic, monetary and social union, followed by the Treaty on German Unity, and finally the election of an all-German parliament as the crowning act of the unification process. The external aspects of unification were managed successfully through the 2+4 process, in which the two German negotiating partners fully participated. The four powers—the United States, Great Britain, France, and Russia (or the Soviet Union until 1992)—had direct legal claims and responsibilities dating back to Germany's capitulation and subsequent postwar occupation, in particular the right to determine Germany's final border and to conclude a peace treaty with Germany. The 2+4 process was a natural result of Germany's special international status after World War II. The two Koreas are fully sovereign already and an international arrangement like the Four-Power Agreement to grant full sovereignty again will not be necessary in the case of Korean unification. Today, more than a decade after unification, German unity is still not complete in every respect. In many ways, post-unification is still an ongoing process. It will take a generation or more until all the remaining disparities, differences, and inequalities between East and West are resolved.

Of course, the time frame for full equality will differ from area to area. For the most part, income equality has already been achieved. The remaining wage differences are minimal and will not last for long. It will take longer to equalize housing quality in the East and West and even longer to repair the enormous environmental damage the GDR regime has caused over the years.

Because West German institutions were basically superimposed on those created in the old GDR during the forty years of communist control, East Germany's representation in the institutions of the united Germany is still a problem that needs to be addressed more aggressively. The only fair East German representation on a national level after more than a decade of unity is the German Bundestag, the national parliament. East Germany's population has at least a fair proportional share of parliamentary seats, but whether it also has a fair proportional weight in decision making is an open question. Fair representation in the

Bundestag cannot make up for judges, lawyers, professors, civil servants, soldiers, union and church leaders, journalists, bankers, and businessmen who have a Western education and family background. This is, of course, no surprise, because political parties, churches, unions, the media, and universities are all enlarged Western institutions at the core.

The political parties extended their reach and amended their local, state, and national structures so that East Germans could join but not take over. Today, more than a decade after unification, all governmental and nongovernmental institutions are in place and working on the basis of the West German system. The task of representing genuine East German interests within the political system of the Federal Republic of Germany fell to the Party of Democratic Socialism (PDS), the former ruling communist party. The PDS made quite successful adjustments to democracy, and the party is now more open and less authoritarian. But, some old thinking still prevails within its rank and file. The long-term prospects of the party are not great. To the degree that unification has been successful, the PDS, with its aging membership, will lose its crucial role as the voice of those who had to suffer from unification because of their ties to the old regime.

The churches, too, simply extended their jurisdiction. Regional church districts had even kept their old names and structures during the German division; therefore, it was not difficult at all to re-create the old all-German administrative church institutions. By maintaining themselves, both the Protestant and the Catholic church provided maximum continuity. The Protestant church profited most from unification as East Germany was predominantly Protestant. However, because of social stress, joblessness, and economic uncertainty, both churches lost membership after unification despite their actively protective—and even heroic—policy toward the clandestine East German opposition.

Unions, too, used the West German model of trade union organization to rebuild trade union structures in the East. Unions lost members in the process of unification because of the disastrous collaboration of East German unions with the communist regime. Reduced to a driving-belt function within a totalitarian system, unions did not have any credibility to represent workers' interests. The trade union movement in the East collapsed along with the old communist regime. Following unification, unions had to start from scratch and reorganize along the lines of the West German industrial unions. Trade union leadership, as a result of sheer membership size, remained in West German hands, with one exception: teachers. Today, their president is an East German, and step-by-step other East Germans will take over leadership responsibility in the German trade union movement.

The Western media, particularly TV and radio, had penetrated the East long before unification. The East German government did not even try seriously to jam broadcasts from the West. There was no language barrier preventing East Germans from participating at least passively—and of course without the right to vote—in the German political discourse. Therefore, in spite of an official ideological hostility in the East toward the West, there was always a certain degree of latent cultural commonality, which was easy to resuscitate once the legal and political barriers to unity were removed.

After unification, radio, TV, and print media played an important role for East Germans in expressing their own feelings and helping them find their own identity in the unified Germany. Not surprisingly, not much of the dominant press and media of the GDR survived. Newspapers were taken over by wealthier West German publishing houses. Radio and TV stations became affiliates of the West German stations. What the East needed most, of course, was a way to express the specific needs of people in the new states of the Federal Republic of Germany. The old guard journalists and media representatives could not do the job. Neither could West German journalists fulfill this task. New faces were needed and indeed many young, aspiring journalists raised in the GDR became successful professional journalists and began to express genuine East German interests, feelings, and perceptions.

The German university system is a case in point where export to the East was not the best solution. Germany missed a great moment to simultaneously reform and modernize its university system in the East and West at the time of unification. New universities were created but they kept their old German structures, imported from the West. The existing East German universities, often old, all-German ones, were simply rebuilt in the West German image. Most of the East German university professors lost their jobs. And this was not only true in areas infiltrated by ideology, such as law, economics, and the social sciences. Radical renewal also took place in chemistry, biology, physics, and mathematics. Even education below the university level—primary and secondary education—underwent major surgery not limited to the substance of teaching and the various curricula. Many high school teachers also lost their jobs and had to take early retirement or—if previously involved with the communist system—had to find new jobs.

Cultural programs and activities can contribute enormously to the establishment of unity between the two Koreas. The states and municipalities administer most cultural activities in Germany. During the unification process, the federal government assumed a part of the cost of cultural programs and activities such as the preservation of monuments and cultural assets in East Germany. Administered by the ministry of the interior, funds were made available to individual artists, as well as museums, institutions for the performing arts, orchestras, and so forth. Some theaters had to close down under financial pressure, while on the other hand political satire and typical Western cultural traditions such as musicals and pop music concerts found a great new market in the former GDR. Joint cultural programs could be particularly helpful in Korea to help make up for the lack of contacts over so many years.

During the pre-unification period both Koreas would benefit from a program designed to help the people of North and South Korea better understand each other by dealing with the past. Textbooks and scholarly research would benefit enormously if experts from both sides could begin to submit their work to the criticism of their counterparts. Germany has used this concept successfully in forging a new relationship with Poland. The often surprising result of the work of textbook committees and symposia on specific historical issues was a new consensus on issues that were subjected to prejudice and stereotypes.

Korea and Germany:
The Economic Burden of Unification

Based on per capita income, East and West Germany were much wealthier when unification took place than the Koreas are today. It would be much more difficult for South Korea to incorporate the North than it was for West Germany to incorporate the East. The economic and social differences of the two Germanys were much less pronounced than those of the two Koreas. The population of North Korea is just half that of South Korea, yet the GDP of South Korea is 20 times greater than that of the North, per capita income is more than 10 times the amount of per capita income in the North, and foreign trade is 126 times larger (see Table 1).

Table 1

South/North Korea (1995) vs. West/East Germany (1989)

	South Korea	North Korea	South/ North	West Germany	East Germany	West/ East
Population, million	44.9	23.3	1.9	62.1	16.6	3.8
GNP, U.S.$ billion	451.7	22.3	20.3	1,207.0	96.0	12.6
Per capita income, U.S.$	10.067	957	10.5	19,283	5,840	3.3
% Economic growth annually, 1990–95	+7.6	–4.5				
Public expenditure, U.S.$ billion	97.1	19	5.1	547.7	61.8	8.9
(as % of GNP)	(21.5)	(85)		(45.5)	(64.4)	
Defense spending, U.S.$ billion	14.3	5.1	2.8	28.5	11.2	2.6
(as % of GNP)	(3.2)	(23)		(2.4)	(11.6)	
Per capita, U.S.$	318	218	1.5	459	675	0.7
Foreign trade, U.S.$ billion	260.2	2.05	126.9	611.1	47.0	13.0
(as % of GNP)	(57.6)	(9.2)		(50.6)	(49)	
Merchandise exports, U.S.$ billion	125.1	0.74	169	341.3	23.7	14.4
Merchandise imports, U.S.$ billion	135.1	1.31	103	269.8	23.3	11.5
Foreign debt, U.S.$ billion	79	11.8	6.6	106.7	22	4.9
(as % of GNP)	(17.5)	(53)		(8.8)	(23)	

Source: Marc Piazolo, "Could South Korea Afford German-style Reunification?" *The Economics of Korean Reunification:* Hyundai Research Institute, vol. 2, no. 2 (1997).

The high cost of German unification, roughly 100 billion U.S. dollars on an annual basis since 1990, must have, of course, a chilling effect on South Korean unification ambitions. German-style unification was, however, highly politicized and amounted to practically a Marshall Plan annually for just 15 million East Germans.[19] Korea does not have to repeat that experience. Without the time constraints of the German case, the speed and timing of economic unity can be more easily managed, wage policy does not have to achieve income equality in just five

---

19. See for instance Ulrich Heilemann and Hermann Rappen, "Sieben Jahre deutsche Einheit: Rückblick und Perspektiven aus fiskalischer Sicht," *Aus Politik und Zeitgeschichte.* B 40–41/1997, September 26, 1997, pp. 38–46.

years or so, and the restoration of property rights does not have to be as hostile to investment as it turned out to be in East Germany.[20]

Substantial savings and reallocations of resources can be realized by the downsizing of the North Korean military forces.[21] The military consumes roughly half of the country's budget. Out of a population of 23 million, North Korea maintains an army of more than 1 million soldiers, the highest proportion anywhere in the world. Likewise, South Korea's military force of some 700,000 could be reduced and savings could be further realized if the military force of the peninsula were reduced to some 400,000 instead of its current approximately 1.8 million.[22] It would be naïve to assume that the military power of the North can simply be added to the economic achievements of the South and another great power in Asia will emerge. Rather, one has to assume that North Korea's extraordinary military strength will present the most difficult hurdle to overcome on the way to national unification. Although South Korea is more than capable of handling the North's conventional forces, the missile technology of the North is a destabilizing factor in the overall military balance. An effective ballistic missile defense would help restore this potential imbalance and greatly contribute to the mellowing of North Korean power.

South Korea's recent economic difficulties and the dismal economic, political, and social conditions in the North make it very unlikely that South Korea will be able to merge with the North anytime soon. To incorporate 23 million people armed to the teeth, while at the same time cope with one of the greatest hunger catastrophes in modern times, should only be attempted after a pre-unification phase of several years, probably even two or three decades, during which time a separate government in control of the North would be necessary in order to prevent an

---

20. For an excellent discussion on the German mistakes see Mo Jongryn, *The German Lessons for Managing the Economic Cost of Korean Unification* in Henriksen and Lho, *One Korea*, op cit., pp. 48–67, here p. 63.

21. See for instance, Charles Wolf, Jr., "How Much for One Korea?" *Asian Wall Street Journal*, October 2, 2000.

22. Don Oberdorfer uses the following figures: 1.1 million for the North and 660,000 for the South. Don Oberdorfer, *The Two Koreas. A Contemporary History* (Reading, MA: Addison Wesley Longman, 1997), p. 2. Some sources use much higher figures for the military forces of North Korea. See for instance Don Kirk, "Stories of North Korean Refugees Turn More Macabre," *Los Angeles Times*, April 18, 1999. According to Kirk the size of the North Korean security forces altogether is about 2 million.

uncontrollable chain of events, such as civil war and chaos. Just a year ago in Berlin, President Kim Dae-Jung declared openly that "the current situation is not suitable for reunification."[23]

Of course, a rapid takeover has many advantages over gradual change and lengthy periods of transition. In the case of Germany, the rapid takeover approach had the advantage of creating the legal, financial, and economic conditions to conduct business immediately. The new federal states that joined the Federal Republic of Germany had a stable macroeconomic environment from the beginning. By contrast, a rapid takeover in the case of Korea would lead to a much greater transformation shock than in the case of Germany. In fact, according to President Kim Dae-Jung, the danger exists that a rapid takeover could lead to war.[24]

However, the cost of Korean unification—based on the German model— is often exaggerated. As Marcus Noland demonstrated, unification will be accompanied by a reallocation of resources throughout the economy that will result in an increase in national income and an increase in tax receipts. The benefit side of the calculus should not be underestimated.[25]

Even if the collapse of the North would not be accompanied by violence, an enormous amount of economic, social, and behavioral differences will have to be overcome as a result of the North's complete isolation and its lack of contact with the South and the rest of the world for a period of more than a half-century. The period of adjustment of living standards would last much longer than it did in the case of Germany. An economic, monetary, and social union like the United Germany created on July 1, 1990, cannot be achieved that quickly. If one would try to close the wage gap between North and South in a short period of time—as in Germany— North Korea would loose its competitive advantage completely. The two Korean economies can supplement each other much better than those of East and West Germany were able to. If the adjustment process is gradual, the North could take advantage of its vast cheap labor pool, making unification much smoother economically.[26]

Because of the rapid adjustment of living standards and a single currency—the German mark (DM)—East Germany's GDP dropped dra-

---

23. Interview with the German newspaper *Die Welt*, August 27, 2000.

24. Ibid.

25. Marcus Noland, *The Costs and Benefits of Korean Unification* (Asia Pacific Research Center, March 1998).

26. On the need for a soft landing see Selig S. Harrison, "Promoting a Soft Landing in Korea," *Foreign Policy*, no. 106 (Spring 1997), pp. 57–75.

matically from day one of the Monetary, Economic, and Social Union. Therefore, it would be advisable not to close the wage gap between North and South Korea too quickly in order to preserve North Korea's only competitive advantage over the South: cheap labor. It would also help to prevent North Korea's currency from appreciating as drastically as the East German Mark did, namely by about 400 percent. As a result East German products completely lost their competitiveness, causing large-scale unemployment in the East. Germany is still struggling with twice as much unemployment in the East as in the West.

By far the greatest challenge of a Korean unification process will be migration. In view of the dismal economic and political conditions in the North, there are already some pressures to emigrate to China and Russia, and some cases of family unification for North Koreans in Japan. An opening of the border to the south could create extreme tension, not only because of the social and economic burden it would place on the South but also because of the South's long-standing political animosity toward the communist system and the brutal conditions of the division of the Korean peninsula.

China is not particularly interested in Korean refugees, and because China, Russia, and Japan have a rather firm control of their borders, the main route of migration would be toward the South. To reduce the migration pressure for the short term, a comprehensive national and international food and nutrition program would have to be launched.

A popular uprising in the North against the present regime would make it difficult to keep the unification process under control. Huge masses would try to move south to find jobs and escape the dismal living conditions in the North. The South could be flooded with political and economic refugees for whom there were too few jobs. Even if supplying refugees with food, clothing, and shelter is manageable, the job situation is going to be desperate.

At first, the German government thought that it would just take a few years to fully integrate East Germany. Chancellor Kohl talked about "blooming landscapes" in the East as if the West's economic success could be replicated in the East in a short period of time. The reality is that migration is still a problem in Germany.[27] Migration from East to West reached an all-time high between 1950 and 1959 of 2.2 million East

---

27. For an excellent discussion of the German migration pressures after unification, see Rainer Münz and Ralf E. Ulrich, "Depopulation after Unification? Population Prospects for East Germany, 1990–2010," *German Politics and Society*, vol. 13, no. 4 (Winter 1995), available at www.demographie.de/info/epub/pdfdateien/depop.pdf.

Germans. The high emigration rates were what prompted the East German government to erect the Berlin Wall in 1961. Migration dropped dramatically after the construction of the wall. In 1989, however, prior to East Germany's slow-motion "collapse" and the opening of the wall on November 9, 1989, migration via reformed communist countries had increased dramatically. In 1989 alone 343,854 people left East Germany though Hungary or Czechoslovakia to settle in West Germany.

For Korea the more interesting period is the German migration following unification, 1990–92. Between July 1989 and December 1992 roughly 1 million people moved from East Germany to West Germany and West Berlin. In 1990, 415,000 people left the East. In 1991 this figure dropped to 150,000, and in 1992 there was a positive trend toward the East. However, during this same period West Germans began to move east in substantial numbers: in 1990: 12,000; 1991: 75,000; 1992: 102,000. Today, migration in both directions is fluid, but this still leaves the East with the more difficult issues to deal with:

—ghost towns in some areas;
—a population older than that of West Germany; and
—a less qualified and less flexible workforce.

In addition, many East Germans commute: They live in the East but hold jobs in the West. In 1992 the number of commuting workers increased to 436,000—more than 5 percent of the working population in the East.

Social integration in Germany turned out to be a much more difficult problem than ever anticipated. It was quite a surprise for Germans to find out that external unification was not a strong barrier at all, although most people assumed that European security needed the division of Germany as a structural component. Internal unification, however, turned out to be a rather thorny and painful issue.

The economic, political, and social difficulties of German unification have been vastly underestimated, as had the extraordinary financial dimension of unification—roughly 2 trillion DM since 1990 or almost 200 billion on an annual basis. This is the equivalent of a Marshall plan every year for East Germany alone. Equally problematic are the differences in lifestyle, mentality, social behavior, work attitudes, and a deep alienation resulting from forty-five years of life under communist rules. Understandably, material and financial aid was the top priority of Western unification policy. Alienation as an issue was not addressed properly.

In the case of Korea, the task of creating equal living standards in the North and South is a very tall order. Even similarity of living standards and living conditions is a much more distant goal than it is in Germany. It will probably take two generations or more to overcome existing differences in income, lifestyle, and the quality of life on the Korean peninsula.

Social expenditures and unemployment compensation were by far the greatest portion of the overall financial transfer from West to East Germany. Only 40 percent of the overall transfer can be considered to be in the form of investments. More than half of the total unification cost consisted of social and unemployment compensation. It would be better for the overall unification success of Korea if the share of investments were higher than it was in Germany's case. Growth in East Germany is still not self-sustaining. More investments in the overall amount of financial transfers would have helped to improve the economic situation. Social expenditures, unemployment compensation, and labor market stimulation programs took up the lion's share in the overall financial commitment of the Federal Republic of Germany for unification. [28]

The high social standards of West Germany were, of course, the main reason behind this enormous financial burden. The German social security system is insurance-based and membership is obligatory, except for federal and state employees entitled to receive retirement benefits from the federal or state government (*Beamte*) and for the self-employed. Membership continues even for those who lose their jobs. A member— even without a job—is still entitled to receive benefits.

By far the most costly commitment of West Germany was the generous access for all East German citizens to the existing social security system (retirement benefits, unemployment compensation, health care, disability insurance, etc.). For example, without having made any contribution to the social security system every East German citizen after unification was automatically entitled to receive retirement benefits. For older people in the GDR this was, of course, a very attractive benefit. Although East German wages were much lower than those in West Ger-

---

28. See Manfred Wegner, "Die deutsche Einigung oder das Ausbleiben des Wunders," *Aus Politik und Zeitgeschichte.* B.40/96, September 27, 1996.

many, retirement benefits for East Germans were based on a putative West German income level minus a small cost-of-living deduction. The result was maximum income equality between East and West along with a huge burden for the social security system supported by West Germans only. In addition, the initial high unemployment rate after unification that resulted from the one-to-one exchange rate for East German marks for individual citizens put severe strains on the system. Since both the employer and the employee make contributions to the social security system (50:50), those without jobs did not contribute to the system but were nevertheless entitled to draw benefits. Also, lower wages in the East (two-thirds of the West German level in 1990, gradually increasing) automatically meant lower contributions. The federal government provided funds for training and retraining purposes. This concept did not work in every individual case. Women particularly had a hard time making a successful transition from the old state-run economy to the West German market economy.

East Germany had one of the highest numbers of women in the work force. Almost 90 percent of East German women worked and held jobs. The GDR government provided a rather generous infrastructure to help working women. Highly subsidized child care was often available on company premises. This generous infrastructure did not survive after unification and a proportionally higher number of women than men lost their jobs as the result of unification. The number of working women dropped dramatically after unification, leaving East German women victims of unification.

Vocational education, training, and retraining will also be an important aspect of Korean unification. South Korean companies with relatively higher labor costs might be willing to move north and profit from the North Korean labor pool. One important precondition is, however, that educational standards be up to the task of modern production techniques. Though the German education effort (vocational education, training, and retraining as well as university education and research) is a useful model for Korean unification, the generous financial commitment that West Germany made to incorporate East Germans into their social security system is not. For the purpose of Korean unification there must be a different way to seek social integration.

Based on the German system, it would have made much more sense to take on the cost of social integration by increasing taxes rather than by making employment more costly. As a result of using the wrong financial instruments to fund social security, Germany became less competitive worldwide and got caught in a bind: global competition abroad and rising labor costs at home.

Conclusion

Even if South Korea's model of democracy is the yardstick for Korean unification, one should leave room for the adjustment of these institutions to new all-Korean realities. More than fifty years of division have created enormous political, economic, and cultural differences as well as different mental attitudes. There is a need for mutual acceptance of the different biographies of people from the North and the South. Not homogeneous equality but rather an "equality of unequals"[29] must be the norm. North and South need to work out a new consensus.

The military sector will be a critical issue. What will be done with the two armies and the military industrial complex of the North? The German model would not work in Korea. In the case of Germany, the East German army was practically dissolved. Only some 30,000 junior officers were integrated into the West German army. In the case of Korea, the solution will have to be more subtle. While unification will be an excellent opportunity to reduce the size of the combined military forces, such a reduction will be accomplished only through integration on the basis of a rough equality. The creation of a joint institution to manage the merger of the two armies will be essential.

No high-level East German diplomat survived German unification in office. The East German diplomatic corps simply vanished. Here, again, the German model does not represent the best way of integrating the two societies. However, North Korea's diplomatic service is currently quite small, so it should be possible to create a joint diplomatic corps, which—out of necessity—will rely more heavily on South Korea's more developed diplomatic service.

How to overcome the mentality gap? If everything from the North is seen as a socialist deformation it will be more difficult and take much longer to overcome the gap. Instead of strengthening ideological divisions, new areas of consensus should be developed to facilitate integration. Obviously, Northern military technology is highly developed and

---

29. Hans-Joachim Veen, "Innere Einheit—aber wo liegt sie?" *Aus Politik und Zeitgeschichte*, B40–41/97, September 26, 1997, pp. 19–28.

does not need to be dismantled in order to be used as a common industrial base in the future. What is necessary is adjustment and a protocol for making the North's military industry more compatible with the future international status of a unified Korea.

The overall delegitimization of the North should be avoided. However, support for basic principles and crucial institutions—democracy, human rights, and market principles—is a must. The North Korean people should be treated as equals. Otherwise, socialization of the people of the North will not succeed.

It will take a long time to create living standards in the North that are fully equal to those of the South. Individuals need to be prepared to accept a certain degree of inequality. To promise too much would be wrong. However, equality of North and South as the common goal of unification is essential. Nevertheless, economic and social equality are not the only criteria of unification. Even with its more developed economy and society, the standard of equality in South Korea is not absolutely equal living conditions, which can be only a long-term goal. Living conditions differ to some degree within every social system. The key is to create an economic system that offers people a potentially better economic future. Korea needs to forge a basic consensus or a minimal consensus that does not subject every social area and activity to strict material equality:

—mutual recognition of biographical differences;
—the adoption of common values, such as basic human rights, pluralism, democratic elections, a market economy, and a common vision of a united Korea's international role;
—the creation of a new political elite.

A unified Korea will need a joint, coherent, and unified political elite within a pluralistic political system. Obviously, it will take time to educate and recruit new political leaders and thus create an elite for the peninsula that is diverse enough to represent the truly pluralistic societal structure of the new Korea but also unified enough to provide good governance and stability even if majorities change as is customary in a democracy. Practically none of the members of the old East German political elite is in a leadership position in the new Germany. East German political leaders either are of the new generation or have had a nontraditional background in the old communist regime. This is true for the PDS as well. An almost complete exchange of political elites in East Germany was unavoidable in the German case.

Obviously, there is a lot for Korea to learn from Germany's unification experience. The most important lesson might be that shock therapy and gradualism are not mutually exclusive. Both are necessary and can be used rather successfully as long as South and North Korea can control the chain of events once the pressure is on to unify. If collapse of the North is the determining factor, then the German experience is a rather interesting model to follow but not necessarily to copy. The economic and financial aspect of German unification in particular could have been managed better. The one-to-one exchange rate was clearly a mistake economically, even though politically, however, it was a benefit to Chancellor Kohl and the electoral prospects of the Christian Democratic Party in the East. Social integration was less successful in spite of rather generous social programs for retirees and the unemployed. Those in need did receive material support. However, the sense of failure and loss among those who grew up under communist rule and depended on the system for their well-being was hard to overcome. This mental hurdle of unification will be much more pronounced in Korea. *Juche* philosophy and a rather broad-based communist party in the North, little exposure to the outside world, and deep wounds from civil war will make the task of internal unification in Korea even harder than it was in Germany.

Korea will need international support for its unification and reconciliation process. Although the German 2+4 example is based on a different legal framework, a four-power procedure to guide the Korean-unification process would be quite appropriate. The United States, China, Japan, and Russia play important roles as crucial partners of the two Koreas. To define Korea's future international role and status through a 2+4 process could help to make Korean unification more acceptable in the region.[30] Since a unified Korea would be an important power in Northeast Asia, an effort to help define its international role could only benefit the stability of the unification process.

---

30. For a discussion of the 2+4 process in the context of Korean unification, see Yeo In-Kon, *Is the German 2+4 Process Applicable to the Korean Peninsula?* a paper presented at the Korean-European Conference, "Change on the Korean Peninsula: The Relevance of Europe" of the Korea Institute for National Unification (KINU), the Friedrich-Ebert-Stiftung, and the EU Delegation in South Korea, Seoul, June 12–19, 2001.

North Korean Defectors: A Window into a Reunified Korea

Kelly Koh and Glenn Baek

Introduction

Since the end of the Korean War (1950–53), defectors from the North, or *talbukja*, have braved bullets, hunger, and stormy seas to reach the South.[1] Once they arrive, however, their arduous journey is far from over. For many North Koreans, arriving in the bustling, cosmopolitan South is like landing on another planet. With just over 1,000 North Korean defections to South Korea since Kim Il-Sung's death in 1994, reports of defectors' problematic adjustment have become increasingly common.

Defectors complain that they are treated like second-class citizens, sometimes worse than foreign guest workers who perform menial labor in South Korea. Yet for both North and South Koreans, adjustment difficulties are surprising. Interviewed North Korean defectors have said

---

In addition to literature reviews and research, this chapter is based on interviews with South Korean government officials and North Korean defectors in South Korea from 1998 to 1999. Defectors' names have been altered to protect their identity. The views expressed in this chapter are those of the authors, and do not represent those of the U.S. government or the Department of State.

1. According to Vladislav Krasnov, the word "defector" came into common use only after World War II. It was used to distinguish Soviet soldiers who went over to the West from the millions of refugees in the West. Those who coined the word apparently sought to suggest that if these soldiers were not quite traitors, there was still something defective about them. To many, defection implies a "defect" or someone who is "defective." For further discussion of terminology, see U.S. Congress, Senate Committee on Governmental Affairs, *Federal Government's Handling of Soviet and Communist Bloc Defectors*, 100th Congress, 1st session, 8–9, October 21, 1987. For the purposes of this chapter, "defectors" are defined as those who have fled communist regimes in violation of the law in order to take refuge in another country. See Vladislav Krasnov, *Soviet Defectors: The KGB Wanted List* (Stanford: Hoover Institution Press, 1986), p. 161.

that they expected acceptance and belonging in the South and were completely unprepared to deal with the reality. South Koreans, on the other hand, assumed that North Koreans would be able to adapt easily given similarities in language, culture, and a mutual history dating back centuries.

No longer feted as national heroes, these days defectors are more often viewed as public burdens or political liabilities. Indeed, opinion polls indicate that South Korea's welcome mat is fraying. A 1998 survey of 2,000 respondents, conducted by the Citizens Coalition for National Reconciliation, in association with *Joongang Ilbo*, reported that 28 percent supported selective admission whereas 22 percent said that defectors should be kept out of the country altogether.[2] Although previously unthinkable, generational change and the reluctance to endure economic sacrifices to support 23 million North Koreans have been reflected in the growing desire to put off reunification. Increasing numbers of young people, lacking the nostalgia and yearning of previous generations, wonder why there must be reunification at all.[3]

Most South Korean scholars and officials concur that the adjustment experience of North Korean defectors in the South offers a preview of the potential problems involved in integrating North Koreans into a reunified Korea. Similarly, the government's difficulty in successfully integrating the 1,188 defectors[4] living in the South reveals some of the challenges likely to arise from larger, more disruptive inflows in the future.

Historically, laws regulating the treatment and resettlement of North Korean defectors have focused on utilizing defectors for short-term propagandistic gain rather than facilitating successful integration into South Korean society. Reports of defectors' problematic adjustment, including increasing cases of unemployment, crime, and suicide, indicate that more needs to be done. While the historic June 2000 summit in Pyongyang and a renewed spirit of inter-Korean cooperation provide

---

2. "Results of the Survey on Citizens' Attitudes Toward Reunification," a report of the Citizen Coalition for National Reconciliation, December 7, 1998.

3. In an essay on the cultural aspects of reunification, Cho Hae-Joang notes that college students have become increasingly indifferent, passive, and doubtful about the eventuality of reunification. She also cites a survey of high school students in which 45 percent said that reunification is no longer a must. "A Discourse on the Cultural Aspects of North-South Korean Unification: The Cultural Homogeneity and Heterogeneity of 'Puk (North) Chosun' and 'Nam (South) Han,' Nationalism and Progressivism," Ministry of Unification, 1997.

4. There are 1,118 defectors living in the South as of December 2000. The White Paper 2001, chapters 4–5, see www.unikorea.go.kr.

hope for improved relations and new possibilities, an examination of the evolution of South Korean government policies toward North Korean defectors, and their adjustment experience, offers a sobering reminder of the formidable challenges that await a reunified Korea.

The Bitter Legacy of Division: Sowing Seeds of Enmity and Mistrust

Cold-war policies and postures of the North and South Korean governments have largely influenced the relations and levels of understanding between the peoples of the two Koreas. In the struggle for legitimacy after the Korean War, both governments marshaled a significant investment of national resources toward demonization of the other side, inevitably affecting the level of trust, kinship, and respect among peoples. Political leaders sought to consolidate their power and control by exploiting the national security issue at the expense of genuine efforts to reunify. In the South, any unauthorized contact with the North was punishable under the National Security Law, including possession of North Korean materials and publications, phone calls, exchanges of letters, and visits. Even little children were indoctrinated with school lessons depicting North Koreans as "monsters" ready to devour the South.

In the post-cold-war era, continuing military incidents involving North Korea—spy cases, seaborn incursions, and a missile launch over Japan—have kept the region on alert. The South Korean media have often reported that North Korea spends 25–30 percent of its GDP expenditures on the military; that a 1.1-million-man army stands forward deployed along the DMZ; and that the regime engages in international terrorism, sales of ballistic missiles, and the development of a nuclear program that threatens the entire Asia-Pacific region. Given a lack of positive representations of the North, some South Koreans wonder why their government should offer food aid to a nation seemingly intent on their country's destruction, or why North Korean defectors should be privileged with more assistance than the poorest and most vulnerable South Korean citizens.

While South Koreans have come to fear North Korea's militarism, they have also come to dread its sudden collapse, especially in the aftermath of the South's own recent economic crisis and the high price tag of German reunification. According to South Korean figures, as the South's per capita income reached the $10,000 benchmark in 1995, North Korea's was less than $1,000. In terms of reunification, the Institute for International Economics (IIE) estimated in 1996 that more than $700 billion would have to be invested in North Korea to achieve some level of income parity with the South and deter massive migration. Furthermore, the IIE forecasted double this figure by the year 2000 and every five years after that. South Korea, meanwhile, estimated that it could afford only about $40–50 billion per year in deficit and private-sector financing without risking its own economic collapse.[5]

Defectors are sensitive to the deeply discrediting effect of this historical legacy. They understand that many South Koreans see little value in the North and fear that after reunification, any North Korean achievements will be discarded. Some conservative thinkers in the South further reinforce the view that North Korean defectors have nothing to offer and question whether they should even be allowed to live in the South, as they did nothing to end military dictatorship or rebuild the economy.[6] On the other hand, scholars such as Cho Hae-Joang have asserted that reunification devoid of mutual understanding and an acceptance of differences can only expect to parallel the disruption and dislocation of the Korean War and herald the beginning of another kind of division.

Background on North Korean Defection

Over the past several decades, defectors have constituted a unique source of information about North Korea's relatively closed systems. They have contributed to the education of South Korean government officials and scholars by bringing to life information on sociocultural customs, intelligence on the North Korean leadership, and the psychology of the people. Though much has been learned about the isolated North, little information is available about the factors and circumstances that have shaped defectors' adaptation, experience, and environment in the South. This

---

5. Projections of reunification costs vary widely according to the assumptions made about the reality of the North Korean situation and the timetable for a merger, among other factors. Hwang Jang-Yop, for instance, estimated that the cost of reunification, had it occurred in 2000, would have been $1.5 trillion, almost double South Korea's projected economic output for that year. See Andrew Browne, "The Frightening Costs of Korean Unification," Reuters, July 10, 1996.

6. Roy Richard Grinker. *Korea and Its Futures: Unification and the Unfinished War* (New York: St. Martin's Press, 1998), p. 253.

section, therefore, reviews basic characteristics and patterns of North Korean defection to South Korea.

Patterns of Defection

Experiences of North Korean defectors show that their adjustment to life in the South is influenced by a multiplicity of factors, including age, marital status, motivation for leaving, size of family, class background, occupation, level of education, and the political, social, and economic conditions in both North and South Korea at the time of defection. As a result, defection may be most usefully considered not just as a single, finite act, but as an ongoing process.

According to the ROK Ministry of Unification (MOU), by the end of 2000, 1,470 North Koreans had defected to the South.[7] Of this number, 282 have either died or emigrated, leaving 1,188 defectors currently living in the South as of December 2000. The latest data available further indicate that in 2001, a record 583 additional defectors have arrived. Figures 1a and 1b summarize the number of defections to South Korea from 1970 to 2000.

MOU statistics also reveal that defectors are becoming younger and more female as a result of greater numbers of family members arriving together.[8] In 1997 the average age of defectors was thirty-two. That same year, fifty-six out of eighty-six defectors came in families. Although being young and arriving with other family members tends to help adjustment to life in the South, the arrival of larger groups has also sparked the fear of mass exodus from the North. In 1996, reports of eighty-four North Koreans stranded at sea, mostly women and children, caused widespread speculation that they constituted the first tide of North Korean "boat people."[9]

North Korean defectors, as a group, are drawn from all walks of life and all levels of education, occupation, age, and motivation, including scholars, scientists, government officials, spies, soldiers, ath-

---

7. MOU White Paper, May 2001. Government data on North Korean defectors are subject to strategic omissions considered necessary for national security. In 1997, for instance, a parliamentary report disclosed that ninety ranking North Korean defectors have been under government "special protection" for decades. The report further stated that their identities would not be made public in keeping with the NIS's "guidelines for personal safety."

8. Sixty percent of defectors arriving in 2000 were male and 40 percent female in contrast to past years when defectors were 90 percent male.

9. Kim Tang, "Over 4 Million People May Escape in Event of Emergency," *Seoul Sisa Journal*, December 19, 1996.

Figure 1a   **Defections by Decade (1970–1999)**

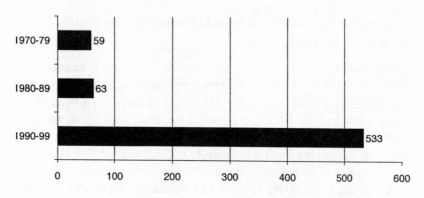

Figure 1b   **Number of Defectors (1990–2001)**

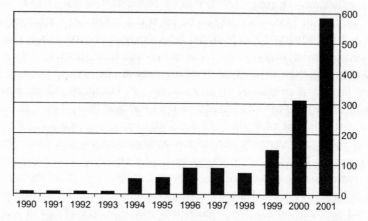

Source: ROK Ministry of Unification, 2000.

letes, and performing artists. A review of defection patterns since 1990 reveals that the number of soldiers and spies, who previously constituted the majority of defectors, declined, whereas the number of government officials, civilians, loggers, and students has increased significantly (see Table 1). From 1948 to 1989, 40 percent (244) of defectors were soldiers and 60 percent (363) were civilians. However, from 1990 to 1997, the number of civilians defecting rose to 94 percent (338), whereas soldiers fell to 6 percent (22).[10] Of the 312 defectors who arrived in

---

10. "More Civilians, Less Soldiers Defecting from DPRK," *Yonhap*, March 8, 1999.

Table 1

Pre-Defection Occupations of North Koreans (1990–July 2001)

Occupation	Numbers	%
Laborer, farmer	463	44.1
Student, unemployed	409	39.0
Overseas trader, diplomat	70	6.7
Party official, instructor	68	6.4
Soldier	37	3.5
Spy/Infiltrator	3	0.3

Source: ROK Ministry of Unification, July 2001.

2000, 49 percent were laborers, 18 percent were students, and 16 percent were unemployed.

A noticeable increase has occurred in the number of high-profile defections. In 1997 the South Korean government was thrilled when Hwang Jang-Yop, the principal architect of *Juche*, became the highest-ranking North Korean official ever to defect to the South. Other high-profile cases of defection include Hong Soon-Kyong, counselor at the DPRK embassy in Bangkok, and the Berlin-based diplomat Kim Gyong-Kil in 1999. Though Hwang's escape required a stay in the Philippines, other North Korean defectors have made their way to the South using routes through Russia, China, Cambodia, Thailand, Vietnam, Hong Kong, and Mongolia.

Defectors offer a variety of reasons for leaving the North: personal and family reasons, hatred of the North Korean system, fear of repression, hope for a better life, pursuit of freedom, and economic considerations (see Table 2). Vladislav Krasnov, in one of the first systematic studies of defection, emphasized that the decision to defect usually involves a number of reasons: ideological and political, religious and moral, ethical and aesthetic, national and personal, noble and petty, altruistic and egotistical, reasons of ambition and vanity, curiosity, and adventure.[11] According to a 1995 MOU study, about 72 percent of North Korean defectors in the 1960s said that they fled for ideological and political reasons.

---

11. Krasnov, *Soviet Defectors,* p. 161.

Table 2

Reasons Cited for Defection to the South

Sample Size of 1,130 (as of July 2001)

Reasons	Number
Difficulties in livelihood	226
Fearful of punishment	219
Disillusioned with the DPRK's system	214
Dependent	194
To seek freedom	168
Aversion to serving in the military	44
"Spy" who turned himself in	41
Committed crime	24

Source: ROK Ministry of Unification.

By this, they mean that they had in some way violated anti-state laws, by either speaking out against the North Korean regime, defacing an image of their leaders, or committing a felony such as fraud or theft. Others say they defected because of an unwitting mistake, for example, accidentally receiving Voice of America broadcasts, committing an error in the construction of a building, being a member of a military group whose leader (and therefore the entire group) is convicted of a crime that would have led them and their families to be imprisoned.[12]

In the 1980s, defectors cited more personal motives, such as ill treatment by the North Korean regime, possessing a faulty background, desire to defect with family members, and fear of punishment. In the 1990s, they gave reasons such as dissatisfaction with their treatment, delinquency, and again, fear of being punished. The most recent flows of North Korean defectors have begun to cite severe food shortages as their chief motivation. South Korean civic groups estimate that as many as 2–3 million North Koreans have died due to starvation and famine-related diseases.[13]

Since 1999, unprecedented numbers of North Koreans have been

---

12. Grinker, *Korea and Its Futures,* p. 266.

13. Chronic flooding and drought, among other factors, have led to severe food shortages, leaving most North Koreans dependent on international humanitarian assistance. See www.wfp.org and www.nis.go.kr for more information about the famine.

streaming into the South. Experts attribute this surge in defections to famine and economic difficulties in the DPRK, a greater willingness by the Kim Dae-Jung administration to accept defectors, more active South Korean civic and religious organizations working to resettle North Korean refugees living in northeastern China, and an expanded number of countries through which one can enter South Korea. Although the MOU estimates that there are 2,000–3,000 North Koreans in third countries, South Korean civic groups contend that there are as many 200,000–300,000 North Korean refugees.[14] The presence of large numbers of North Korean refugees or economic migrants suggests that the number of defections to the South will only accelerate in the years to come. In a survey of 1,383 North Korean refugees in three northeastern regions in China, 82 percent indicated that they wanted to come to the South.[15] Although the ROK government's official policy is to accept all North Korean defectors who apply for asylum, in reality, it lacks the resources to accept them.

South Korean Government Policies Toward North Korean Defectors

Over the years, laws regarding the treatment of North Korean defectors have been amended to reflect changing circumstances, each revision further shaping and impacting the adjustment process of defectors. During the early stages of the cold war, the South Korean government encouraged defections from the North in an effort to gain symbolic advantage over the North. As a result, any North Korean who defected during this era was unabashedly touted as *yongsa* (a national hero) and was accorded the same social status and privileges accorded descendants of Korean heroes who had fought for independence from Japan. According to the South Korean Constitution, North Koreans who defect have their ROK citizenship "restored."

---

14. The number of North Koreans living abroad varies widely according to the assumptions made about their status (i.e., refugee, economic migrant, etc.) and motivations. Further adding to the complexity is the Chinese government's position that North Koreans are illegal immigrants who have temporarily crossed the border in search of food and therefore cannot be categorized as "refugees" according to the 1951 Geneva Convention Relating to the Status of Refugees.

15. Kim In-Ku, "Eighty Percent of North Korean Refugees Want to Come to South Korea," *Choson Ilbo*, February 11, 2000.

The first law pertaining to North Korean defectors, "The Special Law to Protect Those Who Contributed to the Country and North Korean Defectors," was passed in 1962. The law divided defectors into three grades based on prior social status in the North and provided *jung chak geum* (resettlement payments) accordingly. Once defectors are vetted and finish their training at a government-run facility, they are given resettlement payments to cover housing and basic living expenses.

In 1978, the South Korean government passed the "Special Compensation Law for Brave Soldiers" that divided defectors into five grades according to the level of *gongjuk* (merit) each possessed. This expanded law provided defectors with free housing, educational benefits, welfare payments, and medical assistance. It also allowed former North Korean soldiers and civil servants to continue their careers in the employ of the South Korean government.

More recently, numerous factors, including the end of the cold war and the anticipation of mass defections from the North, have led to a decline in the prior attention given to North Korean defectors living in the South. In 1993 the government passed several amendments to the 1978 law. These changes included the responsibility of placing defectors with the Social Welfare Department in the Ministry of Health and Welfare and replacing the phrase "Special Compensation Law" with "Protection Law for North Korean Defectors." The law also stated that defector assistance will be "managed rationally" according to more stringent factors such as "benefit to national interests."[16] The government excluded criminals and those who had resided in a third country for a considerable period of time from protection and no longer provided free housing; instead, defectors became eligible to receive a one-time payment of 8.4 million won ($7,000) toward the rental fee of an apartment. In effect, standard defector resettlement payments were cut drastically from a level of 40 to 50 million won ($30,000 to $40,000) to 17 million won ($14,000)—and then further reduced to 15 million won ($12,500).

This reduced financial support has untethered the social safety net for defectors, dramatically increasing their reliance on public welfare. The Ministry of Health and Social Welfare has estimated that up to 70

---

16. "Special Compensation Law for Brave Soldiers," June 11, 1993, Articles 792.6–792.10, ROK National Assembly.

percent of North Korean defectors are in financial trouble. Some defectors have been forced to subsist on a monthly income of between 400,000 won and 800,000 won ($300 to $600), an amount insufficient to feed, educate, and clothe themselves and their family.

In an attempt to cope with the sharp increase in North Korean defectors since 1994, the MOU sought to "overhaul" defector laws by shifting the focus more toward education and job training than financial compensation. The MOU also conducted a tentative policy review to consider accepting only those North Koreans who did not commit crimes in third countries while awaiting admission to South Korea and whose special "merits" obliged the South to accept them. By May 1995, it was reported that the government considered it "meaningless to unconditionally allow in North Korean defectors as Seoul did during the Cold War age,"[17] indicating there may be further efforts to place restrictions on acceptable conditions for entry.

In 1997 the government passed the "Protection of Defecting North Korean Residents and Support for Their Settlement Act" (Settlement Act). This law entitles defectors to one year of support in a protection facility and two years at their own residence. It also establishes a "Consultative Council of Defecting North Korean Residents" that, along with the unification minister, determines whether a defector is entitled to governmental protection. The Settlement Act places final authority on the unification minister to expedite applications and reach a decision. This law also enables the government to provide temporary protection even before a decision is made and allows defectors to receive their resettlement subsidy in installments instead of one lump sum.

Furthermore, this law also provides for the establishment of *Hanawon*, a university-style camp for 500 defectors where they can be housed, educated, and trained in English, computers, and driving. Defectors will be placed in this facility for an obligatory three-month program and then an optional six-to eight-month job-training course afterwards. Belatedly, this is the first time a training program for defectors will be adapted to take into account individual talent and aptitude, yet graduates have reported that the training they received is useless.[18] This $12-million facility, with an annual budget of $10 million, is based on the government's recognition that the majority of North Korean defectors in the country experi-

---

17. Yi Pyong-Kwan, "Background on the Government's Overall Plan Concerning North Korean Refugees," *Kyonghyang Shinmun,* May 1, 1995.

18. *Choson Ilbo,* "Defectors from DPRK Call ROK Reorientation Center a 'Waste,' "April 27, 2001.

ence language problems, are jobless or have simple labor jobs, and are unable to adapt to capitalist society.

The 1997 law also transferred some of the exclusive powers of the National Intelligence Service (NIS) to the MOU.[19] For more than thirty years, South Korea's intelligence arm has had great latitude and influence on the formulation and implementation of government policy regarding defectors with little possible impact from other government agencies or sectors of society. This law also merged defector-related programs—previously distributed among the Ministries of Education, Labor, Health, and Foreign Affairs and Trade—under the MOU, reflecting a growing understanding that the problems of North Korean defectors require more comprehensive, intragovernmental cooperation. This new interministerial body, headed by the vice unification minister, is empowered to accept or deny applications for asylum from North Koreans who have reached South Korean territory or its overseas missions. It also makes decisions on the length of time North Korean defectors should stay in accommodation facilities before joining South Korean society.

The Settlement Act further states that the unification minister is responsible for administering a settlement facility for regular defectors whereas those defectors that "involve significant hazards to national security" will be kept in a facility operated by the director of the NIS. Specifically, the intelligence agency has purview over defectors who have worked inside the North Korean government or security agencies. This group also includes spouses or relatives of high-level North Korean leaders.

In response to the worsening social and economic problems experienced by North Korean defectors, the South Korean government revised the Settlement Act in December 1998, increasing resettlement funds from 15 million won ($12,740) to 38 million won ($31,845) per person.[20] Although guidelines set the resettlement payments to twenty times the minimum wage (approximately 344,650 won in 1994), this revision reflects eighty times the minimum wage (361,600 won). Those defectors who arrived between December 1993 and December 1998 are ex-

---

19. The NIS was formerly known as the National Security Planning Agency (NSPA) and the Korean Central Intelligence Agency (KCIA).

20. *Handbook on Detection of North Korean Defectors*, published by the MOU, March 6, 2000, p. 3. In addition to the basic resettlement payment, the government provides supplemental payment to those who are under eighteen and over sixty; considered "special care cases"; or disabled. Currently, the first two groups receive $3,000, and the third group receives $6,000.

Table 3

Defector Resettlement Payments (Basic Pay and One-time Housing Subsidy)

Exchange Rate Used: 1,200 KW = 1 USD

Category	1993–1998	1998–Present
A (8+ people)	17,220 + 9,625 = 26,845	48,000 + 13,125 = 61,125
B (5–7 people)	14,350 + 7,000 = 21,350	42,000 + 10,500 = 52,500
C (3–4 people)	11,480 + 7,000 = 18,480	36,000 + 8,750 = 44,750
D (2 people)	8,610 + 7,000 = 15,610	30,000 + 7,845 = 37,845
E (1 person)	5,740 + 7,000 = 12,740	24,000 + 7,845 = 31,845

Source: ROK Ministry of Unification, March 2000.

cluded from eligibility (see Table 3).

Additional government measures include the decision to recognize academic careers and vocational licenses that defectors acquired in the North or in third countries and to send twenty South Korean officials to as many as sixteen former communist states on an annual basis in order to learn more about socialist administration. Government ministries have also begun to support a program that encourages social and religious organizations to form close bonds with defectors. Though the South Korean government has undoubtedly improved some of its policies toward defectors, most of these changes reflect efforts to rectify and stem serious problems associated with them, such as inadequate training, education, acculturation, and financial support. Given that the government's policies may one day shape and reflect the future conditions under which millions of people will coexist, greater foresight, attention, and preparation are necessary.

Challenges of Integration

Despite frequent reports of defection in the South Korean media, few citizens have ever personally encountered a North Korean defector, owing to national security concerns, especially in the past. Until 1990, the government routinely provided defectors with five years of police protection; this has been reduced to a period of two years. While under government custody, defectors were given tours of Seoul's showplaces—high-end department stores, tourist attractions, and productive, efficient factories—then placed in temporary government housing until released. They complained, however, that such tours did little to help them prepare to live independently in the South or find a job. Once this protection ends, some defectors admit to feeling abandoned because they are not well acquainted with South Koreans other than various security personnel.

Although a few defectors have prospered in the South as professors, comedians, singers, and small business owners, the majority find themselves bewildered by their new surroundings and suffer from depression, job failure, and regrets about leaving North Korea. Even defectors armed with some knowledge of the South before arrival experience psychological trauma—feelings of guilt, suicide, and nightmares. Mr. Cho, a former North Korean commando whose mission it was to infiltrate the South, told us that despite years of training, he was shocked by the differences he confronted. Indeed, mental health experts believe that the majority of North Korean defectors experience psychological difficulties that are often left unrecognized and untreated.

Defectors report a myriad of difficulties, from obtaining gainful employment, managing money, and finding marriage partners to deciphering signs written in English or Chinese characters.[21] In an environment where one's life chances are intimately connected to social standing, family background, educational achievement, and school ties, North Koreans find it hard to compete in the South. Several defectors we interviewed were advised to marry as soon as possible in order to accelerate their adjustment, but many defectors feel as if they have nothing to offer either their adopted homeland or potential marriage partners. In encounters with South Koreans, moreover, they confront a range of negative stereotypes and complain of discrimination, enmity, hostility, and indifference. They are also often accused of being without virtue, abandoning their filial responsibilities, and lacking any sense of loyalty.

The adjustment experience for defectors is also compounded by the fear of attack or mistreatment. According to a NIS survey, more than 96 percent of 456 North Korean defectors suffer from lingering fears of revenge attacks, and 65 percent have actually been threatened by unknown people.[22] Moreover, in early 2000, nine defectors sued South Korea's intelligence agency, charging that

---

21. Although Korean is the official language of both North Korea and South Korea, defectors report language difficulties because of English and Chinese characters commonly used throughout South Korea. In the North, use of Korean does not include foreign characters or words.

22. Kim Hyoung-Min, "North Korean Defectors Fear Terrorism," *Korea Times*, October 20, 1998, p. 1.

agents included torture during interrogation sessions after their arrival.[23]

Several defectors we spoke to expressed the desire to leave the South as soon as they are able to do so despite the enormous sacrifices and risks taken to reach its shores. Mr. Kim, a twenty-year-old university student who arrived in South Korea with four other family members after a harrowing journey through China, expressed his hope that by living in the United States or elsewhere, he could escape the baggage of being North Korean and the high pressure to belong and excel. According to a Korean Education Development Institute study of seventy students that defected, 43.1 percent said they wanted to start a new life where no one knew of their origins.[24]

Arkady Shevchenko, a former United Nations undersecretary general who defected from the USSR to the United States, reflects the sentiment of the majority of defectors interviewed for this study in calling for greater understanding:

> [W]e have to understand better the agonizing ordeal of the defector. The psychological state of mind of a person, who has decided to break with his past, his traditions, his family, his compatriots, and his familiarity with his culture, is fragile. . . . Delicate care and tact are needed to help him cross the line and adjust to a new life.[25]

Economic Adjustment

Many South Korean scholars agree that defectors are representative of the North Korean population in terms of their restricted economic opportunities and marketable skills once transplanted to the South Korean context. Although people in the South assume that North Korean defectors are financially well off because of the resettlement payments they receive, data on defector occupations as of July 2001 reveal that more than 20 percent are unemployed (see Table 4).

Although employment and education are guaranteed in Articles 8 and 9 of the 1993 "Protection Law for North Korean Defectors," many have difficulty holding down jobs. Unaccustomed to competition in the workplace, they find it hard to get along with colleagues who often resent the defectors not pulling their weight. Those hired to perform clerical or other

---

23. Calvin Sims, "Life in South Hard for North Koreans," *New York Times*, April 24, 2000.
24. Seo Hyun-Jin, "United in Spirit, But Worlds Apart," *Korea Now*, November 4, 2000.
25. Arkady N. Shevchenko, *New Statesman*, vol. 110, no. 2850 (November 8, 1985), p. 18.

Table 4

Current Occupations of 1,040 Defectors (As of July 2001)

Occupation	Numbers	%
White-collar worker	162	15.6
Researcher	22	2.1
Self-employed	65	6.3
Public servant/military	11	1.1
Student	147	14.1
Laborer	67	6.4
Child	16	1.5
Elderly	81	7.8
Unemployed	228	21.9
Unaccounted	55	5.3
In Training/protection	186	17.9
Total	1,040	100.0

Source: ROK Ministry of Unification.

menial office jobs often lack the necessary language or computer skills. In addition, frequent invitations to give anticommunist lectures have also discouraged defectors from adapting to routine office work. Some have argued that these lecture fees, often higher than regular wages, hamper the development of sound job attitudes. In order to avoid these workplace difficulties and to attain the social acceptance and respect wealth bestows, a number of defectors have started their own small businesses.[26]

Concerned about the high unemployment rate among defectors, in 2000 the government implemented the "Directive for the Job Protection of North Korean Defectors." This plan, implemented by the Ministry of Labor, provides incentives to local businesses who hire defectors by offering up to 700,000 won ($583) or 50 percent of an employee's monthly wages.[27] The government also moved to allow defectors to practice professional skills acquired in the North through a special certification program and provides regular job counseling at forty-six government centers across the country.

---

26. Many of the defectors, who have chosen to start their own businesses, have entered the restaurant industry specializing in "authentic North Korean" cuisine—notably *Naeng-myun* (buckwheat noodles).

27. Kim Min-Hee, "Public Job Centers to Help Out North Korean Defectors, *Korea Herald*, February 25, 2000. To qualify for the plan, defectors must have arrived in the South after 1994 and be employed more than fifteen days a month.

Defectors' adjustment difficulties have been further reflected in the rising number of crimes committed by North Korean defectors. According to South Korean figures, twenty cases of illegal activity were recorded during the 1970s and 1980s. Between 1997 and 1998, however, this number jumped to forty-four, and in 1999 alone, fifty-five crimes were reported.[28] The most desperate and troubled defectors have attempted redefection or have resorted to suicide. Nevertheless, several defectors interviewed believe that North Koreans, as a whole, are a very proud and tough people and would eventually endure. As an example of this tenacity and will to survive, one defector recalled how North Korea imported garbage from Germany so it could recycle every last piece of it.

Not All Created Equal

A number of the defectors we interviewed possessed a strong sense of equality and believed that the government should treat all defectors equally. They resent the South Korean government's "defection arithmetic"—the practice of calculating resettlement payments based on defectors' prior social status and the value of any intelligence relevant to national security. In their eyes, those most responsible for keeping the North Korean regime afloat are the ones most handsomely rewarded by the South after defection, while those with little "value" are given a small payment and then left largely to fend for themselves. This manner of determining compensation led one defector to claim that the same class system they lived in under North Korea has been reproduced among defectors in the South. Defectors report that the practice of ranking defectors into different categories has served to evoke jealousy and comparison. A twenty-two-year-old former North Korean soldier angrily expressed these thoughts:

> How did these elite North Koreans obtain their high positions? They sucked the lifeblood out of ordinary North Koreans, benefited at their expense, and only egged on the South Koreans while in their former positions. They also created and directed the policies we had to follow. Yet they come here and are rewarded more handsomely than those of us who toiled like animals.[29]

---

28. MOU estimate in 1998. See D. Peter Kim, "Death of a Dream," *NEWSREVIEW*, November 7, 1998.

29. Mr. Oh, age twenty-two, arrived April 1994, interviewed by authors, June 20, 1998.

According to Article 40 of Presidential Executive Order No. 15436, dated July 14, 1997, those who supply information deemed valuable to national security can receive up to 250 million won ($210,000) and those who bring with them military equipment can receive up to 150 million won ($125,000). These figures are not fixed, however, for defectors have been given awards in excess of these prescribed sums. Hwang Jang-Yop, for example, was awarded 300 million won ($250,000) and North Korean pilot Yi Chol-Su was paid 480 million won ($400,000) when he defected with his MiG-19 fighter jet in 1996.[30]

The Sunshine Policy and Defectors: Growing Liabilities

In pursuing implementation of the Sunshine Policy, the Kim Dae-Jung administration has been negotiating a delicate balance between affording North Korean defectors their civil liberties and maximizing possibilities of détente with the DPRK regime. Formerly, when North Korean defectors arrived in the South, it had been customary for them to hold an NIS-organized press conference to describe their plight in the North and express gratitude for their newfound freedom. However, under the Kim Dae-Jung administration, this practice has all but disappeared, making it difficult for the press to obtain information or ask questions of new arrivals. Pundits have speculated that this lack of publicity apparently reflects the ROK government's desire to avoid any potential political embarrassment that might upset North-South relations.

After the June summit, one Korean newspaper reported that the NIS "asked" defectors not to give media interviews or cause problems for the peace process. Furthermore, in the June 2000 issue of a magazine published by an association of defectors, an article critical of North Korean leader Kim Jong-Il was pulled at the last minute, but the front-page headline embarrassingly remained when published.[31]

Hwang Jang-Yop, one of the most vocal critics of the North Korean government, has written scathingly about the North since his arrival. Recently, he accused the NIS of restricting his public activities, including contacts with politicians and journalists. According to media reports, the government is loath to let Hwang travel despite his acceptance of an invitation to speak before a U.S. congressional audience. The intelligence agency also reportedly stripped him of his position as chairman of a

---

30. "Forgotten Heroes," *Economist*, February 14, 1998, pp. 42–43.
31. Choi Byong-Mook, "NIS Gags Defectors," *Choson Ilbo*, August 6, 2000.

NIS-run research institute and threatened to expel him from a government safehouse.[32] After more than a week of bitter protest by Hwang and opposition legislators, the government rescinded its decision. His supporters claim that, although Hwang's criticism against North Korea served the government's purposes in the past, it has become a burden to an administration seeking to achieve historic breakthroughs in inter-Korean relations.

Preparing for Reunification: The Role and Participation of NGOs

The NIS's long tradition of managing each defector's debriefing and resettlement process has discouraged civil, church, and social organizations from establishing direct contact with defectors and has served to exacerbate defectors' feelings of isolation. However, as resettlement responsibilities have shifted to the MOU in recent years, more concerted nongovernmental assistance programs have begun to emerge.

South Korean church groups have been among the first to develop programs that assist defectors. Several defectors interviewed said that they or their friends had converted to Christianity because they enjoyed the sense of community found in church. One defector commented that the few times he attended church, the worship and ritual reminded him of. home. Other defectors said that church groups were the only ones interested in getting to know them.

In a 1998 study of 113 South Korean religious, civic, academic, social welfare, and media organizations, researchers found that 11 ran programs specifically geared toward North Korean defectors.[33] These NGOs viewed one of their roles as developing the means to accommodate larger inflows of North Korean refugees as preparation for reunification. The Citizens' Alliance to Help Political Prisoners in North Korea, the leading advocacy organization for North Korean defectors, with 110 volun-

---

32. Charles Lee, "North Korean Defector Sacked by Intelligence Agency," UPI, November 23, 2000. It is probable that Hwang could suffer bodily harm if he leaves the safehouse, as Kim Jong-Il reportedly ordered his assassination after he defected. Hwang's supporters cite the mysterious circumstances of defector Lee Han-Yong's death in 1997 as an example. Lee, a relative of Kim, was found murdered near his home. The assailant has yet to be found.

33. Kim Dong-Bae and Lee Ki-Young, "Situation Regarding Civic Group Support for North Korean Defectors," paper presented at Yonsei University, Conference on Reunification and the Role of NGOs, November 1998.

teers, works to improve the human rights situation of the people in the North as well as those who have fled the country. The types of assistance provided by organizations like these consist of offering material assistance such as food, housing, tuition, and health care, and nonmaterial assistance such as job counseling, matchmaking, and religious guidance. Unfortunately, most of these organizations are poorly funded and overstretched. Moreover, few allow defectors' input into the planning and evaluation of programs.

In the past several years, academic institutions have also begun to serve as a source of facilitating interaction with North Korean defectors through regular discussion groups and retreats. These fora serve to humanize North Koreans and allow defectors to share their knowledge and experiences. They further allow South Korean participants to learn about the differences between the two countries, to separate fact from fiction, and to develop greater mutual understanding.

Conclusion

> *This is a dress rehearsal for reunification. This shows that we can't just tear down a wall like in Germany and let our Northern brethren come streaming across the border. We are not prepared to receive them, and they are not prepared for what they will find on the other side.*
>
> —Professor Lee Sang-Man[34]

Since the June 2000 summit between North Korean leader Kim Jong-Il and South Korean president Kim Dae-Jung, the two Koreas have begun collaborating on a number of joint projects, ranging from construction of an inter-Korean railroad, to incipient military-confidence-building measures, to the reunion of separated families. However, as North and South Korea explore new possibilities for increased cooperation and reconciliation, many defectors interviewed expressed skepticism about the government's commitment and ability to adequately accommodate North Koreans in a reunified Korea. A number of scholars and analysts have also come to doubt the government's ability to integrate millions of North Koreans, especially when it cannot sufficiently acculturate even

---

34. Sims, "Life in South Hard."

a fraction of them. Former ROK Vice Unification Minister Kim Suk-Woo gives voice to this sentiment by asserting that South Koreans "don't even have the right to talk about reunification if we are unable to accommodate the small number of North Korean defectors who exist today."[35]

Therefore, though South Korean government policies toward North Korean defectors have exhibited signs of improvement, persistent and continuing adjustment difficulties indicate that current measures fall short. It is clear that the acculturation of North Koreans into South Korean society will take a concerted and active partnership among all sectors of society—the government, religious and civic organizations, the South Korean citizenry, and North Korean defectors themselves. Moreover, if the adjustment experience of defectors is to improve, it will undoubtedly require greater mutual understanding; a more comprehensive social cushion consisting of sociopsychological and cultural assistance; more active involvement and outreach by community groups; improved collaboration between the government and defectors; and education of the South Korean public. Further research on defectors, both multifaceted and systematic, is also needed.

Numerous questions remain regarding the process of reunification and the practical, step-by-step process of acculturating 23 million North Koreans. Yet these issues need to be addressed in order to insure a reasonable degree of stability and harmony in a reunified Korea. In this process, North Korean defectors can contribute positively by expanding the dialogue and discourse on reunification. Many defectors we spoke with want to assist in the process of reunification, but feel dismissed or marginalized.

Today, though approximately 1,500 North Koreans might seem a small fraction of South Korea's 45 million citizens to be singled out and given the benefit of such attention and study, the government's treatment and understanding of this group will undoubtedly have enormous implications for millions who are likely to face similar, if not worse, adjustment difficulties in the future. The demise of the cold war and the growing numbers of defectors arriving in South Korea necessitate a new vision concerning the role and importance of North Korean defectors, one informed by greater expertise, attention, and sensitivity. It is hoped that in turn this will contribute to the peaceful process of reunification and the positive integration of the two societies and peoples.

---

35. Kim Suk-Woo, interviewed by authors on April 12, 2001, Washington, D.C.

July 1999–June 2001:
A Chronology

July 1999

29　The South Korean Ministry of Unification announces that South Korean professor Kim Soon-Kwon, known as the "corn doctor" for his work on corn cultivation, is currently in North Korea for a one-week visit. His trip had been postponed. North Korea had announced a temporary suspension of visits by South Korean citizens on June 16, immediately after the naval conflict in the West Sea.

August 1999

2　Japan and South Korea hold naval exercises in the East China Sea. The six-day exercise is the first joint military exercise between the two countries.

7　South Korea's Ministry of Unification announces that in this year reunions of families separated since the Korean War are increasingly taking place in third countries. From January to July this year, 122 South Korean citizens meet their North Korean family members, mainly in China.

9　The sixth-round meeting of four-party talks aimed at securing a permanent peace on the Korean peninsula ends without visible progress. The North Koreans re-iterate that the talks deal with their demand for the United States to withdraw its troops from South Korea.

Compiled and edited from issues of The U.S.-Korea Review published by The Korea Society, and from issues of the East Asian Review published by The Institute for East Asian Studies.

11　South Korea's National Intelligence Service confirms that North Korea had purchased 30 or so old MiG-21's from Kazakstan for $40 million.

16　The United States and South Korea begin the joint Ulchi Focus Lens military exercise involving warships, computer simulations, and thousands of soldiers.

17　A North Korean foreign ministry spokesman issues a statement criticizing Seoul's engagement policy, calling it "an absurd anti-national and anti-North intrigue."

23　Visiting South Korean defense minister Cho Sung-Tae and his Chinese counterpart, Chi Haotian, agree to the exchange of military personnel and the expansion of high-level military contacts.

27　A Russian military delegation visits South Korea in accordance with an agreement on the exchanges of military delegations made between the two parties last year.

30　Investigations show that 75.5 percent of displaced North Korean citizens who fled from North Korea to China are women. The displaced women had either been sold as slaves or forced into prostitution, and they had moved far away from the border in order to escape deportation to North Korea, South Korea's *Choson Ilbo* reports.

September 1999

1　The USS *Pueblo*, captured by North Korea on January 23, 1968, for spying off the coast of Wonsan, is now on display beside a bridge on the Taedong River in Pyongyang.

6　South Korean citizens who have met North Korean family members in a third country (usually China) have given an average of $1,345 to their family members, South Korea's *Joongang Ilbo* reports.

14   North Korean foreign minister Paek Nam-Sun visits New York to attend the Fifty-fourth UN General Assembly.

15   After hearing a briefing on the Perry Report, Benjamin Gilman, chairman of the U.S. House of Representatives Committee on International Relations, announces that he will oppose the U.S. administration's move to relax economic sanctions against North Korea.

19   North Korea has effectively completed the sealing up of 8,000 spent fuel rods at a reactor in Yongbyon and the removal of radioactive residue in the water in holding tanks, in conformity with requirements of the 1994 Agreed Framework.

25   North Korea will cease test launches of long-range missiles during talks with U.S. negotiators, according to the Korean Central News Agency (KCNA). The announcement comes on the heels of a much-publicized agreement between the United States and North Korea in which the U.S. eased strict trade, banking, and travel restrictions in exchange for the suspension of missile tests during negotiations. Restrictions against North Korea will be eased on:

- U.S. imports of raw materials and most goods made in North Korea
- Sales of most U.S. consumer goods and financial services to North Korea
- U.S. investment in agriculture, mining, petroleum, timber, transportation, road building, travel and tourism
- Direct financial help from U.S. citizens to relatives or other individual North Koreans
- U.S. transport of ordinary cargo to and from North Korea by ship and plane
- Commercial flights between the United States and North Korea

Restrictions remain on:
- Sales of U.S. weapons and missile-related technology
- Unlicensed export of "dual-use" goods or technology—items that could have military uses
- U.S. foreign aid, including help from the Peace Corps and the Export-Import Bank Act
- U.S. support for other international loans to North Korea
- Unauthorized financial transactions between U.S. individuals and the North Korean government. (Associated Press, *Los Angeles Times*, and USIA)

October 1999

1   The Pentagon, in an abrupt about-face, declared that it would use "whatever resources are available" to investigate whether U.S. infantrymen massacred more than 100 South Koreans in 1950 during the chaotic opening weeks of the Korean War. Although a recent army study found no basis for survivors' claims, Army Secretary Louis Caldera said new disclosures justify a "quick and thorough" study of the actions of 1st Cavalry Division troops at the rural hamlet of No Gun Ri, 100 miles southeast of Seoul. (*Los Angeles Times* & Associated Press)

North Korean leader Kim Jong-Il meets with Hyundai Group's honorary chairman Chung Ju-Yong and his son, Hyundai chairman Chung Mong-Hun.

5   President Kim Dae-Jung says that during the next three and a half years of his remaining term, he will complete the process of democratic development by promoting human rights, rooting out corruption and pushing through political reforms. As part of the drive to establish Korea as a nation advocating human rights and democracy, Kim pledges to carry out judicial reform, revise the National Security Law and the Broadcasting Law, and enact the Human Rights Law. (*Korea Times*)

Chinese foreign minister Tang Jiaxuan visits Pyongyang to join celebrations to mark the fiftieth anniversary of establishing diplomatic relations.

17 South Korean unification minister Lim Dong-Won announces the government's plan to accept all North Korean defectors who have been staying in other countries.

26 The annual South Korea–U.S. combined rear-area field-training exercise, Foal Eagle, begins. The U.S. aircraft carrier *Kitty Hawk*, and some 35,000 U.S. and 300,000 South Korean troops, join the drill.

29 A national rabbit fair and a symposium on rabbit cultivation are held in Pyongyang.

31 Fifty-five South Koreans, mainly high school students, are killed and seventy-five others are injured in a fire that trapped people inside a cramped, illegal beer hall in the port city of Inchon, thirty miles west of Seoul. Authorities say 97 of the 129 known victims were under the age of eighteen, the legal drinking age in Korea. The bar manager reportedly told his staff to lock the doors and not let the customers leave until they paid for their drinks. He then apparently left. The bar owner, Chung Sung-Gap, thirty-four, is arrested on charges of bribing officials and admitting minors into his bar. Following the fire, the National Police Agency (NPA) of Korea pronounces a series of measures to reform the deeply ingrained culture of collusion between police officers and bar/club owners. (*Los Angeles Times*, Associated Press, & *Korea Herald*)

November 1999

9 The FBI plans to open a liaison office in Seoul, FBI Director Louis Freeh says. The FBI was asked to establish a presence in Seoul by its South Korean counterpart, the National Police Agency, which already has a liaison office in Washington. As of late August,

42 percent of 631 South Korean fugitives, believed to be overseas, are in the United States, according to South Korean officials. South Korea and the United States say they have no accurate information on the number of American fugitives in South Korea. (Associated Press)

10 The U.S. Defense Department announces that it has agreed to sell fourteen of the latest Patriot air defense systems to South Korea for $4.2 billion, the *Korea Times* reports.

16 Radio Pyongyang says South Pyongyang Province built more than 1,000 fish farms after the launch of the fish-raising campaign last May.

24 United States intelligence analysts have discovered evidence that South Korea is trying to develop longer-range ballistic missiles while keeping some of the program's key aims secret from Washington, American officials say. After talks with the United States, North Korea shelved its plan to test-fire a more powerful missile, which experts say could reach Hawaii and Alaska. Under a 1979 agreement with the United States, South Korea cannot develop a missile with a range longer than 112 miles. Washington has agreed in principle to lift the ban, allowing Seoul to develop a missile capable of traveling up to 187 miles. South Korea wants U.S. permission to research and develop a missile with a range of up to 312 miles, a distance that would cover all of North Korea. Three days of U.S.–South Korea missile talks in Seoul last week failed to reach agreement on the issue. (Associated Press)

27 North Korea's Korean Central News Agency (KCNA) reports more than 193 million trees were planted during the twenty-day period of the nationwide land-management campaign.

28 South Korea's president has ordered a probe into allegations that a top aide tried to cover up an influence-peddling scandal dubbed "Furgate." The scandal centers around businessman Choi Soon-Young, the chairman of South Korean life insurance giant, Shindongah Group. Choi was arrested in February on embezzlement and other charges. Soon after, his wife told local news media that she had given fur coats and other expensive designer clothes to the wives of the justice minister and another Cabinet minister. The incident was characterized as a lobbying attempt, and both ministers resigned. The internal report, leaked to the media Friday, cleared the ex-justice minister's wife of involvement. That was contrary to findings by an independent counsel, and the opposition accused presidential aides of trying to protect the ex-justice minister, a close ally of the president. (Associated Press)

December 1999

1 The Korean Sharing Movement kicks off a campaign for public donations to buy 20 million South Korean eggs and send them to North Korea.

2 A South Korean clothing firm, Nix, announces that it will deliver 10,000 pairs of blue jeans and 5,000 sweaters to North Korea on November 11. North Korea's Asia-Pacific Peace Committee asked the firm to offer 30,000 pairs of blue jeans on the condition that they be dyed a dark color. North Korea has banned young people from wearing blue jeans because they are regarded as a symbol of capitalism.

3 North Korean party secretary Kim Yong-Sun and Tomiichi Murayama, head of a Japanese delegation, issue a joint statement in Pyongyang urging both governments to reopen talks for normalizing ties at the earliest possible date.

5   President Clinton's half-brother and two dozen South Korean pop stars perform a concert in communist North Korea. Roger Clinton, a singer and bandleader, arrived with thirty-seven South Korean pop stars and organizers to perform in a 2,000-seat concert hall in Pyongyang. The U.S. State Department said there was no official U.S. government connection to Clinton's visit. (*Washington Post*)

9   The new commander of U.S. forces in South Korea takes charge in a ceremony with American soldiers carrying M-16 rifles and Korean army musicians in traditional yellow robes. Gen. Thomas Schwartz assumes control of the 37,000 U.S. troops (Associated Press)

14   The Japanese government announces that it will lift sanctions on food aid for North Korea and resume diplomatic normalization talks.

15   One million people have disappeared from famine-hit North Korea's official population total in a year. Pyongyang has said the population is now 22.5 million, one million less than it revealed last year. Meanwhile, a survey of North Korean refugees in northeastern China has found that more than 70 percent questioned had had at least one immediate family member die of starvation in North Korea. More than 100,000 North Korean refugees are believed to have crossed the North Korean border into northeastern China. More than 60 percent of the respondents had been arrested and repatriated at least once. Last year, Pyongyang allowed a rare random survey of child health under the supervision of UN medical experts. It revealed that 16 percent suffered from severe malnutrition and more than 60 percent had severely stunted growth. (*South China Morning Post*)

Arirang-1, Korea's first observation satellite, was

launched successfully from Vandenberg Air Base in California aboard a Taurus launch vehicle. The 470kg satellite is orbiting at 685km and circles the earth fourteen times a day. (*Korea Times, Choson Ilbo*)

Representatives from Japan, South Korea, the EU, and the United States sign an agreement on delivery of nuclear reactors to North Korea, as arranged for in the 1994 Agreed Framework. The project is estimated to cost $4.6 billion, with South Korea paying $3.2 billion, Japan paying $1 billion, the United States paying $115 million, and the EU paying $80 million.

21 A sixty-two-member North Korean delegation led by a vice-ministerial level official arrives in Seoul for a four-day visit to hold friendly basketball games with South Korean teams.

Red Cross officials from Japan and North Korea sign an agreement on humanitarian cooperation after three days of talks. The two sides agree to resume home visits by next spring for Japanese citizens married to North Korean spouses who had not previously been permitted to leave the country.

The World Food Program (WFP) and twenty non-governmental organizations (NGOs) participating in aid activities in North Korea release a joint statement condemning the North Korean authorities' methods of inspection and delivery of aid supplies, according to South Korea's *Choson Ilbo*.

23 In the next millennium, there will be far more bachelors than eligible women, making the female gender more valued in the process, reported South Korea's National Statistical Office (NSO). In the year 2000, there will be 269,089 more eligible men between the ages of twenty-six and thirty than there

will be women between the ages of twenty-three and twenty-seven. The number will increase to 315,273 the following year, but will even out again by 2006. Until 1980, eligible women overwhelmingly outnumbered eligible men. Abortions of female fetuses became particularly widespread around 1980, leading to predictions that eligible women will be in extreme shortage by the year 2011, according to *Choson Ilbo*.

31   A total of 3,501 prisoners are freed under a sweeping year-end amnesty. They are among 1 million prisoners and criminals punished for minor charges, and who benefited from the special pardon announced by President Kim Dae-Jung. The ministry allowed the release of Shin Kwang-Soo, seventy-one, and Son Song-Mo, seventy, who have spent more than fifteen years in jail on conviction of espionage charges under the National Security Law. The ministry said that there are no more long-term prisoners convicted of spying for North Korea under the strict security law following the release of Shin and Son. Civic groups advocating human rights welcomed the presidential pardon. (*Korea Times*)

January 2000

4   South Korea's Ministry of Foreign Affairs and Trade (MOFAT) releases a report that the United Nations has provided assistance worth $580 million to North Korea since 1995.

13   The National Assembly approves an economics expert as the new prime minister in President Kim Dae-Jung's government. The approval of Park Tae-Joon sets the stage for a partial Cabinet shakeup. Kim replaces seven Cabinet members after Park's approval, to prepare for parliamentary elections on April 13. There were five abstentions or invalid votes. Park replaces Kim Jong-Pil, who resigned to lead one of the coalition parties, the United Liberal Democrats, in the April elections. (Associated Press)

18   Chinese defense minister Chi Haotian visits Seoul, marking the first official visit by a Chinese defense minister chief since the Korean War.

20   There is a saying that if two Koreans live in a desert, they will create three political parties. The one is the ruling party, and the other is the opposition with the third being a coalition. This axiom may be applied to President Kim Dae-Jung who establishes his fifth party. Since 1954, he has worked with eleven political parties. He created the National Congress for New Politics (NCNP) in September 1995. On the NCNP ticket, he won the presidential election in a dramatic coalition with Kim Jong-Pil and realized the first peaceful transfer of power from the opposition to the ruling party in fifty years. Now, Kim is founding his fifth party, the New Millennium Democratic Party, out of his aspirations for political reform and making it a national party. (*Korea Times*)

29   The South Korean defense ministry announces that it has secured a list of 268 South Korean soldiers captured during the Korean War and presumed still alive in North Korea.

February 2000

7   North Korea's KCNA announces that the Reverend Moon Sun-Myung's Unification Church has begun construction of the first automobile plant to be built jointly by South Korea's Pyonghwa Motor Company and North Korea's Yonbong Corporation, in Nampo, North Korea.

9   In Pyongyang, North Korean foreign minister Paek Nam-Sun and his Russian counterpart, Igor Ivanov, sign a new treaty of friendship and cooperation, which nullifies Russia's former obligation to send troops to North Korea in case of war.

22   A delegation of four Australian diplomats visits Pyongyang with a $3 million aid plan to discuss re-establishing ties which have been suspended for the past twenty-five years.

23   North Korea's KCNA blames its "worst ever" power shortage on the United States, criticizing the United States for delays in building the two nuclear reactors under the Agreed Framework.

27   A commentary in North Korea's *Rodong Shinmun* party newspaper labels the South Korean government's engagement policy "a useless, silly dream," noting, "It has been proved that the puppet's engagement policy is a confrontational war scheme aimed at militarily squeezing us to death, in collusion with foreign forces."

March 2000

2   The National Movement for Withdrawal of U.S. Soldiers, a local NGO, launched a drive last month to collect 100,000 "on-line" signatures calling for the early withdrawal of the approximately 37,000 American soldiers stationed here, they said. Another group, the Citizens' Network for Peace on the Korean Peninsula, has been conducting cyber polls on arms reduction on the peninsula. The Ministry of Foreign Affairs and Trade, deciding renewed anti-American sentiment could be detrimental to the largely cooperative ties between the two countries, plans to step up efforts to better inform the public of various bilateral issues, including the revision of the Status of Forces Agreement (SOFA). (*Korea Herald*)

3   The Japanese government decides to donate 100,000 tons of rice to North Korea through the WFP. This is the first food aid from Japan to North Korea in three years, the *Daily Yomiuri* reports.

5   Kim Jong-Il, accompanied by a group of high-rank-
     ing army officers and party cadres, visits the Chi-
     nese embassy in Pyongyang at the invitation of the
     outgoing ambassador.

7   North Korea urges all women in the country to bear
     more children and to bring them up as "lifeguards"
     of leader Kim Jong-Il.

     North Korea Vice Foreign Minister Kim Gye-Gwan
     and U.S. envoy Charles Kartman begin talks in New
     York to prepare for a visit by a high-level North Ko-
     rean official to Washington.

8   South Korean president Kim Dae-Jung, at the Free
     University of Berlin, announces that South Korea is
     willing to engage in economic cooperation with North
     Korea on a government level and urges North Korea
     to accept South Korea's proposal to resume govern-
     ment-level talks.

9   The French aid organization Action Against Hunger
     announces that it had withdrawn from North Korea
     because it was unable to gain direct access to the
     population.

11   North Korea refuses to send more workers to the site
     of the KEDO nuclear reactor project, because it is
     demanding that North Korean workers' wages be
     raised from the current average monthly wage of $110
     to $600.

13   A group of South Korean civic organizations sends
     300,000 yards of textiles and 50,000 pieces of cloth-
     ing to North Korea, the Korean Sharing Movement
     announces.

23   The North Korean People's Army-Navy Command re-
     iterates its claim to waters north of the Northern Limit
     Line (NLL) around the five islands off the west coast.

April 2000

6   Misdeeds by South Korean soldiers during the Vietnam War received scant attention outside Vietnam. In South Korea, rumors their soldiers had killed many Vietnamese civilians circulated for years, but no historical books chronicled the attacks and past governments suppressed open discussion and news reports. The alleged killings, said to have occurred two years before U.S. soldiers massacred 504 Vietnamese in the village of My Lai, became public knowledge in South Korea only recently. Some 320,000 South Koreans fought in Vietnam from September 1964 to March 1973, the largest contingent after Americans. South Korea lost 5,077 soldiers and suffered 10,962 wounded. While U.S. forces coordinated the anti-communist operation in Vietnam, the South Koreans operated under their own command. In 1998, South Korean president Kim Dae-Jung came to Vietnam for the annual summit of the Association of Southeast Asian Nations and expressed regret for his country's role in the war. (Associated Press)

7   North Korea–Japan normalization talks end without agreement, and with North Korea insisting that Japan first offer compensation for wartime actions.

10   South and North Korea announce simultaneously that their leaders will hold a historic summit meeting in Pyongyang on June 12–14.

14   South Korea's governing party picks up additional seats in midterm parliamentary elections. Although it failed to win a plurality, President Kim Dae-Jung's Millennium Democratic Party performed better than had been expected before the government agreed to a summit meeting with the north. Mr. Kim's party was widely expected to suffer a loss of ten seats or more, a blow that in effect would have reduced what had been a reformist administration to lame-duck

status. Mr. Kim produced a coup with the announcement of a June summit meeting with the leader of
communist North Korea, which would be the first
ever between the two heads of state. With almost all
the votes counted, Mr. Kim's party had 115 seats.
The opposition Grand National Party had 133 seats
and remains the largest party in the Assembly, but
both parties made gains. The big loser was the United
Liberal Democrats, whose standing shrank to seventeen seats. In an unusual feature of the election, civic
groups that urged voters to reject eighty-six candidates they described as corrupt did very well: fifty-
eight of the candidates they opposed were defeated.
(*New York Times*)

20   South Korean soldiers and police, observed at times
by U.S. Army officers, executed more than 2,000 political prisoners without trial in the early weeks of the
Korean War, according to declassified U.S. military
documents and witnesses. Large numbers of South
Korean leftists, arrested by the right-wing regime,
were secretly killed as its forces retreated before the
North Korean army in mid-1950, apparently to keep
them from collaborating with the communist invad-
ers. Information about the South Korean government's
mass executions was suppressed for decades under
this country's former military rulers. The AP located
the declassified documents while investigating what
happened at No Gun Ri, South Korea, July 26–29,
1950. (Associated Press)

May 2000

2   North Korea's party newspaper, *Rodong Shinmun*,
strongly demands the withdrawal of U.S. troops from
South Korea, calling the withdrawal "a requirement
for the entire nation and for the times."

3   In Korea, Internet cafes are called PC *bangs*
("rooms"). For $2 an hour, this is where many join

the mellow intensity of the dot-coms. The *bangs* have been a major force in popularizing the Internet in Korea since they emerged in 1998. Nearly 15,000 have sprung up nationwide. Although they earn less than half of Japan's per capita income, Koreans spend more than their richer neighbor shopping online. Cybertrading accounts for half of the exchanges on Korea's stock market. By year-end, nearly a third of Korea's 45 million people may be online. (*Christian Science Monitor*)

4   Amnesty International expresses concern for infringements on human rights by China for sending North Korean refugees back to North Korea and urges a campaign to save the refugees.

6   South Korea's Unification Ministry announces that it will send $58 million worth of fertilizer to North Korea.

9   The South Korean government confirms for the first time that it possesses chemical weapons. The statement follows a local newspaper report, which says that since October, the military had been secretly disposing of hundreds of tons of weapons at a specially constructed plant about 130 miles outside of Seoul. Although no details are released on the grounds of national security, a Defense Ministry spokesman says the government was abiding by the chemical weapons convention. Seoul joined the 172-member convention three years ago. (BBC)

15   The Reverend Franklin Graham, the son of Reverend Billy Graham, visits Pyongyang.

The U.S. House of Representatives, by a vote of 374–76, passes the "Congressional Oversight of Nuclear Transfers to North Korea Act of 2000." The bill stipulates that no nuclear equipment or technology be transferred to North Korea without U.S. congressional review and approval.

19 The downfall of Prime Minister Park Tae-Joon comes after a court ruled this week that he had concealed ownership of properties to avoid large tax payments. Though such concealment wasn't illegal at the time, Park's action is considered unethical and he is required to pay back taxes. Opposition parties and civic groups call on Park to quit and issue a public apology after a court said this week that he put property valued at $5.3 million under the name of his private treasurer to avoid paying taxes. (Associated Press, *Korea Herald*)

23 A twelve-member team of U.S. nuclear and arms-control experts visits North Korea to inspect an underground tunnel in Kumchang-ni. A team that inspected the facility a year earlier found nothing.

24 A 102-member art troupe of the Pyongyang School Children's Palace arrives in Seoul for a performance tour until May 30.

29 North Korean leader Kim Jong-Il makes an unofficial visit to Beijing at the invitation of Chinese president Jiang Zemin, accompanied by a number of top North Korean generals and party secretaries.

30 At their bilateral talks in Rome, North Korea formally demands compensation from the United States for the delay in construction of the KEDO nuclear reactors.

June 2000

1 North Korea closes its border with China from June 1 to 25 as a security measure in order to prepare for the June 12–14 inter-Korean summit talks.

7   Approximately 2,000 villagers and activists clash with South Korean riot police, demanding closure of the Koo-ni range, a U.S. military bombing range southwest of Seoul. Anti-U.S. protests have increased since early May, when a U.S. fighter jet, experiencing engine trouble, dropped six bombs there, the Associated Press reports.

10   South Korea's presidential spokesperson announces that North Korea has asked in an urgent phone call for a twenty-four-hour delay of the summit meeting due to unspecified "technical reasons."

13   North Korean leader Kim Jong-Il welcomes South Korean leader Kim Dae-Jung at Pyongyang's airport. On the following day, a summit meeting is held between the two leaders. After the talks, they sign a five-point "Joint South-North Declaration."

19   South Korea's Ministry of Defense announces that it will abolish the term "Bukkoe" (North Korean puppet) when referring to what the ministry still considers to be South Korea's "main enemy," in order to support the Joint Declaration. On the following day the ministry also announces that it will cancel a military parade and battle-scene reenactment that was to have commemorated the fiftieth anniversary of the outbreak of the Korean War, and will replace them with more peaceful ceremonies, such as photo exhibitions and dinner parties for veterans. On the twenty-fifth, the anniversary date, North Korea holds no ceremonies or other commemorative functions.

20   North Korea's KCNA says the country is suffering from the worst drought in fifty years.

24   North Korea's domestic broadcast network (KCBS or KCBN) stresses that Pyongyang will not accept the Japan-initiated plan for building a six-party re-

gional security body involving the two Koreas, Japan, China, Russia, and the United States, criticizing it as a bid to impede the "independent" reunification of Korea.

26 In a muted ceremony commemorating the outbreak of war on the Korean peninsula fifty years ago, President Kim Dae-Jung of South Korea pays tribute to the soldiers who fought and those who died in the conflict, which continues to divide the North and South. Mr. Kim's remarks appear intended to address widespread criticism over his government's decision to scale back celebrations of the fiftieth anniversary of the start of the Korean War to avoid offending North Korea. The government says that it had canceled all its war commemorations to maintain a spirit of cooperation. (*New York Times*)

29 North Korean leader Kim Jong-Il meets in Wonsan, North Korea, with Hyundai Group's honorary chairman Chung Ju-Yong, to discuss business deals.

July 2000

1 U.S. Defense Secretary William Cohen says that the United States should maintain a military presence on the Korean peninsula even after reunification.

5 The South Korean Red Cross, through a national computer lottery, randomly selects 400 out of 75,000 registered names as candidates for inter-Korean family reunions. The list will be narrowed to 100 and released shortly before the first reunions are to take place on August 15, Korea's Liberation Day.

12 Negotiations over North Korea's missile program end in a stalemate, with the United States refusing to pay Pyongyang to curb exports of missile technology. After three days of talks, the North Koreans restated their offer: $1 billion a year in exchange for a halt to

missile technology exports. They also refused to stop
developing such weapons for self-defense. The talks
were the first in sixteen months, and chief U.S. ne-
gotiator, Robert Einhorn, assistant secretary of state
for proliferation, said no breakthrough had been expected. (Associated Press)

19   North Korean leader Kim Jong-Il and Russian president Vladimir Putin hold talks in Pyongyang.

25   South Korea is gradually lifting its bans on imports
of Japanese popular culture, breaking a long taboo
inherited from a history of colonization. First, it allows Japanese films that had won international
awards, followed by pop concerts in halls that seat
no more than 2,000. Last month, the government
ended the limit on audience size and also allowed
Japanese family movies. Japanese-language CDs remain illegal, however, along with Japanese television dramas. Japanese culture has long been a
sensitive topic among Koreans because from 1910
to 1945, when the peninsula was a Japanese colony,
Japanese authorities forced Koreans to speak Japanese and tried to eliminate Korean identity. Koreans
have stronger feelings about Japan than vice versa,
according to opinion polls. A poll by the Japanese
newspaper *Asahi Shimbun* showed that more Koreans view Japan as an economic rival than vice versa
and more Koreans think historical issues have not
been settled. In surveys over the past fifteen years,
about two-thirds of Japanese have said they have no
particular feelings of like or dislike about South Korea, according to *Asahi*. The number disliking Korea
ranged from 12 to 23 percent. Until the 1996 poll,
roughly two-thirds of Koreans said they disliked Japan; last year nearly half of South Koreans said they
were indifferent. (*Washington Post*)

27   During the Asian Regional Forum (ARF) meeting in
Bangkok, foreign ministers of twenty-two countries

approve North Korea's bid to join the organization, which is a consultative conference on security matters.

31 The two Koreas agree to reconnect a major inter-Korean rail link and re-open border liaison offices.

August 2000

5 Broadcasters and executives of forty-six South Korean media organizations visit North Korea and meet Kim Jong-Il, who invited them during the June summit talks. Kim tells them that he was not serious last month when he offered to scrap his country's missile program in return for U.S. help launching satellites, and that he had made the offer "laughingly" to Russian president Putin. Kim remarks that the idea, made public by Putin, must have given the United States "a bad headache," according to the executives. Kim says, according to an account provided by executives who met with him Saturday in Pyongyang, "Why would I need to [court] bigger countries? If I sit here in Pyongyang, many from powerful nations come to me."

10 Hong Kong–based *Asiaweek* magazine picks President Kim Dae-Jung as the best democrat in Asia in the past twenty-five years. In its twenty-fifth anniversary issue, *Asiaweek* presents a selection of all the best in Asia from food to fashion, business, leisure, travel, pleasure, places, personalities, and more. (*Korea Times*)

14 The two Koreas activate their liaison offices at the border village of Panmunjom, after a four-year hiatus.

15 South and North Korean family members who had been separated for a half-century meet in tearful reunions in Seoul and Pyongyang. Emotional scenes of joyous, weeping men and women hugging and caressing the faces of their long-lost kin grip the Korean peninsula, which is celebrating the fifty-fifth anniversary of the nation's liberation from Japan's

colonial rule. All major South Korean television networks broadcast live the historic, touching scenes from Seoul and Pyongyang. North Korean television also broadcast the meetings. One-hundred North Koreans fly into Seoul in the morning to meet their South Korean relatives in the afternoon at a huge conference room at the Convention and Exhibition Center (COEX) in southern Seoul. The same number of North Koreans meet their families from the South at the Koryo Hotel in central Pyongyang almost simultaneously. The family reunions are only the second of their kind since the two Koreas were divided at the end of World War II in 1945. In 1985, fifty people from each side visited Seoul and Pyongyang. (*Korea Herald*)

18   The North Korean National Orchestra arrives in Seoul to perform at the North-South Grand Joint Concert. It is the first time a large North Korean orchestra has ever visited South Korea.

21   A total of 70,000 military personnel including 12,000 U.S. soldiers participate in the annual ROK-U.S. Ulchi Lens Focus war simulation. The total number of participants is reduced to nearly one-third so as not to impede reconciliation between the two Koreas.

22   In Tokyo, North Korea and Japan resume talks on the normalization of relations.

25   South Korean officials say that the Seoul District Prosecutor's investigation into the illegal dumping of toxic chemicals into the Han River by the U.S. Forces, Korea, is proceeding much slower than expected, mainly because of the U.S. military's lack of cooperation, the *Korea Herald* reports.

September 2000

1   In a breakfast meeting between North Korean leader Kim Jong-Il and South Korean unification minister

Park Jae-Kyu, Kim approves all high-level talks issues, including the establishment of military talks, joint flood control of the Imjin River area, the exchange of letters between separated families, and the size of tourist groups to visit each other's countries.

2   North Korea holds a grand ceremony in Panmunjom to welcome its sixty-three returning POWs who had refused to abandon their communist ideology while jailed in South Korea.

4   South Korea's opposition Grand National Party (GNP) holds a massive protest rally against President Kim Dae Jung's management of state affairs, notably his North Korea policy. The GNP charges that no progress was made during the recent minister-level talks on returning South Korean POWs and abductees now living in North Korea. The South Korean Defense Ministry now believes that a total of 351 South Korean POWs are still alive in North Korea.

6   North Korea's Kim Yong-Nam, chairman of the Presidium of the Supreme People's Assembly and nominally the country's head of state, along with his entourage, angrily turns around and flies home, skipping the UN Millennium Summit of World Leaders, after American Airlines security officers insist they would have to undergo body searches before being allowed to board a connecting flight to New York from Frankfurt, Germany. The State Department and the White House say they regret the incident, which comes at a particularly sensitive moment, as Washington is seeking to persuade the reclusive communist regime to halt its missile-development program and to pursue peace with its neighbors. Kim Yong-Nam would have been the highest-ranking North Korean official to visit the United States or the United Nations since the Korean War. (*Washington Post*)

The U.S. Forces, Korea, announces that it will punish two U.S. civilian employees involved in the illegal dumping of toxic chemicals into a sewer that leads to the Han River.

11   North Korean party secretary Kim Yong-Sun visits Seoul, accompanied by the vice director of the General Political Bureau of the Korean People's Army, General Pak Jae-Gyong, who is escorting 300 gift boxes of pine mushrooms (valued at $800,000) for South Korean officials and media heads who visited Pyongyang in June and August. The mushrooms had been promised at that time. General Pak immediately returns to Pyongyang without meeting with any South Korean military officials.

20   North Korean propaganda leaflets severely criticizing South Korea's opposition party president Lee Hoi-Chang and calling for the withdrawal of U.S. troops from Korea are discovered in Seoul. According to the *Korea Herald*, 300 of the leaflets are discovered at the Shilla Hotel, where the North Korean delegation recently stayed.

25   South Korea Defense Minister Cho Sung-Tae and North Korea Defense Minister Kim Il-Chul hold the first-ever defense ministers' meeting on the South Korean island of Cheju.

The International Atomic Energy Agency (IAEA) issues a resolution during its forty-fourth general conference reiterating its concern over North Korea's nuclear programs and noting it cannot conclude whether North Korea is diverting nuclear materials for weapons.

October 2000

1   Japan's *Asahi Shimbun* says that Japanese prime minister Yoshiro Mori secretly sent a personal letter to

North Korean leader Kim Jong-Il asking for Japanese–North Korea summit talks. The prime minister
is widely criticized for this unofficial initiative.

6   The Japanese government announces that it will con-
     tribute a half-million tons of rice to help North Ko-
     rea and encourage its government to continue
     improving relations with other countries (including
     Japan).

9   North Korean leader Kim Jong-Il dispatches Vice
     Marshal Cho Myong-Rok, his second in command,
     to Washington for talks with high officials and a meet-
     ing with President Bill Clinton. Cho is the most se-
     nior official ever to visit the United States.

     Despite domestic criticism, forty representatives of
     South Korean religious, labor, arts, and civic groups
     and scholars travel to North Korea to attend the fifty-
     fifth anniversary of the founding of the North Ko-
     rean Workers' Party on October 10.

13   It is announced that South Korean president Kim Dae-
     Jung will receive the Nobel Peace Prize for efforts
     toward Korean reconciliation. The prize will be
     awarded on December 10, 2000.

17   Korea and the United States, wrapping up five-year-
     long negotiations, reach a working-level deal in
     Washington on the extension of Seoul's ranges of
     ballistic missiles. The new agreement enables Korea
     to develop and deploy missiles with ranges of up to
     300 kilometers (187 miles), while lifting any limits
     on its space programs, although there are still differ-
     ences on the method of notification. (*Korea Times*)

     Chinese premier Zhu Rongji visits South Korea for
     talks with President Kim Dae-Jung and for the third
     Asia-Europe Meeting (ASEM) in Seoul.

23   U.S. Secretary of State Madeleine Albright visits
Pyongyang and meets with North Korean leader Kim
Jong-Il. Albright is the highest-ranking U.S. official
to visit the North.

25   The United States, South Korea, and Japan agree to
coordinate their policies toward North Korea to prevent Pyongyang from playing one nation off against
the other to win concessions. "Our unity is crucial if
we are to make further gains," Madeleine Albright,
the U.S. Secretary of State, tells a news conference
in Seoul held with the South Korean and Japanese
foreign ministers after her visit to Pyongyang. The
statement comes amid rising concern in South Korea that North Korea is focusing on improving ties
with the United States at the expense of developing
contacts with Seoul.

26   A top South Korean unification policy maker states
that North Korea has sent a memorandum of understanding to the ROK proposing that they slow down
the pace of inter-Korean contacts.

30   Japan and North Korea hold the eleventh round of
normalization talks between the two countries in
Beijing, but fail to reach an accord.

November 2000

1   The United States and North Korea hold talks in Kuala
Lumpur on curbing the North's missile program.

7   With over 16 million South Koreans—more than one-
third of the population—online, the Internet has become an integral part of daily life. For some students,
however, the Internet has become an addiction. In a
survey of 1,930 students between ten and eighteen years
old, about 20 percent said they used the Internet for
more than three hours a day. (Yonhap News Agency)

Since 1990, North Korea has returned the remains of 285 U.S. MIAs from the Korean War, the *Korea Times* reports. The United States paid $6,277,000 in compensation for the joint searches.

28 South Korean film director Im Kwon-Taek's *Chunhyang*, which surprised many by gaining invitations to Cannes early this year and to next year's Oscar Awards, has made headlines again as it snatched the top prize at the Hawaii International Film Festival 2000. (*Korea Herald*)

30 The second reunion of 200 members of separated families takes place in Seoul and Pyongyang.

December 2000

1 A Japanese delegation headed by former Prime Minister Tomiichi Murayama visits Pyongyang to talk about improving relations. In an editorial in North Korea's *Rodong Shinmun*, North Korea refuses a Japanese proposal to normalize relations based on an economic plan (adjusted for inflation) similar to that used in 1965 to normalize relations between Japan and South Korea.

3 In the ROK's Defense White Paper 2000, the Defense Ministry reiterates that North Korea is still the "main enemy" of South Korea.

7 David Morton, the UN resident coordinator in North Korea, announces that the country is suffering its worst food shortages since 1996–1997.

10 A spokesperson for the North's Committee for the Peaceful Reunification of the Fatherland issues a statement demanding that South Korea retract its description of the North as a "main enemy."

13 South Korea's two major labor federations send thirty-two delegates to the unification forum of workers of the two Koreas, which takes place at North Korea's Mount Kumgang.

21 A monument extolling North Korean leader Kim Jong-Il's military-first policy is dedicated on Mount Kumgang. In Pyongyang, a national fine arts exhibition opens at the People's Palace of Culture to mark the ninth anniversary of Kim's appointment as the Supreme Commander of the Korean People's Army, and also commemorating the birth of his mother, Kim Jong-Suk, who, according to North Korean legend, is one of the "three generals" of Mount Paektu.

The South Korean Unification Ministry reveals that 303 North Korean defectors came to the South in 2000, the largest number to date. The previous year 148 arrived, the first time the number had exceeded 100.

28 The United States and South Korea agree on new rules in the Status of Forces Agreement (SOFA) that give the South Korean government broader jurisdiction over U.S. soldiers accused of crimes while stationed in the country. The new SOFA is to be signed on January 18, 2001.

January 2001

5 More than 100,000 Pyongyang citizens hold a rally vowing to carry out the national tasks announced in the New Year's Joint Editorial.

7 The North's domestic broadcasting station announces that the fifth annual exhibition of the Kim Jong-Il flower (Kimjongilia) will open in Pyongyang on February 14 for a seven-day run under the sponsorship

of the North Korean Kimjongilia Federation. Kim's birthday is February 16.

12 The governments of South Korea and the United States hope a statement of regret from President Clinton will end the controversy over the killing of civilians by American soldiers in the Korean War, but survivors of the attack at No Gun Ri said today they are not satisfied. Survivors and their supporters call a U.S. report issued on the incident "incomplete and too late" and complain that even after five decades of denials, the U.S. government appears reluctant to fully confront the incident. But the government in Seoul says Clinton's acknowledgment that American soldiers killed civilians is "a very difficult decision" and appeals for public acceptance. The Pentagon concludes that panicky and ill-prepared American troops had shot at refugees as they huddled under a bridge between July 26–29, 1950. Survivors say more than 300 were killed. (*Washington Post*)

17 North Korean leader, Kim Jong-Il, arrives in Shanghai on a furtive impromptu tour of China's economic capital. He visited Beijing in May 2000 for three days. A newspaper in Seoul, *Joongang Ilbo*, reports twenty high-ranking officials, including Cho Myong-Rok, head of the General Political Bureau of the North Korean Ministry of People's Armed Forces, are accompanying Mr. Kim. Like his previous trip, this one was not announced by China or North Korea until after Kim had returned to his country.

The South Korean foreign ministry announces that the country's new missile policy would allow it to develop short-range missiles with a range of 300 kilometers, capable of hitting targets in most of North Korea.

18 South Korea and the United States have revised a 1979 accord limiting Seoul's development of mili-

tary rockets, allowing it to deploy missiles that can reach the North Korean capital, Pyongyang. The new missile-policy agreement allows Seoul to make and deploy missiles that can travel 300km and carry a 500kg payload. The previous accord limited South Korea's missiles to 180km. North Korea's firing of a missile over Japanese territory in August 1998 buttressed the South's case. (*South China Morning Post*)

31   Apprehension is increasing in South Korea over the approach of the new Bush administration toward North Korea, with key figures in Washington apparently signaling a much tougher line in relations with Pyongyang. The incoming U.S. deputy secretary of state, Mr. Richard Armitage, found himself in the middle of a diplomatic flap this week after reports in Seoul that he had urged the Kim government to drop the name "Sunshine Policy." The policy is a hallmark of President Kim Dae-Jung, emphasizing his desire for closer relations with the prickly Stalinist regime. Some Seoul media reported Mr. Armitage had suggested that the name tag, borrowed from one of Aesop's fables about a man being coaxed into removing his coat by the warm sun, was too soft and should be replaced by the more prosaic "engagement policy." (*Sydney Morning Herald*)

February 2001

11   A North Korean arts troupe including opera and folk music singers makes their first tour of the United States, visiting Los Angeles, New York, Washington, Chicago, and Houston.

12   The UN Human Rights Commission releases North Korea's first report on its human rights situation in sixteen years. The report, however, only describes the North's laws.

26   The two Koreas hold the third round of family reunions.

28 In a joint communiqué issued during Russian president Vladimir Putin's visit, President Kim Dae-Jung sides with Russia in criticizing the United States for falling behind in its commitment to reduce the threat from nuclear weapons. He adopted the Russian view that the 1972 treaty that would ban the United States from erecting a national antimissile shield is a "cornerstone of strategic stability" and that it should not only be preserved, but also "strengthened." (*International Herald Tribune*)

Family members bid farewell to their kin, not knowing if they would ever meet again after the three-day reunions held simultaneously in Seoul and Pyongyang. The third inter-Korean family reunions came to an end, with the relatives having heartbreaking partings. The two Koreas are expected to discuss the issue of holding more reunions at the inter-Korean Red Cross talks, slated for April. They will also discuss the terms for the establishment of permanent meeting points for the dispersed families, which would benefit a greater number of families. (*Korea Times*)

March 2001

7 President Bush tells President Kim of South Korea that he will not resume missile talks with North Korea anytime soon, putting aside the Clinton administration's two-year campaign for a deal and the eventual normalization of relations with the reclusive communist state. Mr. Bush's comments come as a clear rebuff to President Kim. In a brief exchange with reporters after meeting Mr. Kim in the Oval Office, Mr. Bush says: "We're not certain as to whether or not they're keeping all terms of all agreements." But the United States has only one agreement with North Korea—the 1994 accord that froze North Korea's plutonium processing at a suspected nuclear weapons plant. Mr. Kim offered a tepid assessment of his conversation with the American presi-

dent. "The greatest outcome today has to be that, through a frank and honest exchange of views on the situation on the Korean peninsula, we have increased the mutual understanding," Mr. Kim said. (*New York Times*)

12   The South Korean government decides to provide about $6.3 million worth of humanitarian aid, including winter underwear and surplus fruit, to North Korea this month.

13   The fifth inter-Korean ministerial talks were supposed to start today in Seoul, but Pyongyang's top delegate sent a message early in the morning saying that his team could not come. The message simply read, "We are unable to attend the meeting due to various considerations."

15   The South Korean Unification Ministry announced that Uzbek laborers will be hired to replace striking North Koreans at the KEDO nuclear construction site.

20   Chung Ju-Yong, the founder of Hyundai, dies.

28   U.S. General Thomas Schwartz, commander of the Combined Forces Command in South Korea, tells a U.S. Senate budget committee that the North Korean military is getting larger, closer, and more lethal every day, according to a *Choson Ilbo* report.

April 2001

5   North Korea's tenth Supreme People's Assembly (SPA) holds its fourth session for one day. The Assembly adopted budget and policy guidelines presented to them by the party. Guidelines emphasized resolving food shortages and boosting trade and diplomatic relations with other countries. The 2001 budget was set at $9.8 billion.

6   North Korea announces that it has begun construction of 30,000 housing units for Pyongyang citizens.

9   More than forty South Korean civic groups form an alliance to oppose U.S. missile defense programs, claiming that the programs will prevent peace from being established on the Korean peninsula.

10   South Korea's ambassador to Japan has been recalled to protest the publication of a Japanese school history textbook which avoids and downplays Japan's colonial aggressions against its neighbors in the first half of the twentieth century.

15   The Inchon Airport opened as scheduled on March 29. Although some had predicted a multitude of problems, the opening was smooth and relatively problem-free. The airport has the potential to become a major hub in Northeast Asia. Located within three and one-half hours flying time from forty-three cities of a million or more people, it now has the capacity to handle 27 million passengers and 1.7 million tons of cargo a year. Unlike Kimpo Airport, which it replaces for most international flights, Inchon will operate twenty-four hours a day. The new airport is thirty-two miles west of downtown Seoul. (*Korea Herald* and *New York Times*)

May 2001

1   South and North Korean workers hold a joint meeting at Mount Kumgang to mark May Day.

4   The European Union decides to maintain contact with North Korea and to encourage communication between North and South Korea while the Bush administration reviews its policy toward the North. To this end, a delegation led by EU president and Swedish prime minister Goran Persson arrived in Pyongyang on May 1, 2001, to meet with Chairman

Kim Jong-Il. Mr. Persson, the first Western leader to visit Pyongyang, was accompanied by EU Commissioner for External Affairs Chris Patten and Foreign Policy and Security Chief Javier Solana. After two days of meetings, the delegation flew to Seoul for brief talks with South Korean president Kim Dae-Jung. At the meeting in Pyongyang, Chairman Kim told the EU officials that he would maintain a moratorium on missile testing through 2003. (Reuters, *The Wall Street Journal*, and *Washington Post*)

Japan expels Kim Jong-Nam, the eldest son of North Korean leader Kim Jong-Il, for trying to enter the country with two associates on a forged Dominican passport.

16   North Korea's deputy foreign minister Choe Su-Hon, speaking at a UNICEF conference in Beijing, reports major declines in several of North Korea's health indicators between 1993 and 1999. Overall life expectancy declined from 73.2 to 66.8, mortality for children under age five rose from 27 to 48 deaths per 1,000 and vaccination coverage for diseases like polio and measles fell substantially. Mr. Choe attributes the declines to natural disasters, the disappearance of socialist trading partners with the fall of the Soviet bloc, and Western sanctions imposed on North Korea for not ending missile sales abroad. Detailed accounts like this by North Korean officials are unusual, and his figures are close to estimates made by outsiders. (*New York Times*)

June 2001

7   Several North Korean merchant ships sailed through South Korean territorial waters during the first week of June. The most significant intrusions were in the shipping lane between Cheju island and the south coast of the Korean peninsula, as these were the first North Korean vessels to pass through the strait since

the Armistice Agreement ended the Korean conflict in 1953. Foreign merchant vessels are normally allowed the right of "innocent passage" through the strait, as specified by the UN Convention on the Law of the Sea, but North and South Korea are still technically at war and the intruding North Korean merchant vessels were met and escorted through South Korean waters by patrol boats and surveillance aircraft. According to South Korean Defense Minister Kim Dong-Shin, stronger measures were not taken since such actions might have undermined South Korea's image in the international community and brought international condemnation. (Korean Overseas Information Service)

President Bush announced on June 6 the completion of his administration's policy review and his decision to resume talks with North Korea. In an official statement, President Bush said: "I have directed my national security team to undertake serious discussions with North Korea on a broad agenda to include: improved implementation of the Agreed Framework relating to North Korea's nuclear activities; verifiable constraints on North Korea's missile programs and a ban on its missile exports; and a less threatening conventional military posture. Some were concerned that North Korea would balk at the requests for improved implementation of the 1994 Agreed Framework and reductions in conventional forces. (U.S. Department of State, *New York Times*, and *Wall Street Journal*)

11   June 15 marks the one-year anniversary of last year's groundbreaking North-South summit and brings with it a critical examination of President Kim Dae-Jung and his Nobel Peace Prize–winning Sunshine Policy. Most critics acknowledge that the summit was a major breakthrough but feel that the momentum and vision surrounding last year's summit has waned

considerably. Some of the blame falls upon Kim Dae-Jung, with whom disappointment continues to rise. In part this criticism is due to the South's economic difficulties, but many feel that President Kim has been too tolerant of the North and not demanded enough reciprocity. Family reunions have halted. High-level talks have stopped and planning for a railroad link between the North and South is at a standstill. Moreover, North Korean leader Kim Jong-Il has yet to respond to President Kim's requests to visit Seoul to fulfill a promise made during the first summit. North Korea has said that the North-South dialogue would not continue until Washington completes its North Korea policy review. (BBC and *Christian Science Monitor*)

Glossary

Agreed Framework between the United States and the Democratic People's Republic of Korea (DPRK). Also known as the nuclear accord or Geneva accord. Signed on October 21, 1994, in Geneva, the agreement stipulates that the DPRK freeze operations of its nuclear facilities at Yongbyon in return for annual deliveries of fuel oil and the construction of two light-water nuclear reactors by the Korean Peninsula Energy Development Organization (KEDO).

Agreement on Reconciliation, Nonaggression, and Exchanges and Cooperation. Also known as the Basic Agreement. A broad agreement signed by the prime ministers of South and North Korea on December 13, 1991. The agreement has never been implemented.

ASEAN. Association of Southeast Asian Nations.

ASEAN Regional Forum (ARF). An annual meeting of the leaders and top officials of the ten ASEAN members and their thirteen Asian country dialogue partners, convened to discuss security issues. Inaugurated in 1994.

Asia European Meeting (ASEM). An annual meeting of twenty-six European and Asian countries, first convened in 1996, to stimulate dialogue on a wide range of political, economic, and cultural issues.

Asian financial crisis. A loss of investor confidence in Asian economies, resulting in the refusal of foreign creditors to renew loans that had grown to unsustainable levels. The crisis began in Thailand in July 1997 and quickly spread to other Asian economies. In November 1997 the International Monetary Fund reached an agreement with the Korean government to provide a $55-billion rescue package in return for the promise of economic reforms. The reforms resulted in short-term hardship, including devaluation of the currency, bankruptcies, and higher unemployment.

Basic Agreement. See **Agreement on Reconciliation, etc**.

Big Deals. A South Korean government plan, never fully realized, whereby each of the major *chaebol* (conglomerates) would concentrate on only three or four major businesses, swapping other businesses with each other in order to achieve "industrial rationalization."

"Buk pung," or "North Wind," scandal—A scandal exposed in the immediate aftermath of the 1997 presidential elections whereby it was alleged that GNP members attempted to convince the DPRK to stage an incident that would influence the South Korean election to the advantage of the ruling establishment and discredit longtime oppositionist Kim Dae-Jung by stimulating questions about his commitment to ROK national security.

Change through Rapprochement (*Wandel durch Annäherung*). Efforts to change the hostile behavior of the German Democratic Republic (GDR) toward West Germany through closer ties of the GDR with the West.

Cheju-do (Cheju island). A semitropical island seventy-seven kilometers long and thirty-five kilometers wide, lying eighty-two kilometers off the southern coast of the ROK, where it is swept by warm ocean currents. A place of great scenic beauty and the site of South Korea's tallest mountain, Mount Halla (1,950 meters), Cheju is a favorite tourist destination, especially for honeymooners.

Chollima. A generic form of North Korean speed battle, taking the name of a legendary flying horse that could cover great distances in a day. The first nation-wide *Chollima* campaign was launched in the late 1950s in emulation of the Soviet Union's Stakhanovite movement. In 1998 Kim Jong-Il called for the launching of a "New *Chollima*" movement to inspire the people to work harder and faster.

Chun Doo-Hwan. See **Presidents**.

Chung Ju-Yong. Founder and chairman of Hyundai, South Korea's leading business conglomerate. Born in the northern half of Korea before its political division, Chairman Chung visited North Korea in 1989 to explore business opportunities but those activities did not take fruit until after he returned with 1,000 head of cattle in visits to the North in 1998. When Chairman Chung died in March 2001, a delegation from North Korea came South to pay their respects.

Committee for the Peaceful Reunification of the Fatherland (CPRF). An auxiliary organization of the United Front Department of the Worker's Party of Korea. The CPRF was established in 1961 to appeal to "patriotic" Koreans in the ROK and abroad to work for the reunification of Korea along the communist lines proposed by Kim Il-Sung. By using the CPRF and other front organizations to deal with ROK government organizations, the DPRK communicates its view that the ROK government lacks political legitimacy.

Confederate Republic of Koryo. Also, the Koryo Confederation. The name given in 1980 by North Korea's late leader, Kim Il-Sung, to a proposed confederation of the two Koreas based on the principle of "one nation, one state, two systems, and two governments."

Containment. Western, in particular American, policies to prevent the spread of communism worldwide by military, political, economic, and cultural means.

Daepodong (Taepodong). The foreign designation of a multistage rocket known as the "Paektusan" in North Korea. The only launch of this rocket was on August 31, 1998, when a three-stage model failed to put a North Korean satellite into orbit, but did overfly the Japanese islands. The Daepodong 1/Paektusan 1 is estimated to have a range of 2,500–4,000 kilometers. It is believed that North Korea is developing longer-range versions of the Daepodong, which will reach the continental United States.

Demilitarized Zone (DMZ). An area of two kilometers on each side of the Military Demarcation Line, 155 miles long, that forms the border between North and South Korea.

Deutschlandpolitik. West German policy towards East Germany and the management of the division of Germany in an effort to keep the long-term goal of unification open.

East Sea. The sea to the east of the Korean peninsula, also known (outside of Korea) as the Sea of Japan.

Financial Supervisory Commission (FSC) & Financial Supervisory Service (FSS). FSC was established on April 1, 1998, on the recommendation of the IMF. It is charged with overseeing the restructuring of Korean banking, security, and insurance companies to overcome the financial crisis. Also, FSS was established as an implementing arm of FSC by merging three supervisory services of banking, securities, and insurance.

Four-Party Talks. Proposed to North Korea jointly by President Clinton and ROK president Kim Young-Sam on April 16, 1996, the talks are a forum to discuss measures to replace the Korean War Armistice with a peace agreement. As a major combatant in the Korean War, China was also invited to participate. The first meeting was held in December 1997. No discernible progress was made in six rounds of talks, which have been abandoned since August 1999. North Korea wants to negotiate a peace agreement with the United States that would remove U.S. troops from South Korea; the United States insists that a peace agreement must include South Korea, and that the presence of U.S. troops is a bilateral issue between Seoul and Washington.

Grand National Party (GNP). Created by a merger of former president Kim Young-Sam's ruling New Korea Party (NKP) and the minor opposition Democratic Party (DP). The GNP is led by Lee Hoi-Chang. The GNP won 35.9 percent of the vote in the presidential election of 1997.

Gross National Income (GNI). International organizations such as the UN, IMF, and OECD invented GNI in 1993 to modify the existing SNA (System of National Accounts). GNI measures the real purchasing power of income.

Han River (Hangang). The river running through the center of Seoul.

Hwang Jang-Yop. The highest-level defector to date. Hwang was a former secretary of the DPRK Worker's Party of Korea who, along with his colleague Kim Tok-Hong, requested asylum at the ROK embassy in Beijing on February 12, 1997. The Chinese government refused to intervene in the affair, and Hwang was permitted to leave China, traveling first to the Philippines and then arriving in South Korea on April 21, 1997. Hwang and Kim live in a safe house under the protection and control of the ROK's National Intelligence Service. Hwang became chief director of the Service's Unification Policy Institute, and Kim is an advisor. Hwang is also the honorary president of the Association of North Korean Defectors, and Kim has served as its president and advisor. In his writings since coming to the South, Hwang has been a fierce critic of Kim Jong-Il, much to the discomfort of the Kim Dae-Jung government, which is pursuing engagement with the DPRK.

Hyundai Asan. The holding company of Hyundai established to manage relations with North Korea, and the primary counterpart in negotiating the Mount Kumgang and Kaesong Industrial Park projects.

Inter-Korean (Kyongui or Seoul-Sinuiju) railway project. A project to relink the Korean railway across the DMZ between the South Korean border town of Munsan and the North Korean city of Kaesong. Construction for the project began after the summit and an agreement was negotiated (but not yet signed by the North Koreans) to allow construction inside the DMZ. The North Koreans halted work on their side in late 2000.

Juche (Chuch'e). North Korea's paramount ideology, first articulated by Kim Il-Sung in 1955, *Juche* can best be translated as Korean nationalism and self-reliance. As such it serves as an official guide in all areas of North Korean life, as in *Juche* literature and *Juche* military strategy.

July 4 Joint Communiqué. On this date in 1972, following a series of talks, the two Koreas signed an agreement to reduce tension and promote cooperation according to the "three principles" of "independent efforts" (i.e., without U.S. interference), "peaceful means," and "great national unity" transcending the difference of political systems. The agreement, which was signed by the director of the South Korean Central Intelligence Agency and the director of the Organization and Guidance Department of the North Korean Workers' Party, was never implemented.

June 15 Joint Declaration. At the conclusion of the inter-Korean summit of June 13–15, 2000, in Pyongyang, President Kim Dae-Jung and

Chairman Kim Jong-Il signed a five-point agreement calling on the two Koreas to "independently" achieve unification, harking back to the July 4 Joint Communiqué of 1972. According to the Declaration, the two Koreas would promptly resolve humanitarian issues, promote economic cooperation and exchange, and prepare for a visit of Kim Jong-Il to Seoul "at an appropriate time."

Kangsong Taeguk. Translated as "a strong and prosperous great power," the phrase was introduced by the DPRK in August 1998 as its national goal. The theme takes on meaning in the context of contemporary events: the convening of the tenth Supreme People's Assembly, the adoption of the new socialist constitution, the reelection of Kim Jong-Il as chairman of the National Defense Commission, the launch of the DPRK's Daepodong1 rocket, and the campaign to promote Kim Jong-Il's "military-first" policy.

Kim Dae-Jung. See **Presidents**.

Kim Jong-Il. The eldest son and successor to DPRK founder Kim Il-Sung. Known as the "Dear Leader" and "the respected and beloved general." Kim was officially designated as successor in 1980 and was named chairman of the National Defense Commission (NDC) in 1990, supreme commander of the KPA in 1991, and general secretary of the WKP in 1997. In 1998, he abolished the position of DPRK president held by his late father and had himself reelected NDC chairman, at which time it was announced that "the NDC chairman is in charge of the whole of our political, military and economic powers, and is the top post of the republic."

Kim Young-Nam. After the proclamation of the 1998 socialist constitution, Foreign Minister Kim was named to the newly created ceremonial post of chairman ("president" in the DPRK's English-language version of its constitution) of the SPA Presidium, in which position he represents the DPRK in international forums as head of state.

Kim Young-Sam. See **Presidents**.

Korea Asia-Pacific Peace Committee (KAPPC). The DPRK united-front organization that serves as the de facto counterpart for inter-

Korean economic cooperation projects including Hyundai's Mount Kumgang tourism project and the Kaesong industrial zone.

Korea Land Corporation (KOLAND). South Korea's state-run property and holding company responsible for managing national real estate projects.

Korea National Tourism Organization (KNTO). South Korea's state-run organization devoted to the promotion of tourism.

Korean Peninsula Energy Development Organization (KEDO). An international consortium established by the 1994 U.S.-DPRK Agreed Framework to build two light-water nuclear reactors for the DPRK in return for the freezing and eventual dismantling of the DPRK's graphite-moderated reactors, which were capable of producing bomb-grade plutonium. Seventy percent of the estimated $5-billion construction cost is to be borne by the ROK; Japan has agreed to contribute $1 billion, with the remainder coming from other participating countries.

Korean Workers' Party (KWP). See **Workers' Party of Korea**.

Military Armistice Commission (MAC). A commission of ten senior military officers, five representing the United Nations Command and five representing the DPRK and China. As provided for by the Korean Armistice Agreement of July 27, 1953, the role of the commission is to supervise the implementation of the Agreement, assisted by the NNSC. In order to further its goal of replacing the Agreement with a bilateral peace treaty with the United States, the DPRK in April 1994 notified the United States and the United Nations of its decision to withdraw from the MAC and close down the operation of the NNSC, thus requiring disputes along the DMZ and MDL to be resolved by ad hoc meetings.

Millennium Democratic Party (MDP). Formerly known as the National Congress for New Politics (NCNP), President Kim Dae-Jung's party. In the 1997 elections, the NCNP won 39.8 percent of the vote.

Mount Kumgang (Diamond Mountain). A mountain of great beauty located in the southeast corner of North Korea, just north of the DMZ.

Hyundai founder Chung Ju-Yong negotiated a deal with a North Korean organization to allow Hyundai-operated cruise ships to bring in South Korean tourists. Hyundai agreed to pay $942 million in monthly installments for exclusive tour rights until the year 2005. The first group of tourists departed on November 18, 1998, and by the end of June 2001 more than 400,000 visitors had toured the mountain.

National Assembly. The ROK's unicameral legislative body, whose members are elected to four-year terms. The Assembly has often served as little more than a rubber-stamp congress in the face of strong presidential power. Under the presidencies of Kim Young-Sam and Kim Dae-Jung it has played a larger political role, but it remains much weaker than its U.S. counterpart. As of 2001, the Assembly had 273 members: 227 elected directly and 46 chosen in proportion to party popularity in the last election. The opposition GNP is the majority party.

National Intelligence Service (NIS). The ROK national intelligence organization. It was established as the Korean Central Intelligence Agency (KCIA) in 1961 under the direction of Kim Jong-Pil, and was renamed the Agency for National Security Planning (ANSP) in 1981. In 1998, as part of President Kim Dae-Jung's reform to halt the agency's meddling in domestic affairs, it was given its new name. Its old slogan, "Working in the shade, heading for the light" was changed to "Intelligence is national strength."

National Missile Defense and Theater Missile Defense (NMD/TMD). The Clinton-era designation of two proposed defense programs to protect the continental United States or a more limited region (such as U.S. forces in Northeast Asia) from limited ballistic-missile attacks. Strategists in the George W. Bush administration prefer the more inclusive term "Ballistic Missile Defense" or BMD.

National Security Law (NSL). Enacted in South Korea in 1948 to control the activities of "anti-state" organizations, primarily those advocating the policies of the DPRK. The law became the principal tool of successive military-oriented governments to punish political dissidents. It was amended in 1991 to limit offenses to those that would "endanger the security of the nation or basic order of liberal democracy." In 2001, it remains in force and is still targeted at North Korea, but it is coming under increasing criticism as a violation of free speech and a barrier to national reunification.

Neutral Nations Supervisory Commission (NNSC). A four-nation commission (Switzerland and Sweden chosen by the UN Command; Czechoslovakia and Poland chosen by China and the DPRK) established by the Korean Armistice Agreement of July 27, 1953, to oversee the Agreement. To pressure the United States to replace the Agreement with a bilateral peace treaty, the DPRK expelled the Czech contingent in March 1993 and the Polish contingent in February 1995, and blocked the Swiss and Swedish contingents from access to the Joint Security Area of the DMZ.

Nordpolitik **(Northern Policy).** A policy of dialogue and engagement with socialist countries (in the manner of West Germany's *Ostpolitik* strategy to improve relations with East Germany), including the USSR, PRC, and the DPRK, first launched on July 7, 1988, by ROK president Roh Tae-Woo. Using momentum gained by Seoul's hosting of the 1988 Summer Olympics, President Roh's *Nordpolitik* policy normalized ROK relations with the USSR and the PRC and established six rounds of prime-ministerial-level dialogue with the DPRK between 1990 and 1992.

Northern Limit Line (NLL). A maritime extension of the Military Demarcation Line (MDL) separating the two Koreas. The NLL was unilaterally declared by the United Nations Command in 1953, and over time it has become recognized as the de facto boundary, which ROK naval forces are committed to defend and DPRK forces have usually honored, even while disputing its legitimacy.

On-the-spot guidance. The term given to carefully arranged visits by Kim Il-Sung and Kim Jong-Il to sites in North Korea for inspection and instruction. According to North Korean statistics, the senior Kim made approximately 8,000 guidance visits during his lifetime, and through 2000 the junior Kim had made almost 4,000 visits, beginning with a visit to a film reprinting factory in 1963. Inspection tours have a long tradition in Chinese and Korean culture. Many of North Korea's economic campaigns were launched or named for the date or location of these visits, including the August 3 Consumer Goods Movement, the Taean factory-work system, and the Chongsan-ri farm-management method.

Park Chung-Hee. See **Presidents**.

Presidents.
Syngman Rhee, 1948–60. Forced to resign by student demonstrations against the rigged April 1960 election.
Chang Myon, 1960–61. Became prime minister after a cabinet system was adopted. Deposed in a military coup by General Park Chung-Hee.
Park Chung-Hee, 1961–79. Park ruled first as head of a military junta and from 1964 as president. Assassinated by the chief of the Korean CIA in 1979.
Choi Kyu-Ha, 1979. Resigned after a military mutiny staged by Generals Chun Doo-Hwan and Roh Tae-Woo.
Chun Doo-Hwan, 1980–87. Became president under martial law and was then reelected by the presidential college in 1981.
Roh Tae-Woo, 1988–93. Handpicked by his military colleague Chun, Roh narrowly defeated Kim Young-Sam and Kim Dae-Jung, who split the opposition ticket.
Kim Young-Sam, 1993–98. Kim Young-Sam merged his party with the government party, thereby winning the endorsement of Roh Tae-Woo and beating out his rival, Kim Dae-Jung.
Kim Dae-Jung, 1998– . Kim Dae-Jung joined forces with conservative Kim Jong-Pil (the third of the perennial "three Kims" presidential contenders) to win a narrow victory.

Rajin-Sonbong Foreign Trade and Economic Zone. A trade zone in the northeast corner of the DPRK bordering Russia and China. In 1991 it was declared a zone for joint-venture and international enterprise operations within a larger development area designated by the United Nations Development Program. Rajin-Sonbong has failed to generate much interest among foreign investors because of its poor infrastructure and the hostility of the North Korean government to capitalism. After the cities of Rajin and Sonbong merged in August 2001, the zone was dubbed "Rason."

Resettlement money. Government grant to assist North Korean defectors in their assimilation to South Korean society, often covering their basic necessities such as housing and food.

Security Consultative Meeting (SCM). An annual meeting of the United States and ROK secretaries of defense, first convened in 1968.

Socialist Constitution. The revised constitution of the DPRK, adopted by the SPA on September 5, 1998. Referred to in its preface as the Kim Il-Sung constitution in memory of the DPRK's founder, it is similar in most respects to the 1992 revision.

Speed battle. The term given by the North Korean propaganda organs to any kind of hurry-up campaign. Speed battles typically last for 70 or 100 days to achieve a specific economic goal, such as road construction. Longer speed battles such as the "Speed of the 1980s" and "Speed of the 1990s" are virtually synonymous with the Chollima campaign.

Sunshine Policy. Kim Dae-Jung's policy of engagement with North Korea that was designed to replace cold-war confrontation with inter-Korean reconciliation and cooperation on the basis of mutual trust.

Supreme People's Assembly (SPA). The North Korean unicameral legislative body. According to the socialist constitution, the SPA is the highest organ of state power and is to be convened at least once a year, with members elected for five-year terms. In reality it is a rubber-stamp congress whose only meaningful function is to ratify decisions made by Kim Jong-Il. When the Assembly is not in session, its Presidium (standing committee) carries out legislative functions.

Talbukja. Most commonly used term for "North Korean defectors" living in South Korea. It literally means someone who discarded the North. A little more politically correct term would be *Buk Han Yee Tal Ju Min*, the resident who discarded North Korea.

Trilateral Coordination and Oversight Group (TCOG). A meeting of State Department representatives of the United States, the ROK, and Japan at the assistant secretary level to coordinate policy toward the DPRK. The group has been meeting several times a year as needed since June 1999.

Tumen River. The river separating the northeast corner of the DPRK from Russia and China. The Tumen River Project refers to a zone designated by the United Nations Development Program (UNDP) in 1990 as a cooperative international development area involving China, North Korea, South Korea, Mongolia, and Russia. The DPRK's part of the zone is the Rajin-Sonbong economic zone.

United Front Tactics. A traditional communist tactic to rally diverse organizations in countries targeted by communism, such as the ROK, in order to destabilize the government and support the struggle for communism.

United Liberal Democrats (ULD) led by Kim Jong-Pil, who abandoned his presidential candidacy and formed a coalition with the NCNP; Kim became prime minister in the Kim Dae-Jung government.

West Sea. The sea to the west of the Korean peninsula, also known as the Yellow Sea.

Won. The Korean unit of currency. In October 2001, the South Korean won was trading at approximately 1,300 to the dollar. The DPRK government's fixed rate of exchange for the North Korean won is 2.2 won to the dollar, but it trades on the black market at between 150 and 230 won to the dollar (an ordinary North Korean laborer earns a monthly salary of 100 won).

Workers' Party of Korea (WPK or KWP). Official communist party of the DPRK.

Yasukuni Shrine. Tokyo shrine honoring Japan's war dead, including the handful of officers who were convicted of war crimes after the Second World War.

Yongbyon. The site of North Korea's major nuclear facilities, ninety kilometers northwest of Pyongyang.

Yongsa ("hero"). Before the surge in the number of defectors in the mid-1990s, the South Koreans referred to North Korean defectors with the glorified term, *Buk Han Gwi Soon Yong Sa*, a North Korean hero who "submitted."

Suggestions for Further Readings and Web Sites

The End of History, the Rise of Ideology, and the Pursuit of Inter-Korean Reconciliation

Korea Focus. Magazine on current affairs published by the Korea Foundation.

Moon, Chung-in, and David Steinberg, eds., *Kim Dae Jung Government and Sunshine Policy: Promises and Challenges* (Seoul: Yonsei University Press, 1999).

Oberdorfer, Don. *The Two Koreas: A Contemporary History* (Reading, MA: Addison-Wesley, 1998).

Web sites

www.chongwadae.go.kr. Official site of the Blue House.

www.hannaradang.or.kr. Official site of the main opposition Grand National Party.

www.hyundai-asan.com. Official newsletter of the Hyundai-Asan Corporation.

www.koreaherald.co.kr. English-language newspaper, covering Korean news and events.

The Economic Outlook for Reconciliation and Reunification

Chopra, Ajai, Kenneth Kang, Meral Karasulu, Hong Liang, Henry Ma, and Anthony Richards, "From Crisis to Recovery in Korea: Strategy,

Achievements and Lessons," presented at the IMF-KIEP Conference on "The Korean Crisis and Recovery," May 17–19, 2001, Seoul, Korea.

Eberstadt, Nicholas, "Prospects for Economic Recovery,"*Joint U.S.-Korea Academic Studies,* vol. 11 (2001).

Korea Development Institute, *KDI Review of the North Korean Economy* (*in Korean*, various issues).

Lee, Doowon, "South Korea's Financial Crisis and Economic Restructuring" in *Korea Briefing 1997–99: Challenges and Change at the Turn of the Century,* edited by Kongdan Oh (New York, M.E. Sharpe, 2000).

Lee, Jong Wha, and Yung Chul Park, "Recovery and Sustainability in East Asia," presented at the IMF-KIEP Conference on *The Korean Crisis and Recovery,* May 17–19, 2001, Seoul, Korea.

Yoon, Deok-Ryong, "Integration and Direction of Investment Market of the Two Koreas: Gradual Integration Approach," *Korea Unification Studies,* vol. 4, no. 2 (2000).

The New North Korea

Bermudez, Joseph S., Jr. *The Armed Forces of North Korea* (New York: I. B. Tauris, 2001).

Buzo, Adrian. *The Guerilla Dynasty* (Boulder, CO: Westview Press, 1999).

Downs, Chuck, and James M. Lee. *Over the Line: North Korea's Negotiating Strategy* (Washington, DC: The AEI Press, 1999).

Eberstadt, Nicholas. *The End of North Korea* (Washington, D.C.: The AEI Press, 1999).

Hunter, Helen-Louise. *Kim Il-Song's North Korea* (Westport, CT: Praeger, 1999).

Lee, Hy-Sang. *North Korea: A Strange Socialist Fortress* (Westport, CT: Praeger, 2001).

Noland, Marcus. *Avoiding the Apocalypse: The Future of the Two Koreas* (Washington, D.C.: Institute for International Economics, 2000).

Oh, Kongdan, and Ralph C. Hassig. *North Korea through the Looking Glass* (Washington, D.C.: Brookings Institution Press, 2000).

Snyder, Scott. *Negotiating on the Edge: North Korean Negotiating Behavior* (Washington, D.C.: United States Institute of Peace Press, 1999).

South Korean Government Publications

A Handbook on North Korea, 1st Revision (Seoul: Naewoe Press, 1998).

Peace and Cooperation: White Paper on Korean Unification (Seoul: Ministry of Unification, 2001).

White Paper on Human Rights in North Korea, 2000 (Seoul: Korea Institute for National Unification, 2000).

Periodicals

Asian Survey

East Asian Review

International Journal of Korean Unification Studies

The Journal of East Asian Affairs

Korea and World Affairs

The Korean Journal of Defense Analysis

Vantage Point (Yonhap News Agency)

Web sites

www.kcna.co.jp—North Korean Central News Agency

www.cnn.com/specials/2001/korea—CNN coverage of Korean relations

www.koreascope.org/english/index.ht—Koreascope

www.nkchosun.com/english/index.html—*Choson Ilbo*'s North Korea site

www.unikorea.go.kr/eng/index.php—South Korea's Ministry of Unification

www.washingtonpost.com/wp-dyn/world/asia/eastasia/northkorea— *Washington Post* coverage of North Korea

www.yonhapnews.co.kr/english—South Korea's Yonhap News Agency

China, Japan, and Russia in Inter-Korean Relations

Eberstadt, Nicholas, and Richard J. Ellings, eds. *Korea's Future and the Great Powers* (Seattle: University of Washington Press, 2001).

Hahn, Bae Ho, and Chae-Jin Lee, eds. *Patterns of Inter-Korean Relations* (Seoul: The Sejong Institute, 1999).

Kim, Dalchoong, and Chung-in Moon, eds. *History, Cognition, and Peace in East Asia* (Seoul: Yonsei University Press, 1997).

Kim, Samuel S., ed., *North Korean Foreign Relations in the Post–Cold War Era* (New York: Oxford University Press, 1998).

Kwak, Tae-Hwan, ed. *The Four Powers and Korean Unification Strategies* (Seoul: Kyungnam University Press, 1997).

Kwak, Tae-Hwan, and Melvin Gurtov, eds. *The Future of China and Northeast Asia* (Seoul: Kyungnam University Press, 1997).

Lee, Young-Sun, and Masao Okonogi, eds. *Japan and Korean Unification* (Seoul: Yonsei University Press, 1999).

Park, Kyung-Ae and Dalchoong Kim, eds. *Korean Security Dynamics in Transition* (New York: Palgrave, 2001).

U.S. Policy Toward the Inter-Korean Dialogue

Cummings, Bruce. *Korea's Place in the Sun: A Modern History* (New York: W.W. Norton, 1997).

Dong, Wonmo, ed. *The Two Koreas and the United States: Issues of Peace, Security, and Economic Cooperation* (Armonk, NY: M.E. Sharpe, 2000).

Henriksen, Thomas H., and Kyongsoo Lho, eds. *One Korea? Challenges and Prospects for Reunification* (Stanford, CA: Hoover Institution Press, 1994).

Jung, Ku-Hyun, Dalchoong Kim, Werner Gumpel, and Gottfried-Karl Kindermann, eds. *German Unification and Its Lessons for Korea.* (Seoul:Yonsei University, 1996).

Kang, Myoung-Kyu, and Helmut Wagner, eds. *Germany and Korea: Lessons in Unification* (Seoul: Seoul National University Press, 1995).

Oberdorfer, Don. *The Two Koreas: A Contemporary History* (Reading, MA: Addison-Wesley, 1997).

Park, Tong Hwan, ed. *The U.S. and the Two Koreas: A New Triangle* (Boulder, CO: Lynne Rienner, 1998).

Web sites

www.fes.or.kr—Web page of the Seoul Office of the Friedrich Ebert Foundation. Here, in particular, the documentation of the conference "Change on the Korean Peninsula: the Relevance of Europe," June 17–18, 2001, Tower Hotel, Seoul.

www.fes.or.kr/K_Unification/K_Unification-index.html—The conference was coorganized by the Friedrich Ebert Foundation, the Korea Institute for National Unification and the Delegation of the European Commission in South Korea.

North Korean Defectors: A Window into a Reunified Korea

In English

Grinker, Roy Richard. *Korea and Its Futures: Unification and the Unfinished War* (New York: St. Martin's Press, 1998).

In Korean

Chang, Yŏng-Ch'ŏl. *Tangsindŭri kŭrŏke challassŏyo?* (Are You Really That Great?) (Seoul, Korea: Saho p'yŏngnon, 1997).

Chun, Woo-Taek, and Lee Man-Hong. "Pukhan t'albukjadŭl ŭi namhan sahoe chŏgŭng e kwanhan yŏngu" (Research on Adjustment of North Korean Defectors in South Korea). *Journal of Korean Neuropsychiatric Association* vol. 36, no. 1 (January 1997).

Jung, Yu-Son. "Kwisunja ŭi namhan sahoe chŏgŭng kwajŏng kwa ilsang esŏ ŭi silch'ŏn pangsik e kwanhan yŏngu" (The Adaptation Process and Everyday Practice of North Korean Defectors in South Korean Society: An Anthropological Case Study), Department of Anthropology, Seoul National University, August 1998.

Oh, Hye-Chŏng. "Kwisun pukhan tong'po ŭi namhan sahoe silt'ae" (The Reality of Defectors' Adaptation to Southern Society). M.A. Thesis, Department of North Korean Studies, Sogang University, 1995.

Tto hana ŭi Munhwa, ed. *T'ongiltoen ttang esŏ tŏburŏ sanŭn yŏnsup* (Learning to Live Together in a Unified Land) (Seoul: Tto hana ŭi Munhwa, 1996).

About the Contributors

Glenn Baek is a foreign affairs analyst in the Bureau of Intelligence and Research at the U.S. Department of State. At the time of research and writing for *Korea Briefing 2001–2002*, he was research associate and Korea project director in the International Security Program at The Center for Strategic and International Studies (CSIS) in Washington, D.C. His articles on East Asian political affairs have appeared in the *Washington Post*, *Far Eastern Economic Review*, and other major publications. He received his M.A. in International Relations from American University.

Dieter Dettke has been Executive Director of the Washington Office of the Friedrich Ebert Foundation since 1985. Prior to coming to Washington, he served as political counselor of the SPD Parliamentary Groud of the German Bundestag (1974–84). He was a research associate at the German Society for Foreign Affairs in Bonn from 1969 to 1974. As a specialist in foreign and security policy, Dr. Dettke has published widely on security issues, East-West relations, and U.S. foreign and domestic policy. He is the author of *Allianz im Wandel,* a book about European-American relations in the Nixon-Kissinger era. Among his most recent publications are *Zwischen Hegemonie und Partnerschaft: Zum Wandel amerikanischer Deutschland- und Europa-Politik nach dem Ende des Ost-West Konflicts* in *Revue D'Allemagne et des Pays de Langue Allemende* (2001); *Militärische Optionen;* and *Amerikanische Strategien in der Auseinandersetzung mit dem transnationalen Terrorismus* in *Gerwerkschaftliche Monatshefte* (11/12 2001). He is General Editor of International Political Currents, a Friedrich-Ebert-Stiftung series published by the Washington office. He received his Ph.D. in political science from the Free University in Berlin.

Ralph C. Hassig is the principal of Oh & Hassig, Pacific Rim Consulting, where he specializes in North Korean studies. He is also Adjunct Associate Professor of Psychology at the University of Maryland University College, where he teaches social and political psychology. He spent six years in Asia teaching for the University College's East Asian

Division. He earned his B.A. in psychology at Albion College in 1968 and his Ph.D. in social psychology at UCLA in 1974. He also earned an MBA in marketing at the University of San Francisco in 1986. His co-authored publications include *North Korea through the Looking Glass* (2000) and "Guessing Right and Guessing Wrong about Engagement" in *The Journal of East Asian Studies* (Spring/Summer 2001).

Samuel S. Kim is Adjunct Professor of Political Science and Senior Research Scholar at the East Asian Institute, Columbia University. He received his B.A. from Rhodes College, and M.I.A. and Ph.D. from Columbia University. He served as Fulbright Professor of International Relations at Foreign Affairs Institute, Beijing, China (1985–86), and taught at the Woodrow Wilson School of Public and International Affairs, Princeton University (1986–93). He is the author or editor of eighteen books on East Asian international relations and world-order studies including, most recently, *China and the World: Chinese Foreign Policy Faces the New Millennium* (1998); *North Korean Foreign Relations in the Post–Cold War Era* (ed., 1998); *Korea's Globalization* (ed., 2000); *East Asia and Globalization* (ed., 2000), *The North Korean System in the Post–Cold War Era* (2001), and *The Two Koreas in the Global Community* (forthcoming). His articles have appeared in *American Journal of International Law*, *China Quarterly*, *International Interactions*, *International Organization*, *International Journal*, *Journal of Peace Research*, *World Politics*, and *World Policy Journal*.

Kelly Koh is Program Manager for Minority/National Affairs at the American Psychiatric Association in Washington, D.C. She received her B.A. from Wesleyan University in Psychology-Sociology and her M.A. from Yonsei University in Asian Studies. She has worked for a number of years with leading South Korean NGOs on numerous international projects. As former Assistant Director for the Conflict Resolution Program at The Atlantic Council of the United States and Legislative Director of the Korea Church Coalition, she specialized in North Korean affairs. In 1997, she participated in an Atlantic Council delegation to North Korea.

Doowon Lee is Associate Professor of Economics at Yonsei University, Seoul, Korea, where he is also the Program Chair for the study of transitional economies in the Institute for Korean Unification Studies. Dr. Lee received his B.A. in business administration from Yonsei University in 1987 and his Ph.D. in economics from Northwestern University in 1991. He was a visiting scholar at the Graduate School of International Relations and Pacific Studies at the University of California, San Diego, from 1991 to 1993. His special fields are economic development, international trade and transition economies including North Korea. His recent publications include "Economic Developments of Korea and China" in *The Korean Economic Review* (January 2000); "Causes of Trade Conflict" in *Journal of International Trade and Industry Studies* (June 2000); and *Comparison of Korean and Chinese Economic Development* (1999).

Kongdan (Katy) Oh is a Research Staff Member at the Institute for Defense Analyses and a Non-Resident Senior Fellow at the Brookings Institution. She received her B.A. in Korean language and literature at Sogang University in 1971, her M.A. in the same subjects at Seoul National University in 1974, and her Ph.D. in Asian studies at the University of California, Berkeley in 1986. Her recent publications include *North Korea through the Looking Glass* (2000) and "The Korean War and South Korean Politics" in *The Korean War and the Peloponnesian War: A Comparative Study of War and Democracy* (eds., David McCann and Barry Strauss, 2001). She is the editor of the 1997–99 edition of *Korea Briefing*, and a member of the Korea Task Force of the Council on Foreign Relations, the Korea Working Group of the United States Institute of Peace, and cofounder and codirector of The Korea Club in Washington, D.C.

Edward A. Olsen is Professor of National Security Affairs at the Naval Postgraduate School, Monterey, California. He has been on the faculty there since 1980. Previously, he served as a political analyst on Japan and Korea at the U.S. Department of State (INR). He earned his B.A. in History at UCLA (1968), M.A. in East Asian Studies at UC–Berkeley (1970), and Ph.D. in International Studies at The American University, School of International Service (1974). He has numerous publications in Asian politics, security, and U.S.-Asian relations, including *U.S. Policy and The Two Koreas* (1988). Another, *In Due Course: Normalizing U.S.-Korean Relations*, is forthcoming.

Scott Snyder is Representative to the Korea Office of The Asia Foundation in Seoul, where he directs a program focused primarily on strengthening South Korea's international relations, supporting nongovernmental efforts to increase women's political participation, and supporting training efforts for North Koreans in the areas of law, business, health, and agriculture. Previously, Snyder was an Asia specialist in the Research and Studies Program of the U.S. Institute of Peace, and was a recipient of the Abe Fellowship, a research program administered by the Social Sciences Research Council. Prior to his work at the U.S. Institute of Peace, Snyder was Acting Director of the Contemporary Affairs Department of The Asia Society. Snyder received his B.A. from Rice University and an M.A. from the Regional Studies East Asia Program at Harvard University. He is an active writer and commentator on Asian security issues with a special focus on Korea, and is the author of *Negotiating on the Edge: North Korean Negotiating Behavior* (1999). He was the recipient of a Thomas G. Watson Fellowship in 1987–88 and attended Yonsei University in South Korea.

Index